150

MAN

The Bridge Between

TWO WORLDS

MAN
The Bridge Between
TWO WORLDS

Franz E. Winkler, M.D.

HARPER & BROTHERS   NEW YORK

This book is dedicated to my late friend Russell W. Davenport who toward the end of his life found the inner security which he had so fervently sought. Once his doubts in a higher purpose in life had vanished, neither pain nor the certainty of impending death could mar the serenity of his last months.

There was just one question which he asked himself time and again. Would his book, The Dignity of Man, *fulfill its objective? Would it stimulate others to take up the torch he wanted to light, would it inspire psychologists, philosophers, educators, and especially the average intellectual to participate in an all-out effort to translate the great American ideals into a language the world could understand? Would it contribute to the renaissance of modern civilization as a whole, which will need for its survival a spiritual as well as a material foundation? In such a renaissance, he felt, lay the mission of his country, whose fate would be decided by its fulfillment. To Russell Davenport the United States was in truth God's own country, blessed with tremendous spiritual and material gifts but also charged with the fateful responsibility of leading the world to God.*

If this book should contribute just a little to the eventual realization of Davenport's dream, it will have fulfilled its purpose.

FRANZ E. WINKLER

NEW YORK, JANUARY 1960

Contents

MAN

The Bridge Between

TWO WORLDS

A PERSONAL NOTE

My interest in the mysterious world of psychology dates back farther than my knowledge of the term itself. When other children were fascinated by *what* an adult did, I was more concerned with *why* he did it. Today, in retrospect, the response of adults to this peculiarity of a fifth-grader seems tragic as well as comical. While in public they made fun of the boy, secretly they used every occasion to tell him their woes, ranging from love affairs to material problems, and even suicidal tendencies. Although their affairs were far from comprehensible to me, their thoughts and emotions seemed almost self-explanatory phenomena on a strange but utterly real plane.

High school gave additional incentive to this "hobby" which, surprisingly, roused more interest than ridicule in my classmates, some of whom joined heartily in its pursuit. Judging by the experience of that time, I believe that many youngsters are naturally endowed with intuitive perception of psychological phenomena, a faculty soon to be thwarted by a lack of understanding on the part of teachers and parents. Encouraged by my enthusiasm, a group of eager students of psychology emerged, bent on testing their hunches on unsuspecting adult victims. In school our experiments covered a broad field. Assignments ranged from soothing the mood of a teacher at the beginning of a class and rousing his wrath just before the ringing of the bell made it ineffectual, diverting his attention where necessary, and much else. In short, we were busily engaged in psychology applied to useful means. Such experiments often ended in minor disasters; but they gave us a chance to test our insight into human nature in a scientific and, if successful, extremely enjoyable manner.

In medical school and during the years of internship and residencies I had ample occasion to observe and interview many patients of Vienna's famous psychoanalytical schools. Although some had benefited greatly by a release of their pent-up tensions, or from a genuine compassion on the part of their physicians, the whole concept of modern psychology appeared the more doubtful to me, the longer I watched ultimate results on those who chose to remain under my care for physical ailments in the years to come.

Almost invariably an increasing indifference to other people's needs, a shifting of symptoms into serious psychosomatic ailments, and a deep-seated unhappiness replaced the emotional conflicts and struggles which had been "cured." Moreover, to my observation at least, the actual phenomena of human soul life showed no semblance whatever to the theories of a predominantly animalistic psychology.

Feeling that it would be preposterous to trust my own impressions rather than the opinions of accepted authorities, I looked for answers to the great men of various ages and nations. Although not professional psychologists, most of them had built their work on a definite concept of man, a concept which was less a product of speculation than of immediate, intuitive experience.

Let us for a moment forget the Middle European schools of nonmaterialistic psychology which, paradoxically, I came to know better only at a later time in my life, and to which I have given credit in the latter chapters of this book, and point here to the universally accepted geniuses of all times. Of these Plato, Aristotle, Lao-Tzu, and Buddha, and the thinkers of the West such as Emerson, Keats, Coleridge, and William Blake are just a few. True, everyone is still paying lip service to the greatness of these men and their peers. But, while putting them on a special pedestal, our generation is turning a deaf ear to their messages, seeking guidance instead from those who have strayed

farthest into the unwisdom of an age that has all but lost its vision. And then we are genuinely surprised at the triumphs of
communism, as if they were anything but the outgrowth of an
animalistic psychology!

Fortunately, whatever can be reactivated of the dwindling
intuitive perception of modern man bears out the spiritual
concepts of human nature as they have emerged in various
forms in the teachings of history's sages.

I hope that those words will make it sufficiently clear to the
reader that I have no intention of imposing on him a new
philosophic teaching. Probably all the facts presented in this
book have been voiced before, in one way or another. But I
adopted them neither by virtue of authority nor by loyalty to
any school. No statement has been made which is not based on
personal conviction; for I believe that only what has become
one's own hard-won possession can be of true benefit to others.

While the ideas presented in this book have not originated
with me, the methods used for psychotherapy have. It took
more than seven years to translate some of these methods,
time and again tested in personal consultations, into the written
word. In this process it became clear to me that some of the
traditional rules of nonfictional writing had to be abandoned,
among them the tenet of following a strictly premeditated out-
line. This rule, essential as it is otherwise, did not seem prac-
ticable in working toward an objective which belongs to the
sphere of healing rather than of information.

Healing—and who of us is not in need of it—depends on a
process of inner activity, a process involving not only the intellectual part of man but his whole being. It can be stimulated
by a sequel of thoughts, a sequel determined by associations
rather than by preconceived patterns. Naturally, these associations must not be arbitrarily selected but should emerge from
the observation of other people's responses. When, as in the
lonely business of writing, such observation is impossible, the
recollection of a large number of individual reactions to his
ideas must serve as a substitute.

A few other rules commonly accepted as essential for the
success of scientific writing had to be shelved. In brief they may

be phrased thus: every concept used should immediately be clarified by definitions; once this has been done, one thought ought to lead to another along the shortest possible connecting line, with a minimum of gaps or repetitions. The author himself should speak either entirely from a personal angle or else disappear entirely behind the message of his work.

These and similar rules were pounded into the heads of those who, like myself, served an eight-year term in a Middle European "Gymnasium." To be fair, they proved of great value in our academic professions. However, life imposes at times rules of a different kind. Definitions are the lifeless replica of living thoughts. While indispensable in logic, mathematics, and science, in psychology they may restrict rather than further man's ability to grasp reality. Since all words and concepts are inadequate in that sphere, I have avoided too strict definitions in the hope that the reader will gradually sense intuitively what cannot be fully expressed in intellectual terms.

Living processes never move along straight lines; they weave in spirals and helices, and thoughts intended to strengthen the vitality of psychological activity must move accordingly. And so, I hope that the repetitions in this book represent corresponding points on a spiral staircase rather than identical dots on a circle. In certain places minor gaps had to be left between thoughts, challenging the reader to bridge them in active participation.

The technique of interspersing impersonal statements with personal remarks was, rightly or wrongly, adapted from life experience, where I found it helpful in the difficult task of making the right contact with another individual.

Now a few more words about the purpose of this book. Our generation's consuming interest in psychology has a good reason indeed. It originates in the feeling that orientation within the intricacies of modern life is possible only through self-knowledge. Since it is believed today that understanding of the healthy self can best be attained by a study of pathological deviations, psychiatry has gradually assumed a leading role in the sphere of psychology. I do not believe, however, that its methods can actually uncover the roots of the emotional agonies of modern man. While paralyzing inferiority complexes, overpowering sexual conflicts, and many other facts play an unquestionable part in emotional maladjustments, to me they are symptoms rather than causes. Every human being has to bear his load of suffering, frustration, and unfulfilled desires. Yet, almost three decades of medical experience have taught me that this load will cause neuroses or emotional disaster only to the degree in which a person has lost his innate sense for the existence of purpose and meaning in life.

Personally, I am deeply convinced that we are living in a moral universe, in a universe which holds not only meaning for evolution as a whole, but for every single individual in his struggles through life and death. And where is the proof for such an optimistic view? In immediate experience. It has grown dark in the sphere in which experiences of such kind occur. In their longing for inner light many today turn to drugs or seek illumination in artificially induced ecstasies. My own experiences with a great number of such seekers after truth are unfortunate. Short periods of rapture and "certainty" are only too soon followed by spells of doubt and despair, as if a weak but still living spark had been whipped into a blinding flame, to be burnt to extinction soon thereafter. No, inner vision, at least for modern man, is not the gift of drama and ecstasy, but the hard-won fruit of patient labor.

There is more than one kind of vision. The type most valued today is acute sense perception illumined by keen intellect. Another, often called intuitive, is the source of all religious and artistic inspiration. The third, almost unknown in our day, is man's vision of himself. Neither grossly sensual nor purely intuitive, it represents a mysterious spark of consciousness that emerges when these two forces attain a state of balance. It has grown so dim that modern man has become uncertain of his individuality, and tries in vain to discover himself in the dark depths of his unconsciousness or in the remote heights of a not-yet-reached superconsciousness.

Unfortunately, there are no words which can adequately describe the self or human spirit; it must be experienced. Such experience is vital to mental health, since it permits man to protect his mind from disintegrating forces which threaten to split his personality. Self-awareness can be strengthened by specific mental exercises. Basically, these exercises are designed to bring to consciousness two opposite poles of a psychological polarity. Since adequate words and definitions for these poles do not exist, their discussion will almost inevitably lead to misunderstandings. Nevertheless, if the book succeeds in stimulating awareness of only one of the innumerable polarities in the human psyche, it has fulfilled its purpose.

As soon as we have learned, for example, to observe the polarity between a sense perception and an intuitive experience, or between creative and analytical activities, we have already entered the road to self-knowledge. For, if in the course of time we learn to trace the two poles further toward their meeting place, that hidden core of our consciousness will gradually emerge before our inner eye in an imagery which brings to mind the enchanted castle of the fairy tale.

Many have tried their hand at this type of psychotherapy, only to be ridiculed and scorned; because man wants to hear fascinating facts about himself, or be encouraged to invent them on the soft couch of an analyst. He dreads true knowledge, especially if its attainment requires mental activity; and yet, in the depth of his heart he longs for it.

One of the great masters of true psychotherapy was Socrates: his questions and dialogues had no other purpose than to rouse in man vision of himself and of his place in a meaningful universe. There is no Socrates today, but the need for his kind of healing is greater than ever. Thus ordinary people must try to meet that need as best they can. Results, however, are harder to achieve in writing than through personal contact, and may not be attained at all, unless the reader will co-operate in a spirit of sympathetic understanding. In private talks concepts unfamiliar to a person can be explained, evasive links repeated until they are finally remembered. This being impossible in writing, the only hope of achieving the desired goal lies in the willingness of the reader to study rather than to scan the contents of a book, and to reserve judgment on details until the end. If, then, in retrospect some or even most of the views presented here are rejected, it will not matter too much, for by then the mental exercise should have achieved some of its desired effect: the heightening of the reader's awareness of his own elusive self.

CHAPTER II

PSYCHOLOGICAL UNDERCURRENTS IN OUR TIME

Our generation is faced with a crisis unequaled in history. The cold war, the horror of nuclear weapons, and, above all, the menace of Communist power have destroyed all vestiges of the pride and complacency marking the beginning of our century. Historians of the future may see in this plight the shock treatment of destiny, the storm scattering the dense fog of intellectual conceit and spiritual confusion which has caused our civilization to drift from one disaster to another. Corrective actions of a purely external nature do not suffice. The revolution which exiled the Kaiser did not prevent Hitler's rise to power, nor did the military defeat of fascism prevent the spread of authoritarianism in the world. Although these experiences should not make us abandon action when freedom is at stake, they should nonetheless induce us to ponder the distinctions between cause and effect, between disease and symptom.

Our world is one organism, in which an illness may present its first symptoms in specific geographic or ethnologic areas, while remaining dormant in others; but no major ill, such as communism, could have spread so far and persisted so long without a serious breakdown of the defense mechanism of the whole. Thus, even if radical means could stem communism's further progress, social diseases of a similar character would be bound to recur, unless a primary cause is recognized and

9

amended. This cause, however, must be sought in the only denominator common to all mankind: in the individual. There it
is hidden, and there it defies and will continue to defy any
measures directed toward the improvement of outer conditions
alone.

How can we hope to discover the root of the evil and thereby
gain an indication for its cure? Although innumerable books
have been written on this subject, there seems room for one
springing entirely from one man's efforts to cope with the actual
questions and psychological problems of people under his care;
for in the small world of an ordinary man may be found the
germs of the countless conflicts which determine the fate of
whole civilizations.

Surely social, economic, and military conditions as well as
fear and terror have played an important part in the world's
division into peoples who cherish their freedom and those who
have abandoned it. But is this division not also a reflection of
the split within the modern individual's soul, of the conflict between his longing for freedom and the fear of the responsibilities
involved? All these problems do not lie deeply hidden. They are
acted out on the stage of everyday life; and, when illness inter-
rupts the rush of his existence, man may pause to think about
his conflicts and to formulate them into questions. If at such
moments he finds a friend in his physician, his problems will
come to the open, without need for a laborious search of his
subconscious mind.

It would be as absurd to deny the influence which sex and
other biological factors exert on the human psyche, as to deny
the role which the elemental forces welling up from the interior
of the earth exert on a tree or a flower. Nevertheless, we do not
dig shafts toward the center of the earth in order to study
the individual plant, but are satisfied with finding its well-
defined roots; for, although a plant is nourished and influenced
by all the forces from the depths of our planet as well as by the
air and sunlight above, it still is an entity of its own. In like
fashion man, although sustained by supra- and subconscious
forces, must be primarily considered within the sphere in which
his consciousness holds sway, the sphere which we shall call his

self. Possibly the future will bring forth scientists great enough to study the spiritual conditions that arouse the genius in man as well as the biological powers that kindle his earthly desires. Such scientists would indeed understand psychology better than we do today. Yet even now one thing is certain: so long as we try to explain the human mind from the depths alone, we shall by necessity arrive at a distorted picture of human nature. And it is this tragic distortion, this caricature of humanity, which is the main subject of modern psychological investigations.

The true spark of humanity is an elusive element which can be reduced, on occasion, to a state of impotence. Such a state occurs in severe alcohol and drug addictions, in epileptic equivalents, and in "unmotivated" crimes and obsessions. At times, for medical reasons, it is actually necessary to bring about conditions of dimmed self-consciousness through hypnotism and the half-sleep induced by psychoanalysts. However, while such experiences may prove beneficial for some patients, conclusions drawn from them have wrought havoc with our philosophical concept of man's true nature. For what comes to the foreground when the light of man's self-consciousness pales is not his psyche. On the contrary, it is the manifestation of all those forces which sustain as well as challenge the ego but are as different from it as the substance of a candle is from its flame. Modern psychology is intensely interested in these forces, and rightly so. But it is in error when it considers the human ego to be on the same level of existence as biological instincts. The former is too elusive for the rather coarse methods of modern psychology, where the latter, being far more robust, will come to the fore. No wonder our psychologists have largely ceased to believe in a spiritual core of the human soul, for it is indeed missing from their sphere of research.

In many years of practice in the field of psychology and medicine, we have come to accept as fully reliable only those revelations of human nature which are given in clear consciousness, at a time freely chosen and without prompting by psychological investigation. Naturally, one must not minimize the importance of the part which medical psychology plays in the treatment of patients requiring that particular kind of help.

On the contrary, the growing inability of modern man to master his subconscious impulses makes analytical treatment a frequent and real necessity. However, a fateful mistake is made when the psychologist fails to distinguish between the human spirit and the forces which challenge it. We find false and misleading that well-known simile of the iceberg whose visible tip is likened to the conscious part of the human mind while its submerged bulk is likened to the subconscious. Man's psyche should rather be compared to a lantern whose fuel is composed of all the material and biological processes of nature which are seeking, as it were, purification and sublimation in its flame.

At times it is necessary to turn the flame low, if the fuel is to be cleansed from ingredients too explosive or too heavy for its flickering light. However, what emerges from such a dimmed state of consciousness is not yet part of the human ego. If hauled up from the depths, it shows the universal aspects of Jung's "Unconscious"; if taken from the already glowing wick, it appears in the form of Freud's "Subconscious."

The physician who is interested in the problem of healing and not merely in the treatment of symptoms finds himself earlier or later confronted with the relationship between disease and moral evolution. No matter how disinclined a doctor may be to consider this problem, he would be a poor observer indeed were he to overlook its existence. For almost every physical illness can bring about an advance in self-recognition which, in turn, can enhance man's chance for moral freedom and spiritual strength. Yet this potent gift of illness may be fleeting and short-lived unless met with sympathetic attention; and as a rule it is the physician in whom the patient confides, provided he can expect more of him than drugs. Deep down in his heart, the patient senses that he will not find real healing unless an illness leads to clearer self-recognition and to moral progress; and instinctively he knows that, without such progress, his mental or physical disorder, although it may become dormant for a time, will return later in an even more serious form.

The physician himself will be amply rewarded for the additional effort which attention to the whole human being requires, for he will be permitted glimpses into the true nature of man, a benefit even greater to him than to his charge. Shown this kind of interest, many patients will become a doctor's life-long friends, thereby giving him the opportunity to observe significant changes in the same individual through long periods of time. Thus a place is reserved for the physician on the grandstand of life from which, more distinctly than any other human being, he can observe its unique game. But even the keenest observer of life must become a student of its rules, if he aspires to be more than a passive witness. He must ask himself if there is a problem common to all men, a question that con-sciously or unconsciously affects everyone, the criminal no less than the well-adjusted.

If such an issue exists not merely as a philosophical but as an actively psychological problem, it should be expected to sur-face under the impact of disease, fear, and recovery. And when a physician remains deeply interested in the psychology of his patients without interference or prying, he will surprisingly often hear such questions as: "Doctor, I want to live because of my obligations, my family, and the pleasures I find in life. But if I had never been born, none of these would exist—and would it really matter? In your profession you are constantly in touch with life and death. Do *you* think there is purpose and meaning in life? Priests and ministers say there is, but is it not their duty to say so?"

Even in adolescence, when the child's mind becomes capable of conscious reflection, this question takes shape in his soul, never to leave him to the end of his days. The adolescent can receive great help from religious education, provided his in-structor lives what he preaches; but in most cases no serious effort is made to tackle the problem of adolescence on a plane other than that of sex. Contrary to all Freudian teachings, however, the teen-ager's gravest problem is fear of life rather than libido. He does not want to follow the pattern of his elders, whom he mercilessly condemns for their errors in in-dividual and public life. But while earlier generations in a simi-lar mood were eager to take the wheel of history into their own hands, modern youths entertain little hope that the world can be improved at all. Consequently, the mood prevailing among the young today is cynical rather than revolutionary. Their reactions vary according to upbringing, character, and temperament. Many have become resigned to an existence of purely physical comfort. Among these are regular churchgoers and eager participants in denominational study groups, determined to utilize all the emotional support which they may obtain from religion. These are the average citizens of the future. But owing to an underlying lack of conviction, they are forced to hide their insecurity in a state of reduced consciousness achieved through alcohol and tranquilizers; and, while they may remain stanch supporters of our way of life, they are utterly incapable of active leadership.

Others are less docile. They express their instinctive rebellion against a life devoid of deeper meaning, either by seeking morbid thrills and "experiences" or by unmotivated crime and vandalism. The history of modern wars, with their underground and antitotalitarian uprisings, has shown that wherever a modern youth is confronted with a nonmaterial and clearly discernible challenge, he is fully capable of rising to the occasion in a spirit of self-sacrifice and initiative, equal to the greatest examples of the past. But, especially in areas where no such challenges exist or where revolutionary changes seem impossible, the youth of our time has all but lost interest in his own future. If human existence has none but biological aims, why not seek pleasures in sex unrestrained, in narcotics, or in the thrills of crime?

As a rule, no good will come of an adult's frantic efforts to gain the confidence of an adolescent. The initiative must be largely left to the youth. But we have not yet found the one who, given time and opportunity, will not raise the question about the meaning of life. This event must be patiently awaited and, when it comes, met with infinite caution and self-control. For the average adolescent of today mistrusts the adult, and hates to confide his secrets to him. When, in spite of himself, he does ask for help, his plea rarely takes the form of a polite and respectful inquiry, but is often camouflaged behind boisterous words or aggressive actions. The more perverted and negative

such pleas, the stronger are his neurotic and criminal tendencies. We have always doubted the sincerity of such an adolescent
when his questions about the purpose of life appeared to be too
docile or devout. Usually, when an inner conflict seeks its solution, a violent outburst occurs with little if any regard for the
amenities of life. And as one in danger of drowning may call
for help and still fight his rescuer to the last, the youth in inner
distress may appear most defiant when actually pleading
for aid.

Frequently it is the physician who has to face these crises
occurring so often in the wake of a physical illness or injury.
In an age which places physical health and natural science above
all else, medical judgment counts highly, even in matters of the
spirit. This trend adds greatly to the difficulties of the modern
doctor who, far from being a metaphysician, would fain be left
to his medical chores. Yet he cannot shun spiritual responsibilities, for illness is more than cellular pathology, and the act of
healing more than science.

The physician need not be a genius, for his call is to restore
rather than to create; and still he cannot heal without recourse
to art, since the object of his labor is nature's greatest wonder.
What is a work of art? It is matter wed to spirit, and its prototype is man. Into the organism of man a power greater than
ours sends its life-sustaining forces and, regardless of what we
may call it, we cannot doubt its existence. Although the physician cannot create, he must learn to sense the creative idea behind man's physical organism: without this, he can no more
heal a human being than a house painter can restore the Sistine Chapel. Knowledge of man lifted into the sphere of art
opens our inner eye to the meaning of life. Lacking this insight, we may become craftsmen, but never healers.

Helmholtz, the great representative of nineteenth-century
science, once complained about the inadequacies of the human
body. And indeed, of all physical organisms, man's is the least
perfected. Far less completion is shown in man than in a pure
crystal, a beautiful tree, or a wild animal. But here we may be
reminded of the great painters who have sacrificed photographic likeness to give life and soul to their portraits. The

physiological imperfections of the human organism represent myriads of tiny pores through which filter the rays of the spirit: disease widens these holes and thus spiritualizes the human entity, whereas too vigorous suppression of illness makes of man a grosser being. When a process of physical dissolution remains unchecked, an excessive spiritualization—death—will occur. If, on the other hand, modern medicine ever realizes its dream of preventing all disease and prolonging life indefinitely, a race of robots or living mummies might emerge to populate the earth.

Man's existence oscillates between the forces of life and of death, between alternately closer relationship to matter and to spirit. In his moral development every illness plays a certain and intelligible role. It does not make him, automatically, a better being. Yet physical dissolution liberates forces in the human soul which *can* be used for greater self-knowledge and moral strength.

The problem of health and disease, although but one of the countless aspects of life, offers a singular opportunity for attaining a glimpse into destiny's workshop. The knowledge gained from such a glimpse is not a matter of faith; it is an inner certainty born of observation of the human being as a whole. Its truth is beyond intellectual proof, as is the reality of beauty, of inner freedom, or of God. But at some time in life every man is given a chance to share to a varying degree in this experience.

Artificially induced self-recognition is an undertaking far more hazardous than most analysts seem to realize. Although alert to psychiatric dangers, psychologists often pay but little heed to the moral hazards of their treatment. They fail to observe that complexes do not stem from ignorance alone, but represent frantic efforts to lock into the dungeons of the subconscious mind powers which the human self does not yet dare to face. "Successful" treatment brings them to the surface, where after a short battle they may well devour the individual, transforming an overconscientious businessman into a level-headed thief, or a neurotic housewife into a contented adulteress. As the fairy tale would put it: the wolf swallowed the grandmother and lived in her guise happily forever after.

None of us is wise enough to control the forces we so jauntily release, and until we have attained this wisdom we must allow life to remain the master psychologist, and the physician his humble apprentice. Quite as rain and snow, heat and frost, are essential to the vegetation of the earth, so is every joy and every trial, every experience and every illness, a power that releases a seedling in the human soul. In this continuous birth process, as we see it, lies the deeper meaning of life: man's opportunity to create in himself a strong and harmonious personality.

But destiny gives us no more than an opportunity; whether we make use of it, dis- or misuse it, depends on our free will. The real tragedy of our time is that the tiny seedlings of the soul are not recognized for what they are and therefore are left, without care, to degenerate or die. Prevention of this tragedy is the true mission of psychology, a mission which must be shared alike by parents, teachers, and physicians. To fulfill it we must come to understand the working of destiny or life— whatever we prefer to call it. How does it challenge man to moral choice?

For an example let us turn once more to the problem of adolescence. Although gradual in coming, the full transition from childhood to adolescent consciousness is a dramatic event. The child, unless spoiled by faulty upbringing, lives within the *qualitative* aspect of the world. He is still so much a part of the inner life of his environment that he responds emotionally and even physically to the psychological atmosphere of his surroundings. Living in its center, he looks outward, at the periphery of existence, where his attention becomes focused on the mechanics of nature and life, as reflected in his perpetual questions. This phase of consciousness changes radically at some time in his early teens when the child suddenly experiences himself as an individual, as an outsider to his family and friends. Now he turns his gaze inward, toward the center of existence, and scrutinizes the inner life of those who surround him. This is the stage when his insight into the soul life of others is unusually clear—and woe if he finds it wanting!

Without mercy the adolescent probes into the souls of his elders, seeking in them the meaning of life. Small wonder that his parents, whenever they can, dispatch him to boarding school! And the youngster remains lonely, disenchanted, and bewildered. According to his character and temperament, he either resigns himself to a prosaic, cattlelike existence or seeks emotional fulfillment in power, money, and sex. Life, the master psychologist, has broadened his consciousness, has endowed him with a capacity for moral reflection, and heightened his individual freedom. But these gifts too often go to waste or even to evil, when not understood and cared for by adult helpers.

True, psychological help is hardly necessary for the adolescent who can revere his parents and teachers. The hero worship natural to youth finds fulfillment in such a case, bringing security and contentment into a youngster's life. But the less fortunate child needs help from outside. Deprived of it, he will seek in the depths what he cannot find in the heights; for the juvenile craves a kind of leadership that is firmly rooted in inner reality. Mere decency and traditional virtue hold little if any meaning for the adolescent who, himself part of a changing world, has no use for the static. On the other hand, it is possible for him to find a stark and dynamic reality in destructiveness and depravation, promising thrill where weak moral leadership has left an emotional void. Thus it happens time and again that teen-agers, in spite of their usually keen psychological instincts, become slaves of the morally depraved. Yet even such danger can be averted by an appeal to the qualities of moral leadership that are dormant in almost all young people.

In adolescence, as in every critical period of life, an inner birth process takes place. Whether its fruits will ripen, die, or grow into monstrosities, depends on wisdom and free will. Moral evolution requires a supreme effort of will, seldom undertaken unless its purpose and meaning are made clear by a friend or a teacher. And the youth in particular, ever plagued by a sense of inferiority, will seek in others the leadership he should develop in himself. But once he finds unobtrusive understanding for the inner torments of his age, and once he learns the meaning of these labor pains, he will rarely shun the fight for a rich inner life.

The average juvenile is proud, secretive, and suspicious, hating adult inquisitiveness, pity, and advice; and yet, whenever he senses inner strength and security in another, he longs to share in it. Then the time has come for the psychologist to tell his own story, the story of the errors, loneliness, and disappointments of his own adolescent life—and of his discovery that these are but the bitter seeds of freedom. And none will agree more heartily than youngsters that virtue and decency in themselves are no signs of moral freedom. Does not every animal obey the moral rules of its kind? Man alone can be free, but only when he is either creating new values—or destroying them. Moral freedom is man's supreme gift, its raw materials supplied by life itself. For the adolescent especially, these materials are loneliness, disenchantment, and sexual desire; he more than an adult has the ability to transform loneliness into compassion, disenchantment into will for moral leadership, and libido into love. Youth leaders all over the world know how capable juveniles are of self-sacrifice and sublimation, provided they are given a worthwhile cause. And surely we may discover the strength of youth's real longing in the history of romanticism, of religious creeds, and of epic fights for freedom.

It is the all-powerful influence of modern psychological philosophy that fails the teen-ager. Told that propagation is the true meaning of life, and repression of libido harmful, he throws himself into the ocean of eroticism, despising himself and his elders for it. What the juvenile feels but dimly in his heart, the psychologist should know and teach. Self-abandonment to libido brings to the human spirit neither emotional peace nor the healing of conflicts. On the contrary, too many of those who have dived into its bottomless pit too early or too deeply, have come back drained of their physical and mental stamina, or obsessed by abnormal compulsions.

Puritanical sex negation is contrary to nature, but sex indulgence without love weakens the human ego. The juvenile, hardly yet capable of true affection for the other sex, merely wastes his will forces in erotic thoughts and actions. Permanently weakened, he will only too easily break under the stress and strain of later life. No, the sex problem of the adolescent cannot be solved by self-indulgence, but only by a deep understanding of life's supreme challenge to man. Nature presents this challenge early in life when the purity of childhood, the strength and idealism of youth, are still powerful forces.

It is rare indeed that an adolescent will discover the meaning of this challenge by himself, for he lacks the kind of wisdom which life experience alone can give. Yet his faculty for responding intuitively to truth is far greater than it is in later life. And once made aware of a reality, he will soon confirm it by an inner experience of his own: in the maturing of his glands, in the tempest of his blood, nature pours into man her greatest gift, her supreme power of proliferation, which no creature save man can sublimate into capacity for love.

Naturally, it would be naïve to expect all youngsters to become saintly on the strength of ideas such as these, for neither intellectual nor even intuitive knowledge necessarily leads to moral progress. Still the most tragic of all juvenile tragedies, those caused by ignorance, may be prevented; and, even if thoughts of this kind fail to influence a youngster's actions, they will at least decrease the danger of complete self-abandonment to subhuman instincts.

The exact timing, and the choice of words that will actually be helpful to an individual, depend on an intimate knowledge of his personality, his stage of development, and his needs. Certain generalities, however, may be gleaned from practical experience.

One of the major problems for the maturing personality lies in the development of the right kind of self-assurance. Here again it is the adolescent who must shoulder the heaviest burden. Usually starting out with a sense of inferiority, he tries to overcompensate for his self-consciousness by defiance, conceit, and braggartism. One of the props he uses is national or racial pride, a tendency exploited to the full by political schemers. Even in people as level-headed as, for instance, North Americans, this shortcut to self-assurance is not entirely missing; and, though apparently less dangerous here than elsewhere, it interferes with the development of truly strong personalities. To be born in this country with its wonderful tradition is indeed a privilege conducive to complacent self-assurance. Yet this very complacency endangers the nation's future, for the qualities which have made the United States the greatest country in the world are no longer fully alive in the hearts of the younger generation. Our generation may still be strong enough to win another war, but how long can it endure the subtler danger of a lasting peace? Let us search a little further for thought habits and ingrained sentiments that block the emergence of a strength adequate to meet the needs of our age.

In antiquity, man's consciousness was more influenced by racial or national affiliations. When a Roman legionary faced superior forces in his campaigns, he often emerged victorious, not because he was stronger, more courageous, or better armed than his enemy, but because he conceived of himself as part of invincible Rome. Let us not be deceived today. We may still build a spurious self-assurance upon family, racial, or national stamina, but such self-assurance might crumble at the first serious test.

The future of our civilization rests entirely on an increase of individual strength, and on the development of qualities that must be nursed to real greatness, and extricated from the weeds that threaten to suffocate them. Such a process of growth, hampered by ignorance, is threatened further by a deeply ingrained mental inertia which makes us seek frantically for reasons to excuse our lack of spiritual initiative. A whole group of such excuses can be classified under the heading of "religious optimism." This optimism is often displayed in a manner either unctuous or aggressive, even when aired in some of those entirely spontaneous confidences from which all the examples in this book are taken. In general, the tenor of these uneasy convictions can be summarized thus: All the individual has to do is to live a decent life. God in turn will take care of His own and bring about changes in our civilization to protect the righteous from the wiles of the wicked. An intense search on the part of the individual for a new approach to life is uncalled for and even sinful. Soon a fresh religious impulse, a kind of universal revivalism, will come to change the hearts of men and the course of history.

Unfortunately, history does not encourage such expectations, having proved appallingly unsentimental as to the fate of whole civilizations. Nor can we reasonably put too much faith in the sudden emergence of a new religious impulse, since such an impulse requires a degree of spiritual perception far beyond the scope of modern man.

If mystical optimism tends to paralyze initiative, its counterpart, philosophical pessimism, can prove an even worse stumbling block. Strangely enough, the two are often teammates in the human soul, for it is well known to psychology that opposing sentiments do not necessarily neutralize or exclude each other: both can remain active in different strata of one and the same personality. The atheist, for instance, frequently poses as a philosophical optimist. Having given up all hope in the very existence of a human soul, he pretends to a glowing faith in man's innate goodness. So it becomes possible for Communists to believe that, aided by dictatorship, and by thought control and conditioning, the human race will blossom into a healthy and contented breed of highly intelligent cattle.

But today even the religiously inclined among modern intellectuals are strongly influenced by pessimistic undercurrents. Although their doubts may remain subconscious during the major part of life, sooner or later they come to the surface of consciousness. This is especially true in the case of the person confronted with a critical operation or a fatal disease: unless he finds someone in whom to confide, he is only too often in serious danger of an emotional breakdown. The fear of complete extinction finds many forms of expression, but all may be summarized thus: Perhaps there *is* a supreme wisdom ruling the universe. Yet what possible interest could such cosmic, transcendental power take in the strife and follies of a microscopic being crawling on the face of this tiny speck of dust called earth? Would it not be naïve to attribute to humans a part greater than the one played by the myriads of other species in the universe? A flickering of life, attainment of some specific gifts, and then decline and extinction.

It is difficult, if not impossible, to refute such doubts on strictly logical grounds. While logic is an essential instrument in the quest for truth, it can only blaze a trail through the jungles or remove obstacles from the path, without carrying too much conviction of its own. Therefore it is not necessary to engage in endless dialectics when dealing with problems arising from a true inner need. Once logic has removed mental blocks, it will be an inner response that decides the issue.

From what we have learned from confessions of the seriously sick, almost every individual in close proximity to death has an immediate experience of his own immortality. But when the emergency passes the memory of such experience dwindles fast in our days of sedatives and frantic diversions.

What is man? Is he really the crown of creation—or a pygmy in the universe? This question can be answered only by another question: is the vast universe, with its awe-inspiring harmony, a really greater miracle than the mind existing in that tiny creature, capable of grasping its wonders? For of all incarnated beings known to us, it is man and man alone in whose mind creation may rediscover itself in conscious thoughts. The fact that homo sapiens as a physical being is but a minute entity in the limitless expanse of the universe makes his true significance appear even greater, for his mind knows no limits.

Ancient thinkers, although deeply awed by the miracles of the universe, did not lose their respect for the human being; on the contrary, they saw the full majesty of the "macrocosm" reflected in the "microcosm" of man. Ironically, it is just modern man's inane pride in his doubtful achievements in the world of matter which, in his own sight, has reduced his place in the universe to utter insignificance. Conceited where he should be humble, he has become abject where he should be proudly aware of his potential greatness.

Seen as highly evolved animals, we have indeed no cause for pride. But what about the potentialities of our mind? Our mind cannot be dwarfed by the immensity of physical distances; it is not bound by time and space, and it is great enough to embrace the whole universe within its world of thoughts. Only man among all creatures known to us can reflect upon both himself and his Creator—only man can choose between good and evil. How, then, can he be insignificant?

If thoughts like these can stir even a faint response in a human being, if memories can be roused of some great moment in his life, a moment in which he had grown beyond himself, a grave danger can be averted. If he cannot muster that self-respect which does not depend on material success or failure, no man can retain full sanity; nor can he die without fear.

Even with the danger of psychogenic melancholy averted, another question plagues the conscious or subconscious mind of modern man. Granted that the human soul has to be credited with innate greatness, what has become of it? Can there be any meaning or purpose in evolution, when millenniums have failed to make man a better or wiser being? Although few people will admit this problem has even occurred to them, let alone plagued them, it is ever present in the routine of our daily life whose emptiness can be borne only with the help of intoxicants; and it is still more clearly reflected in juvenile rebelliousness, cynicism, and delinquency, almost never failing to be revealed when a juvenile brings himself to confide in an adult. And indeed, what is there in our present civilization to stir youth to enthusiasm and self-control? How many in this generation still believe that suppression of wars will bring peace to the world, that shorter working hours will bring happiness to people already tormented by boredom? The young generation of today is suffering from a supposed lack of higher purpose in life, and without such a higher purpose youth cannot exist. The blame for this plight rests with us, with the educators, scientists, and philosophers of our generation, who have failed in the interpretation of historical evolution.

Is it really so difficult to find meaning in history, just because we are forced to admit that modern men as individuals are neither wiser nor better than their ancestors? Wisdom and goodness are not among the gifts historical evolution can bestow; as a matter of fact, they cannot be gifts at all. History has implanted a variety of seeds into the soul of mankind, and thus provided a greater freedom of choice; it has given man great power to act, and thus made it easier for him to see the consequences of his actions. But goodness and wisdom belong to the sphere of individual striving and individual freedom. If they could be gained and strengthened by such evolutionary means as selection and survival of the best, or by beneficial mutations, and handed on from generation to generation by heredity, their true nature would be lost. For then goodness and wisdom would mean no more than desirable qualities in a breed of cattle.

No, history has never been a breeder of good and wise human beings, but neither has it been prone, as so many modern philosophers claim, to run forever in circles. For, the saying that history repeats itself is simply not true. There have never been H-bombs before. There has never been another age when the decision of a small group of people, indeed of one individual, might save or destroy the world as a whole. True, there have been single personalities holding tremendous concentrations of power in their hands, but none of them could have endangered the very survival of the human race. Only in our day has it become possible for one person to determine the fate of the world. He need not even be a dictator, nor the chosen leader of a great country. One officer on a strategic mission might well start the ball of destruction rolling.

In these exaggerated signs the Era of the Individual throws its distorted shadows ahead of itself. Its shadows are distorted, for they fall against the weird background of modern materialism. And deep in his soul, man knows that he has come of age, that he must accept the responsibility for the future of his race to a degree unequaled in history.

Where can he find the spiritual strength and the wisdom needed for such a gigantic task?

Psychological reaction to this dilemma varies greatly, depending on temperament and character traits. Some, probably the majority, carry on their lives as usual and, on the surface, seem to succeed well enough; but the tremendous demand for tranquilizers, alcohol, and narcotics, as well as the shockingly high rate of psychoneuroses, tell a sad story of unassuaged fear and frustration. Others, despairing of a worthwhile goal, seek satisfaction in merely sensual pleasures; but a large part of the free world's population turns again to traditional religion.

Naturally, it is not only the search for a meaning in life that makes people revert to their churches. It is also a profound longing for religion itself, an unconscious nostalgia for the glowing faith of the Middle Ages, a faith that bears little if any resemblance to the vague spiritual emotions of our days. This lack of fulfillment which haunts modern man is the price he must pay for his growing but still immature scientific outlook on life. For, strenuously as we may try to hide the feebleness of our religious convictions, we are unable to accept fully what does not readily fit into our intellectual world picture.

There is another problem. We pride ourselves on our respect and tolerance for other people's faith. Yet these qualities—no doubt excellent in themselves—have brought the masses into closer contact with the highly contradictory theological conceptions of various civilizations. And which of these conceptions are right? Or are so-called revelations no more than shadow pictures of unfulfilled longing? Such doubts, undermining the religious convictions of our age, have strongly influenced the present philosophy of education. John Dewey, referring to religions, wrote: "The differences among them are so great and so shocking that any common element that can be extracted is meaningless."[1] An American philosopher has thus opened a split between religions and scientific convictions, a split we cannot bridge by merely denouncing the untoward results of "progressive" pedagogy. But we may gain some useful clues from a short excursion into the history of human consciousness.

The attitude of the pagan world toward the then even larger multitude of creeds was quite different from ours. Without necessarily being tolerant, the enlightened priest of the pre-Christian era was not perturbed by the apparent conflicts in theological conceptions. To him different creeds merely indicated racial, national, or tribal predilections for various aspects of divinity. Did not the traditional legends and myths of different cultures bear a surprising similarity to one another, pointing to preindividual eras, when revelations had been of a more universal character? For there were such messages wherever the light streamed through the pure, untainted soul windows of great seers and prophets. As evolution moved toward the heightening of individual characteristics, those visions became more and more colored by the personality of their recipients. Consequently, revelations were still radiant but already broken down into various colors and shades, attracting some ethnological groups and repelling others. Yet no pagan considered foreign deities as mere illusions. Not until late in history did individualism become so powerful a force as to blind even leading personalities to the true nature of religious perception. Had the medieval seers been aware of the unconscious influence their own egos had on their spiritual experiences, persecution and bloody religious wars for the protection of the "pure" word of God might have been avoided. When the individuality became so strong that the windows of man's heart lost their transparency and revelations disappeared almost entirely, all existing creeds were frozen into well-nigh unchangeable doctrines. They still inspire the souls of millions but do not fully satisfy the minds of even a few. For all that lives is in motion, and what was right for yesterday cannot possibly be right for today, unless it has kept pace with evolution.

It is not absolute truth that grows and changes, but its reflection in the changing needs of evolution. Creeds all over the world have recognized that truth does not look the same at all times and to all kinds of peoples. Christianity acknowledged the truth of the Old Testament, Judaism added the wisdom of its medieval scholars to its old traditions, Buddhism accepted essential parts of Hinduism, and so on. Only with the beginning of our own intellectual period did medieval concepts become rigidly confined within the structures of our religious creeds.

The psychological conflicts arising from this fact are obvious to all, but the remedies applied are inadequate. They consist chiefly of two extreme attitudes taken by various religious authorities. One is the truly modern trend of passing lightly over uncomfortable doctrines. Its policy is that, while tradition is too sacred to be tampered with, it must not be allowed to confuse the seeking soul. What actually matters is an honest, charitable life, and belief in God; religious convictions beyond these are considered mere crutches for those who have remained childlike in their thinking. The progressive would no more dispute the picturesque rituals or concepts of various creeds than he would ridicule Santa Claus in front of children. But, like all "enlightened" people, he considers them lingering residues from eras long past, eras untouched by the wisdom of modern science. How easy it is for such people to see the common element in all creeds, after having dismissed all elements of religious "phantasy"! The price for such tolerance is high, for unwittingly it discards religion for humanism. Humanism, however, is only the *shadow* of spiritual truth, beneficial to modern man but incapable of giving him the strength and inspiration he so desperately seeks. The opposite trend in religious upbringing insists on the vital significance of rigid doctrine. If the mind rebels, silence it! There are enough matters of secular importance where it may find its task and satisfaction.

However, both trends are heedless of the fact that religion can fulfill its mission only when it becomes the prime mover of heart and mind alike. If it is permitted to pervade only one part of the human soul, it is likely to form powerful undercurrents, which must eventually emerge as fanaticism and pseudo-religion. For man's need for spiritual security, although less conscious, is as great today as it was in the Middle Ages. Consciously he may scoff at it, subconsciously he longs for it with all his heart.

In the Middle Ages, when the human soul was almost entirely sustained by the forces of feeling, intellect was of minor importance. The vast majority of men never doubted the existence of God, and regarded intelligence merely as a tool to be used in His service. But now when intellect has become a full partner in man's inner and outer life, religion can fulfill its mission only if it is capable of satisfying the mind as well as the heart. Since it has failed to do so, a split has opened in the human soul which is one of the major causes for the paralysis of modern spiritual life.

Modern psychology, possibly with the exception of Jung's, has not fully appreciated this fact, owing to its preoccupation with sexual conflicts. Volume upon volume has been filled with theories, diagnostic details, and alleged causes of various diseases. Yet, however sincere our sympathy for the man who lives in frustration and turmoil because as a child he was not permitted to kill his father and possess his mother, we cannot help wondering how mankind could have managed so well before Freud discovered his "Oedipus Complex." Previous generations seem not to have been as neurotic as ours, even though widespread psychological crises did occur, affecting the individual as well as whole civilizations. In any case, these crucial periods could not threaten the survival of mankind, as do our own, for the world was not so intricately interwoven as it is today. If one civilization sickened, there was always another, young and healthy enough to replace it.

Those earlier crises had at least one important factor in common with our present one, in that they developed when the religious ideal characteristic for a specific type of civilization had lost its hold on the hearts of the people. In our age, too, unfulfilled religious longing has played a major part in the emergence of national catastrophes. Fascism and nazism displayed their mysticism openly, using it as the most effective weapon on their rapid march to power. Not until they had reached political control did their real difficulties begin, for only the unfulfilled goal could keep alive the mystical longing in the hearts of their followers. Therefore, these false prophets could not stop, but had to create ever new aims; eventually they evoked ancient barbaric rites of blood sacrifice, which led to torture chambers, to war, and finally, to the twilight of their gods. Naturally, there were social, political, and economic motives too, but we must not forget that the success or failure of revolutions has always depended on the idealist, the mystic who for himself demands nothing but ecstasy.

In Russia conditions were more complicated. The end of the old regime was long overdue, and the lost war simply swept away a culture that had outlived itself. The Russians, probably the most religious and mystically inclined people in the world, had grown deeply despondent when in the last century they saw their beloved Church degenerate, and turn more and more into a political instrument. Russian folklore, music, and philosophy reflected the profound melancholy pervading a people who had been disillusioned in their most fervent longing. Thus it was easy for the intellectuals to stir the masses to action. But the revolution, after effecting certain political and economic changes, would have faded had it not been for a handful of determined men who had found the key to real power, and used it ruthlessly.

Materialism in itself with all its intellectual doctrines lacks the power to stir man's imagination. Nor can it generate vital energies on its own. Yet it does something else: it makes man doubt the reality of his spiritual ideals, and thus cuts off his soul forces from their legitimate aims. Those pent-up energies when denied their proper outlet soon break the restricting walls of a merely materialistic existence and create explosions that sweep away new and old systems alike. The Bolsheviks, regardless of the ruthlessness of their methods, could never have conquered the country had not, at the beginning at least, a vast number of their countrymen given them support. Lenin and Stalin—unlike their predecessors, the Socialists and Mensheviks—were not naïve materialists. At their command was an intricate knowledge of human nature, which they put relentlessly to use. Only too well did they know that the average Russian needs religion more than he needs his daily bread. Through exploitation of the shortcomings of the Church, materialistic propaganda, and falsification of scientific facts, many Russians could be made to forsake their God, but never their mystical longings. Stalin, the son of a deeply devout mother, and himself a one-time pupil in a theological seminary, resembled the high priest of a pagan cult rather than the head of a modern state. More than this, he eventually assumed prerogatives which shocked the free world but inspired those who craved to serve a god on earth.

In decadent creeds there had been gods demanding human sacrifices, a barbaric rite strangely fascinating not only to their followers but to their victims as well. The Supreme Soviet hierarchy demanded of its worshipers body and soul; it repaid them with the promise of a future heaven on earth in whose wonders they could never hope to share. It openly declared as truth what was publicly known to be false, and then reversed its decision at will. Whenever a dogma was nonchalantly dropped, after many had been imprisoned and killed for doubting its truth, to be replaced by another which heretofore had been heresy, the Western world hoped for an awakening of the masses. Yet, contrary to all expectations, these actions strengthened the Stalinist regime. For who but a god could make and unmake truth? Speaking of different stages of Stalinist developments Charles W. Lowry says:

The first was the virtual deification of Stalin in his own lifetime and the elaboration of a definite cult for his worship and praise. This may have been a deliberate design for holding the miserable masses by drawing toward the living leader the unchanged religious ardor of the Russian soul.[2]

The Bolshevik fanatic worshiped his idol as the pagan priest of a decadent creed worshiped his god-king. This half-divine, half-sacrificial being was credited with supernatural power but eventually sacrificed to bring victory and riches to the tribe. One or the other of his modern counterparts escaped violent death behind impregnable walls of a self-imposed prison and remained "divine." Mere flattery cannot account for these words as they appeared in *Pravda,* in 1936:

O great Stalin, O leader of the peoples,
Thou who broughtest man to birth,
Thou who purifiest the earth,
Thou who restorest the centuries,
Thou who makest bloom the Spring,
Thou who makest vibrate the musical chords.[3]

Could any man not affiliated with perverted mysticism tolerate such deification? But most of the misled idealists of Stalin's era never reached a position of power at all. They toiled like slaves for a utopic goal, fully aware that life was likely to end in a trial in which they might have to act as their own accusers.

And still they kept coming, mystics serving an earth-bound cult. Stalin's heirs are of a different breed. They are cold, calculating men, who want to convert communism from its present pseudo-religious state into a sober political institution. Let us hope they will succeed; for if they should, communism must eventually lose its mystical hold on the Russian soul.

None of the powerful political movements of our era were born in the hearts of the masses. They arose in the souls of small groups of individuals, individuals whose minds rejected spiritual concepts of traditional religion but whose hearts were full of mystical longing. The result of such inner conflict is by necessity some form of illness. The masses in their subconscious hunger for the spiritual merely followed the individual fanatic as they would have followed a truly great leader. Thus the problems of our time cannot be solved by political, economic, or social reforms alone: they are deeply rooted in the unfulfilled and often hidden longings of the human soul.

CHAPTER III

THE THREE DIMENSIONS OF REALITY

The plight of modern man, torn between materialistic thought habits and an innate spiritual longing, is at last finding growing recognition in sermons, appeals, and publications. Many eminent personalities, such as Toynbee, Myers, and Du Noüy have devoted their lives to proving that science and religion need not contradict each other. Much has been achieved, and yet the general trend toward materialism, with all its dire consequences, is still gaining, and drawing additional strength from many and varied sources. There are powerful political interests determined to further their own objectives by making use of man's unfulfilled spiritual longing; there are well-intended but confusing philosophical doctrines hiding errors in logic behind a screen of unintelligible terms; and there is the deep-rooted intellectual conceit in the minds of the too highly specialized. But the greatest obstacle blocking the way to inner security is man's ignorance of basic psychological principles which could serve as keys to the crucial problems of humanity.

Without such keys the countless well-meant efforts to bring man back to a more spiritual understanding of life are of theoretical rather than of practical value; for they are likely to show the goal without pointing out the path which leads to it.

Current religious endeavors can be roughly divided into two categories. They work predominantly either on man's emotions or on his intellect.

The emotional approach finds its expression in revival movements as well as in many sermons and admonitions. Yet exhortations "to be more spiritual" somewhat resemble a doctor's advice to his patient to hurry up and get well. If the doctor has made the correct diagnosis and selected the right remedies, such an appeal may be very helpful; if not, it can bring only temporary relief, often followed by frustration and despair. Sermons and exhortations are of great value to those who seek them; they can do little for the growing number of people who accept guidance only from the intellect. Nor can they really heal the ever-widening rift between faith and reason, a rift which threatens even the deeply religious.

Although in the free world a resurgent interest in religion and an unprecedented rise in the membership of churches exist, we must not forget that religion today is still confined to the realm of emotions and has little influence on the trend of materialistic thinking and the conduct of everyday life. If someone were tactless enough to stand up in church to protest the unscientific attitude of the Bible with its references to angels, visions, and supernatural interferences, a storm of indignation would arise and put the offender in his place. But what would happen if on an ordinary weekday a faithful parishioner were confronted by a stranger who believed without question in the existence of angels, archangels, and supernatural events? Would he not consider the man feeble-minded, to say the least? Yet such an attitude reduces his Sunday consciousness to the level of hypocrisy or superstition, and thus widens the split in the subconscious reaches of his own mind.

On the other hand, intellectual efforts to reconcile modern thought habits with religion vary greatly in usefulness and understanding. Some of them are rather naïve, some highly scientific and elaborate, but almost all try to subordinate spiritual concepts to the dictates of present-day thinking, and to fit them into the scope of an intellectual world picture.

True, modern man has reached a state of evolution in which the voice of faith must be corroborated by reason, but this cannot be attained by despiritualization of the spirit; nor can it be achieved by setting up our limited intelligence as the final measure of truth. Unfortunately, this is exactly what so many intellectual religionists try to do. Even theologians, professing deepest reverence for the spiritual giants of the past, unwittingly reduce them to the level of charlatans by implying that they used medical or other scientific means to trick their less educated fellow men into believing in miracles. It is ironical that the same type of materialistic reasoning, so strongly opposed to the acceptance of ancient miracles, seems only too ready to expect divine influence on modern man's material life. There are reports of businessmen who expect greater prosperity to result from the practice of taking Bibles to their offices, and similar reports of executives gathering for weekly meetings, under a clergyman's guidance, to pray for good business. Steps of this sort are frequently hailed as indications of a religious renaissance but, in our opinion, it would be better to reject religion entirely than to make it a servant of egotistic aims. Surely subservient and diluted spirit is not spirit at all; it is a slow-acting but deadly poison. And the use of spiritual forces for selfish reasons may prove an extremely poor investment in the end.

Many otherwise highly intelligent personalities have shown themselves more inclined to reduce religion to the level of our present-day intellect rather than to make an all-out effort to raise the standard of thinking to the heights of spiritual reality. Yet it is helpful to know that a growing number of truly great scientists find nothing in modern science which contradicts their own religious convictions. "To pursue science is not to disparage the things of the spirit. In fact, to pursue science rightly is to furnish a framework on which the spirit may rise."[1]

Science of history is founded on acceptance of the records of various original sources so far as these recorded events can be verified by traceable effects on the evolution of consciousness. It is scarcely honest to accept historical evidence only as far as it confirms one's own predilections and, regardless of our intentions, the practical results of such inconsistency have proved disastrous to modern education. This is not surprising; for if we imply that metaphysical traditions are merely a residue of an ignorant past and permit the average man to take on the responsibility of modifying or rejecting some or all of them, he will hardly refrain from censoring God Himself. Remodeled and reshaped, even God will become man's creation rather than his creator: a deity habitually in accord with oneself and one's own views, but a stern judge of others. The Nazi philosophy with its concept of a deity favoring the physically strong is just one example of the dangerous potentialities of this approach to truth.

The dilemma which confronts us is not easily solved. For if we accept all religious tradition as unalterable truth, we may discover in our soul an unbridgeable chasm between faith and reason. If we admit that part or all of such tradition is untenable in the light of modern knowledge, we destroy the very foundation of a building whose erection has taken millenniums of labor and suffering. Should this building fall, all that is left of inner security will fall too, and man's inherent longing for the spirit will flow into entirely subjective channels. Then the gates will be opened even wider to the victory of half-mystical, half-political ideologies whose triumph might seal the fate of man.

Yet the dilemma can be solved. Its clue lies in a quest for truth that may and must be undertaken by every man. It lies in thought. Unquestionably there must be leaders, men who have the time and the ability to prepare the ground for an edifice of thought accessible not only to professional philosophers but to all who are endowed with common sense. But these leaders should not be accepted on authority alone, nor by virtue of an awe-inspiring, unintelligible language. What we need today is a common-sense philosophy accessible to all who search for truth.

In earlier periods of civilization the attitude of intelligent people toward their great philosophers and prophets was subtly but significantly different from ours. They knew better than we that even the most profound words of wisdom are but inadequate symbols. Differences in doctrines seemed as natural to them as various images of the same object, seen through different mediums. If the system and the teachings of a philosopher made a particular appeal to a man, he was more than willing to cross half the known world to become his pupil; seeking not infallible answers, but help in attaining a greater capacity for cognition.

Today we are still willing to accept ideologies, provided their phraseology is complicated enough to give us a valid excuse for not reading them, their conclusions simplified enough to be learned without effort, and their truth guaranteed by the social or academic position of their authors. We are inclined to forget that it is the struggle for knowledge, rather than knowledge itself, which gives wisdom. Modern man, in fact, does not like to think; he prefers to pay others to do his thinking for him. Overly impressed by the importance of material objects, he does not really consider the world of ideas essential for his well-being on earth.

Yet there he is mistaken. Ideas *do* exert a tremendous influence on our lives; even in world politics their power is greater than force of arms or economic strength. During the critical periods of the past, Americans have often blamed themselves for military unpreparedness and lack of political vigilance, but they could have traced their real failure to an almost contemptuous attitude toward ideas, and to an unwillingness to formulate for their own benefit and for the good of the world the basic principles of an American philosophy. Removal of trade barriers, political leadership, and, at times, even military interference by the world's greatest nation are necessary. Still all material help is deeply resented as an offense against human dignity unless it is matched by spiritual contributions; and so far our spiritual gifts to a world starving for ideals have been meager indeed. The public is so disinterested in ideas and diffident as to their significance that it has become possible for a handful of men to label as "American" those concepts which are diametrically opposed to all this nation stands for. While Americans have proved time and again that they would not only spend their wealth lavishly, but fight and die for the sake of ideas, their spokesmen have convinced the world that this nation believes in nothing but material values.

And still we neither can nor should silence our philosophers. We cannot even blame them for obvious mistakes, for all human beings err; it is we ourselves, the average citizens, who are not truly awake. For the time is long past when the public could leave the quest for truth to a few seekers. Half the world's population has already lost its freedom, owing to such mental apathy: Hitler rose to power, and communism gained sway over hundreds of millions, not on the strength of superior weapons but on that of blindly accepted doctrines. The fate of democracy itself hinges on the independent thinking of the greatest possible number of individuals.

True, there are many intelligent people who have fully realized the significance of ideas, but they are in the minority. While some do not feel competent to struggle with the complicated terms and the bizarre ways of philosophy, others are too deeply impressed by the undeniable achievements of great personalities to weigh and evaluate their opinions. Here much harm has been done, for greatness in itself is not proof against error.

Regardless of whether a man is great or not, whether he is liked or disliked, and regardless of the quality of his achievements, his ideas must be accepted or rejected solely on the strength of their own merits. A human being who refuses to assume full responsibility for his own independent judgment in dealing with ideas is actually destroying the groundwork of his freedom. Purely emotional acceptance or rejection of any ideology, even one of apparently little significance, weakens the power of discrimination and makes the individual an easy victim of political dialectics.

By way of example, let us consider the champion of progressive education. We know that John Dewey liberated pedagogy from its lingering medieval confinements and brought joy and light into stuffy schoolrooms. It was primarily he and his pupils who freed the artistic abilities of the child, and opened the eyes of many a teacher to dormant talents that might have been doomed by abstract educational methods. Yet, while this modern method of education has given freedom of expression to the small child, its philosophy has weakened the very foundation of freedom for the adult. For if we accept the views of

John Dewey, who states that "habits . . . are the sole agents of observation, recollection, foresight, and judgment, and that a mind or consciousness or soul in general which performs these operations is a myth,"[2] we may as well abandon all belief in man's capacity for freedom.

None can doubt that attainment of good habits is highly beneficial to any form of community life; but even the best of habits are no more than casts into which man's will may flow. Essentially rigid, and truly useful only as props for the routine affairs of social life, they must be overcome—regardless of whether they are good or bad—whenever an act of freedom is required. Beings actually governed by habits could no more conceive of freedom than could robots.

Freedom is lost not by political upheaval but by uncritical acceptance of prefabricated concepts which paralyze individual thinking and thus prepare the way for dictators. The citizen of the still free world is dimly aware of such danger and mistrusts ideas altogether. Furthermore, he has all but stopped reading, and thus remains blissfully unconcerned with the quickly changing philosophic trends of his time. He is unaware that every single ideology, known or unknown to him, is capable of exerting a subtle but decisive influence on his personal life; and he does not realize that, in today's crucial struggle between freedom and slavery, every individual must take an active part in shaping a world concept for his age.

Failing in this participation, he will eventually become no more than a puppet, controlled by a small group of puppeteers. Lack of initiative in thinking creates a mental vacuum into which alien concepts flow unchallenged. In newspapers, radio, television, movies, and popular-science magazines, our time has countless channels through which such concepts can enter a person's subconscious mind, evading his mental defenses; thus thought habits could indeed become "the sole agents of foresight and judgment," and thereby replace man's ego in the shaping of his destiny.

Whether the concepts determining our cultural life are correct or not is scarcely the point; for, right or wrong, such views are manifestations of someone's longing for truth or enmity against it. What matters is the manner in which they are absorbed. Every piece of information we receive, be it factual or conceptual, is but a challenge to our innate sense of truth. This sense may be warped, but can, if persistently excercised, become a reliable means of experiencing reality.

Yet, does reality exist at all, and if so, is it accessible to the human mind? As we all know, a battle has been raging on this issue with devastating results on the ideological, political, and psychological life of the last centuries. But to us such a philosophical conflict appears as futile as the "Schoolman's" famous dispute on how many angels find room on a needle's point. Since an angel is by definition a supernatural being and a needle a material object, it is hard for modern men to understand how it was possible for brilliant minds to waste their intelligence on such an illogical question. But our own philosophical squabbles on truth and reality are no less foolish, for they try to prove or disprove intellectually what is accessible only to intuitive perception. Such perception has always existed in man, and is responsible for all his great religions and ideas. Today it has grown faint and needs training if it is to fulfill its all-important mission in human existence.

Such training, however, can be successful only if based on a threefold quest: the quest for self-knowledge, for scientific penetration of the outer, and for intuitive insight into the inner world. "Know thyself" was the inscription over the portals of ancient temples. The world of the spirit was a perceptible reality not only to the seers and prophets of old, but also to the greatest philosophers of all times. Thales, Plato, Aristotle, Hippocrates, Plotinus, Thomas Aquinas, Jacob Boehme, and Johannes Kepler are only a few of the many who never doubted that man is a spiritual being and that a world of intangible realities exists which, however elusive, has never been entirely inaccessible.

Yet our ancestors, though far more interested in the supersensible than we are today, rarely denied the realities present in the world of the senses, to which the human organism belongs. Even Plato, the greatest idealist, who saw ultimate truth only in the world of ideas, did not minimize the significance of earthly life. To him, the world of matter was the reflection of a higher truth; although inferior to it, it was nonetheless patterned according to the eternal laws of the intangible. This Platonic philosophy has no intrinsic similarity to later forms of idealism denying the very existence of an external world (acosmism or immaterialism) which weakened man's hold on the physical reality without stemming the tide of materialism.

It is true that the sources of modern skepticism and philosophical defeatism can be traced far back in history, even to the fifth and fourth centuries B.C., but they must not be sought in the systems of the great masters of philosophy. Trends of this kind were usually born in schools not too much concerned with the search for truth, but devoted to ulterior motives— such as the Sophists' desire to train young people for fast and easy political careers.

In his search for truth, ancient man did not have the problems of our day. Although we may deem his intellectual outlook on life less advanced than ours, we must remember that at least he knew his spiritual origin to be divine rather than biological. This knowledge has faded from consciousness during the course of history. Modern man, while discovering the secrets of his own physical organism—as well as that of the world—has almost lost himself. Today he has awakened to his plight; and all the conceit and self-assurance of the last century have given way to fear.

How can he rediscover himself without losing the fruits of intellectual evolution? By starting his search at the only solid base available to him: at his own nature as it manifests itself in the routine conduct of ordinary life.

What are the basic principles on which life is carried on? One is an unquestioning belief in the existence of physical realities. The food we eat and the money we earn are real to us, as are our physical gains and deprivations. We may find a second principle in our trust in the existence of intangible realities: love, friendship, loyalty, even hatred and lust for power. And the third basic principle in life is our self- or ego-consciousness. Even the philosopher-to-be starts in the second or third year of his life to refer to himself by the unique term, "I," and from then on remains aware of his selfhood.

Any form of philosophic speculation denying the reality-in-principle of any of these three points of psychological orientation does not understand earthly man as he is and acts, but refers to a being of an abnormal mentality. Such speculations, influencing modern thought habits, undermine even further the already badly shaken balance of the human mind.

Let us consider a few examples of that conflict between the demands of daily life and the powerful philosophic undercurrents which influence our thinking.

We all agree that our time calls for the development of strong, self-assured individualities—of people who can judge and act for themselves, as well as defend themselves against mental and moral hazards. In a time when mental illnesses have reached an unprecedented peak, when the disintegration of personality, obsessions, amnesia, and unmotivated, compulsive acts have become daily occurrences, man's discovery of himself as an individual spiritual entity should be more than ever the goal of mental hygiene and education. Here, indeed, lies the only protection against the mental and moral dissolution brought home to us day after day in the never-ending reports of crimes, increasing alcoholism, and drug addiction. Yet our present educational system, challenged as it is by an ominous increase in juvenile delinquency and youthful schizophrenia, is inclined to undermine rather than to strengthen the human self. It still holds, if no longer to the methods, so at least to the ideology of a system which has unwittingly undermined the very foundation for spiritual self-affirmation. John Dewey, referring to the basic functions of human psychological behavior, writes: "The doctrine of a single, simple, and dissoluble soul was the cause and the effect of failure to recognize that concrete habits are the means of knowledge and thought."[3]

Then there is the problem presented by intangible realities. Politically, we are pledged to defend our freedom at any price, even at the risk of total destruction; but, while we are raising a generation which may have to sacrifice its physical existence for the sake of an idea, we are turning our whole civilization into a cult of material values.

Paradoxically, this cult does not prevent us from doubting the very reality of our sensual world. Whether or not the well-known reasons for such doubts are valid, will be discussed later. From the viewpoint of practical psychology such ideologies as post-Kantian idealism, acosmism, immaterialism, et cetera, are extremely harmful since, unobserved and unchallenged by individual consciousness, they have penetrated into present-day intellectual life to add further to modern man's growing sense of bewilderment. Living in a world of movies, television, advertisements, and propaganda, all designed to "make-believe," he has come dangerously close to losing all ability to distinguish between fact and illusion. And unless modern youth is given the strong conviction that there are basic realities in the physical world, as there are in the world of ideas and in the human self, the trend toward instability will grow still further.

Some optimists feel that no great harm can come from such doctrines which, while denying reality in one sphere, stress its existence in another and thus balance their ultimate effect on human psychology. Unfortunately, this is not so; for it is much easier to destroy convictions than to create them. Moreover, in all radical doctrines there is one common factor capable of a cumulative effect on human thought life, and that is doubt. Whether such skepticism concerns the physical world or the reality of ideas is of less importance than the spreading conviction that nothing is real except the satisfaction of personal desires. For example, pure idealism did nothing to stem the tide of materialism: it helped only to liberate modern man from his sense of moral responsibility to his physical surroundings. Craving for power and sensual enjoyments is not diminished by a denial of physical realities, but the feeling of responsibility toward one's fellow creature definitely is.

Man is a spiritual as well as a physical being. He lives in a world of ideas and in a world of tangible objects. If he loses confidence in the reality of one of them, he automatically destroys the validity of the other. What remains is chaos.

The purpose of this study is not to evaluate individual

philosophical systems but to search everywhere for the fragments of truth which are dispersed all through the various doctrines. There seems to be a strong urge to separate such fragments from the whole, to appropriate them, and build around them edifices of speculation that serve self-glory and the establishment of ideological factions. Any attempt to collect those dispersed building-stones for the eventual erection of an edifice of truth faces not only opposition from ideological fanatics, but also the frustrating influence of speculative skepticism which poses as the voice of science. Too many of our modern skeptics not only know little of modern science, but are prone to neglect the primary rules of logic whenever these interfere with their own inclinations.

True, an absolute proof for the existence of any reality is impossible. Yet so is proof for the very existence of human consciousness, without which man could not reason at all. Lacking consciousness, no human being can either prove or disprove anything whatever; and still—

Consciousness cannot be defined; we may be ourselves fully aware what consciousness is, but we cannot, without confusion, convey to others a definition of what we ourselves clearly apprehend. The reason is plain. Consciousness lies at the root of all knowledge. Consciousness is itself the one highest source of all comprehensibility and illustration![4]

There are some fundamentals in human psychology which must be accepted as archphenomena, subject neither to proof nor disproof. Just as it is impossible for a photoelectric cell to disprove the reality of the light whose presence or absence it registers, so is it logically untenable for the human mind to *deny the laws under which it operates*. As human beings we are endowed with certain primary gifts which are our only available tools for cognition. We cannot make use of them for the purpose of denying their existence. In doing so we would unwittingly destroy the postulates necessary to reach a logically valid conclusion. Any human being making a statement proves by his very action his belief in reality. For if he

were actually convinced of the nonexistence of reality, why
would he state his views which, according to his own reasoning,
could hold no truth? The materialist who preaches the nonexistence of absolute truth and of God, seems unaware of the
fact that in so doing he himself is making metaphysical statements which he, too, considers as absolute truth. Only the person who has never expressed an opinion at all may be an honest
skeptic. Unfortunately, we are in no position to know his views.

To protect the sanity of his generation and to assert his own
freedom of thought, the average individual must become capable of defending the principles of common sense against ideological indoctrination. Common sense cannot survive, however,
unless the individual can maintain the fundamentals of mental
existence: trust in inner and outer realities, and in his own
self. For what holds true in the actual conduct of everyday life
must be reflected in the philosophical outlook of man; otherwise the already existing rift in the human soul will be widened.

In personal life, sincere doubts regarding the existence of
reality constitute a symptom of mental illness. A person losing
the conviction of his own self-existence is as ill as the patient
to whom objects of the outer world appear unreal. In political
life, doubts concerning the existence of absolute realities are
conducive to the introduction of "subjective science" on the
one hand, and to interference with religious freedom on the
other. The political history of nazism and communism should
at least convince the world of the powerful effects that philosophical ideologies may exert on the lives and liberties of
millions.

As was said before, many people may never have heard of
philosophical systems which deny the existence of objective
reality in the world of the senses or in the world of intuition.
Nevertheless, philosophical skepticism has penetrated through
countless channels into the conscious and subconscious minds of
all. We have also mentioned the paralyzing effect which philosophical indoctrination has on the development of free thinking. Its effect is even worse when a whole generation is brought
up in a pedagogical system whose underlying philosophy denies

the existence of metaphysical reality. For here not only freedom of thought is endangered, but also freedom of moral decision.

In any serious moral conflict the voice of our intangible conscience is hard put to overcome the vivid sensations of aroused emotions. Unless education succeeds in implanting into the child a deep respect for, and an acute awareness of, spiritual reality, the scales will automatically tip in favor of desire, hate, lust for revenge, or other forms of immoral satisfaction. Even if the fear of reprisal or punishment should suffice to prevent action of a criminal nature, such restraint in behavior would not represent a moral achievement.

If morality is nothing but "an endeavor to find for the manifestation of impulse in special situations an office of refreshment and renewal,"[5] why should not crime be committed when the result appears more refreshing to the criminally inclined? In his *Psychology* John Dewey writes:

He [man] will have himself good. The reason that he will is, that he will. Only the ideal of himself as good will satisfy him. If we ask why this ideal alone is satisfactory, we can get no other answer than this: he wills to be satisfied in that, and in that alone. It is willed because it is satisfactory because it is willed as that the man would be.[6]

This rather involved statement leaves no room for moral choice since it degrades morality into a quest for satisfaction not much different from an animal's search for its appropriate food. Moreover, since some obviously find satisfaction in evil, such a concept would divide men into different species, some of them harmless—or good, if we chose to call them so—others ferocious. Nor is it likely that habits could actually change "bad" people into "good" ones, since centuries of civilization, not to mention decades of "progressive" education, have failed to check the increase in criminal trends.

Only when we stop speculating and simply observe the archphenomena of our own psychological attitude toward life can we see that every single one of our mental activities depends on unquestioning acceptance of three categories of reality: one material, the second intangible, and the third which is part of both and a bridge between them.

For centuries philosophical arguments have raged over the nature of man's consciousness: whether it depends on sense perception in its relation to the outer world, or consists of man's awareness of his selfhood and the world of ideas. Monism and dualism have been the battle cries of whole generations, and their conflict has had tremendous effects on the history of culture and on the evolution of science. Yet the chasm between them, now possibly wider than ever, is not due to an actual incompatibility between two opposing realities, but to man's tedious habit of drawing party lines where they are least appropriate—in the sphere of cognition.

Leaving aside all the countless forms and aspects of those two conflicting world concepts, and turning only toward what is experienced, we must admit that at the first glance man appears as a twofold being. His body consists of matter; his primitive instincts are animal-like, and his very existence depends on the same natural factors which sustain the life of other creatures. Thus he unquestionably belongs to a world ruled by the laws of matter and of biological processes.

Man is also a spiritual being. His thoughts may depend for their manifestation on the structure of his brain, but neither their origin nor their contents lies in the realm of matter or physical energy. Still, however intangible they may be, thoughts are realities. Often defying biological purposes, they can cause man to sacrifice his life, the life of his offspring, and even the life of his whole race, for the sake of ideas.

So long as only these two aspects of human nature are considered, a dualistic world concept is prone to emerge. However, the dualist makes the mistake of disregarding his own selfhood which closes the gap between the world of senses and the world of ideas, the realm of biology and the realm of the spirit. He fails to see that man's ego, his unique capacity for merging physical and spiritual consciousness into the oneness of self-awareness, closes the apparent rift of dualism and confirms the world concept of monism, which believes in only one fundamental reality. And yet a human being cannot comprehend himself and his greatest gift, freedom, unless he learns to contemplate the oneness of creation in its various aspects, which in man are threefold.

Actually, the history of human consciousness could be rewritten from the viewpoint of man's attitude toward the three aspects of reality—the intuitive, the sensual, and the bridge between them: his ego. During the classical eras of some nations, especially of ancient Greece, there were great personalities, the artists among them in particular, who knew that human culture must rest on these three facets of reality, which find their expression in religion, science, and individual freedom. What they built survived the ages and added lasting values to the spiraling course of historical evolution. Yet the classical periods were short-lived and not really rooted in the consciousness of the masses. Thus every historic epoch labored to build the edifice of its culture on one single aspect of human nature, while neglecting the others. No wonder that none of them could withstand the tempests of history for long. Necessary as it was for civilizations to die, the fruits of their labors could have survived better and their foundations been firmer.

But as it was, cultures predominantly rooted in mysticism paid scant attention to the physical needs of men, and fell into fanaticism and unworldliness.

Eras like ours, preoccupied with materialistic science, inevitably misdirect man's unfulfilled longings into pseudo-religious ideologies, powerful enough to threaten civilization as a whole.

Civilizations overemphasizing individualism only too often neglect spiritual aims and physical realities, and consequently become easy victims to self-worshiping tyrants. Only when man will learn to be less one-sided, and to build his life and that of his nation on the principles of individualism, spiritual values, and physical realism alike, will the edifice of human culture grow until it spans the world.

To our mystically inclined ancestors the world was important chiefly insofar as it furthered man's spiritual life. Now the scales have tipped toward the other extreme. Religion has become merely the more or less valued servant of material existence; and art, once the sacred messenger from superhuman realms, is seldom more than exhibitionism.

This shift of values, at first almost imperceptible, became obvious in the late Middle Ages, when vigorous efforts were made to check its progress. Exhortations were followed by attempts at persuasion by fire and sword. Both methods met with failure, for unknowingly the defenders of an antimaterialistic consciousness were as much affected by creeping materialism as were their foes, the protagonists of a more earth-bound trend. How else could they have conceived of halting a universal change of consciousness by threat of physical punishment?

In retrospect, the emergence of a materialistic era seems to have been inevitable, and thus a part of human destiny. And since materialism affected the vast majority of men, involving even those who hated and feared it, it would be more realistic to study its meaning than to condemn it as the cause of all our troubles. But this discussion must be left to a later chapter.

The historical change in consciousness manifested itself mainly in man's growing interest in the world of the senses. This interest could be satisfied only by a widening of the sphere of sense perception with the help of instruments, and by intensification of the type of thinking best suited to interpret the results of physical research, which is intellectual analysis. Such thinking is concerned for the most part with the analysis and classification of observed facts, together with investigation into the laws and processes that connect one natural phenomenon with another. Once these factors have become known, they can be reshuffled to bring about changes in natural objects and processes to suit man's needs. This activity, in the last analysis, is technical science.

The tremendous influence of analytical intellect on practically all classes of the world's population marked a new state of historical evolution, and enhanced man's opportunities for technical progress. This progress, however, has exacted a steep price, since it had to be won at the expense of important faculties of intuition.

If the average denizen of the twentieth century were for once to interrupt his ceaseless activities to take a close look at his mental life, he would find it almost entirely occupied with the digesting of sense perceptions. To keep his mind well supplied with stimulating impressions, modern man pursues them during every waking hour of his life. His restlessness is not due to overwhelming will forces which find their expression in physical activity—a view held by many pragmatists— but to his mind's craving for stimulation. If the pragmatists' "universal will of nature" actually found its true expression in an irresistible urge to ceaseless activity, how could we explain the well-established practice of sitting motionless for hours in front of television sets and movie screens? Apparently it is not the need for activity as such, either physical or psychological, that determines man's fundamental behavior, but his need to maintain consciousness. For our generation is in mortal danger of losing the faculty of stimulating consciousness from *within*. It takes very little self-investigation to discover that today's ceaseless striving for sensory stimulation is motivated less by a positive longing for happiness than by subconscious fear of mental collapse. The foreboding symptoms of such crises— boredom, depression, and anxiety, setting in as soon as outer stimulation ceases—indicate the barrenness which prevails in whole areas of our soul life.

It has not always been so. Our ancestors were more capable than we of drawing strength from within, and were less dependent on persistent stimulation from without. We must remember that, even in regard to external achievements, the truly great feats of culture owe their origin to man's intuitive-creative activities, rather than to his intellectual experiments. Many inventions which have actually made life happier and more worthwhile, rather than longer and emptier, can be traced back to a more intuitive era. Whether we look at the great art of the past or only at the simple household implements of medieval craftsmanship, we shall detect in all of them the unmistakable signs of true creativeness.

Should we need further proof of the great difference between our own consciousness and that of our forefathers, we shall find abundant examples in literature through the ages. One, chosen at random, may suffice. Gregory of Nyssa (331–396 A.D.) writes of his countrymen:

In all places, clothes merchants, money changers, and grocers alike argue unknowable questions. If you ask a man how many obols you owe him, he expresses his ideas about the begotten and unbegotten. If I inquire the price of bread, the baker answers that the Father is greater than the Son. If you try to find out whether your bath is ready, you are told that the Son was made out of nothing.[7]

If we call the sum total of sense impressions perceived by man his "outer or sensual experience," we may call all that has no tangible source "inner or intuitive experience." As we have said before, the type of thinking best suited to deal with the world of senses is analytical intellect. The spiritual activity connected with inner experience may be called "intuition."

The concept of "selfhood," for instance, can never be reached by means of intellect alone and is, therefore, frowned upon by modern psychology. And, indeed, where do the borders of our self lie? In our body? Hardly, for many parts of it can be destroyed or surgically removed without noticeably affecting our self-consciousness. In the mind? What happens, then, to the continuity of our self in sleep? What of our subconscious mind? Intellectually, these questions are unsolvable. Nevertheless, selfhood exists. In his second or third year, every sane child undergoes an inner experience of utmost significance, an experience which radically changes his mental life. From that moment on he ceases to refer to himself in the third person and conceives of "I." Some endowed with an unusual memory will recall this event later and will consequently not easily be swayed by philosophers and psychologists who deny the reality of selfhood. But they who do not remember the critical moment of selfhood-awakening should keep in mind that the test of a theory lies in its application.

Let those who disbelieve in the integrality of the human ego apply their skepticism to themselves, and observe its effects on their own mental life! Our institutions are filled with the unfortunates who for physical and psychological reasons have lost awareness of their integrated self.

Man's awareness of himself as an indivisible entelechy is based on the experience insofar unique as it requires a certain co-operation between an intuitive and a sensual form of cognition.

The Occidental has become so intellectual and extroverted that he is in danger of losing himself to the multiple external phenomena.

The Oriental whose consciousness is still predominantly intuitive, cannot yet see that the emergence of a strong ego, though separating man from union with the divine, marks a new and essential phase on the path of evolution.

All qualitative judgments on right and wrong, good and evil, beauty and ugliness, as well as belief or disbelief in the existence of God, are based on man's conscious or unconscious reliance on intuitive experience as an archphenomenon of his mental life. In short, every single philosophical utterance, including those denying the validity of intangible realities, proves rather than disproves their existence. Other examples of intuitive or inner experience lie in the fields of art and religion. The creative musician often experiences original music without the aid of his physical ear; the painter frequently conceives of a picture before he attempts to put it on canvas; and all creeds in which we profess to believe trace their origin to visions and inspirations, not to sense perception and analytical thinking.

We must not believe that modern man has lost entirely the gift of intuition. It is rather that his interest has become so exclusively focused on the outer world, his mental activities so completely occupied with analytical thinking, that he has lost the full appreciation of intuitive experience. Thus he neglects one of the indispensable principles of his psyche, which must be rebuilt by an acceptance of a world of intangible truth.

On the other hand, such trust in the world of ideas must not lead to the negation of physical reality. Even the "immaterialist" disproves the concepts he professes. Scoffing at the objective validity of sense perceptions, he ignores the fact that the sound of his own words and the letters of his own books themselves depend on sense perceptions and are consequently, according to his own views, unreal. By the very action of uttering opinions, or publishing books, or giving lectures, he proves that he himself does not fully believe in the veracity of his theories. Our conscious life, every moment of it, is an irrefutable testimony of our dependence on realities in the sphere of senses and in the sphere of ideas, and in the integrality of our selfhood. It is not decisive whether our sense perceptions are correct or defective, whether our intuitive experiences are revelations or illusions, whether or not modern psychology doubts the existence of our ego: the confidence that somewhere within the reach of our senses is a world of objective material existence, that somewhere within the reach of our inner groping lies an intangible but real world of truth, and that they are reflected in the mirror of a really existing self, is indispensable to human nature. They are the three dimensions of reality.

TRAINING FOR TRUTH

In ordinary life a question concerning the reality of the physical world or of man's potential ability to perceive it is hardly ever raised. For the industrialist, businessman, scientist, or any other levelheaded realist, only one problem exists in regard to physical reality: how reliable is the *person* charged with its observation and interpretation?

Since our whole civilization is dependent on people who are capable of accurate observation, a great deal of attention has been given to human psychology in regard to accuracy and error. Scientific investigations of this kind are too complex to be discussed here, except for their basic principle. According to this principle, the following three qualities are necessary to make a person a reliable mediator of physical reality: keenness of sense perception, clarity of analytical thinking, and capacity for self-criticism. The last is of great importance, since even the interpretation of a scientific experiment can be tainted by an investigator's hidden prejudices.

Unfortunately, the sober efficiency distinguishing our modern approach to the problem of outer experience is conspicuously missing in our attitude toward the problem of inner experience: of intuition. This lack stems from the present trend to ascribe less reality to the world within than to the world without, and also from the misconception that inner phenomena can be grasped by methods appropriate to natural science. In fact, it is usually the least erudite who is closest to an intuitive understanding of another creature and especially of his fellow man. Only he who has experienced in his own heart the sufferings and joys, the longings and frustrations of another individual, knows that person. And the better he knows him the less will he feel tempted to describe in intellectual terms what can be expressed only through art. On the other hand, a generation such as ours, which has reached a low in human understanding, is most prone to fill libraries with volume upon volume of psychological books. But while intellect can never rule in a world of intuition, it can guide man on his way to it. What, for instance, does the word "intuition" mean? Its root is the Latin *intueri*, which means "to look in." In other words, it denotes a form of perception. As we need physical senses for the observation of the outer world, so must we possess certain faculties for perceiving the world of intangibles within. The composer who conceives of music never heard before must have some sort of capacity for experiencing it. Naturally, he is not hearing physical sounds; he is perceiving, rather, the very essence of music. And yet, although intuition is a process of inner perception, the creative artist is not merely a transmitter of supersensible realities. Brahms said: "But don't make the mistake . . . of thinking that because I attach such importance to inspiration from above, that that is all there is to it. . . . Structure is just as consequential, for without craftsmanship inspiration is a 'mere reed shaken in the wind.' " [1]

In a later chapter we shall discuss the relationship between intuitive perception and creative self, but here we want to stress the all-important fact that there is an inner world accessible to man through nonphysical perception, as there is an outer world manifesting itself to his physical sense organism. We chose the artist as an example, since he is endowed with an acute awareness of inner realities which is now largely lost to the great majority of men.

Goethe, the universal genius, was capable of remaining sufficiently aloof from both inner and outer perception to observe and re-create the messages received from either. It was he who spoke of *anschauende Urteilskraft* when referring to the activities of the spirit as contrasted to the activities of the senses.

Urteilskraft, "the power to judge," obviously refers to an activity of the will, to an effort to interpret correctly, while *anschauend,* "looking on," can indicate only the perception of objective events. Artists of lesser individual strength could be crushed under the impact of their intuitive experiences. This tragic fate befell many a Romanticist, overwhelmed by visions and waking dreams, and subsequently losing their mental balance. What came into the world in this manner is undoubtedly art, but art that borders on insanity, since it threatens to sweep aside the human self.

The great Russian composer Tchaikovsky wrote: "Music is no phantom but a revelation"; and, referring to the act of composing: "One forgets the whole world, becomes almost insane, all shakes and trembles within, there is hardly time to make notes."[2] Even in his childhood a world of unearthly sounds breaks in on him, often waking him from sleep in terror and despair. His teacher Marya Markovna does her best to reassure the crying child but has to admit that she cannot hear the music which to him sounds so real. When only five years old he listens to "sounds no human ear could perceive" and at times "he could hardly bear them, these tunes audible to him alone."[3]

Richard Wagner once said to Humperdinck:

I wish to say that inspiration is a very evasive, a most elusive subject, which is not easily defined . . . and about which we know very little. Few indeed there be who know how to tap the source whence it flows, and this undoubtedly is the reason why there has been so little written about it. . . . I am convinced that there are universal currents of Divine Thought . . . and that anyone who can feel those vibrations is inspired, provided he is conscious of the process and possesses the knowledge and skill to present them . . . be he composer, architect, painter, sculptor, or inventor.[4]

Can we really deny that man possesses an inner organism which perceives the physically imperceptible, just because it cannot be found in autopsies? If so, we shall have to deny our own consciousness as well, since it too will elude the microscopes and test tubes of pathologists.

Naturally, there is no reason to assume that faculties of inner perception are the sole property of the highly artistic. Even a noncreative person who truly loves and appreciates music hears more in a symphony than mere sound. But, by disuse, this inner ability may become dormant or entirely atrophied, as physical vision may be lost during a long confinement to a dark cell. This is exactly what is taking place in our time. Not only religion, but such ideas as freedom, brotherhood, and truth are becoming abstractions, respected shadows of realities we can no longer behold and therefore do not really comprehend. Small wonder then that the foes of freedom and truth dare to call slavery "freedom" and dialectical materialism "truth."

We said earlier that an observer of outer events is the more trustworthy the keener his senses are. But we all know that even a man who starts as a poor observer may be trained to become very reliable in his perceptions and interpretations of outer events. Here again we find a similarity between sensual and intuitive experience which may shed light on some of our problems. An artistic person is born with keen organs of intuitive perception, while the average man may be entirely lacking in them. But, if the latter will diligently expose himself to the influence of great art, he can gradually cultivate an inner sense capable of discerning the inexplicable difference between the work of a genius and the often very pleasing products of mediocrity. Thus, capacity for intuitive perception can be developed to recognize inner realities, as our sense organs can be trained to become dependable messengers of outer events.

Art, however, is neither the sole nor the highest form of intuitive experience. By their tremendous influence on the moral evolution of the world, the prophets and saints who founded the great religious movements have proved the existence of realities surpassing all other known values. These men were endowed with a clarity and an acuteness of inner perception far beyond the faculties of ordinary men. At a time when intuition was more powerful, and considered of more weight than the observation and analysis of outer facts, relatively great numbers of people were able to confirm the important experiences of religious leaders by lesser experiences of their own.

Contemporary literature and the records of early Christianity contain sufficient proof of this.

But when the focus of man's consciousness shifted outward, his intuitive life became neglected, and in consequence religion disappeared as an experience. Transplanted from its native soil of intuition to the alien ground of intellectualism, it soon began to lose its vitality, and could cast but a shadow of its former greatness.

This was not the case in the youth of Christianity. At that time the light of religious experience was still shining so brightly that it outshone the light of the senses. To the early Christian, personal property, power, and ambition seemed unimportant, compared to the realities experienced within. This fact alone explains why the most powerful organization of the time, the Roman Empire, crumbled before those who could neither be tempted by physical rewards nor swayed by threats of torture and death.

But when religion lost its feeding ground in the human soul and, with it, its self-sustaining strength, it began to need external protection from the smallest deviation of thought and word. During several centuries it was this need which brought about the most rigid thought control ever established over human beings. It would be unfair to blame the Church for the means she used to keep Christianity from complete disintegration; for it was man himself, whether he wore the clerical habit, the knightly armor, or the rags of a serf, who desperately tried to preserve the residues of a great past. Not that the Middle Ages were entirely lacking in individuals endowed with inner vision. There were still saints and seers; there were painters who transferred to their canvasses some of the supernal glow of their visions; and there was faith—not the uneasy belief of today, but the vivid memory of revelations.

Yet the change in human consciousness took its course. Immediate knowledge of God turned into creed, and creed into a code of morals. But codes, even the most venerable ones, are unable to meet the longings in the human soul. So it was that mysticism, turning earthward, ultimately came to worship at the altars of Trotsky and Lenin. Will it find a lasting ful-

fillment there? Certainly not, for the dream of a world-wide
brotherhood lies shattered in the blood-drenched streets of
Budapest, and the spirit of self-sacrifice so appealing to Russian
mysticism is bound to lose the very ground for its existence
once the U.S.S.R.'s military security and economic wealth will
be assured.

Thus bolshevism, at least in Russia, may be self-defeating,
since it was founded on a longing which it cannot fulfill. But
what will come after its fall? Possibly there will be an interval
of rejoicing, to be followed by more unrest. For man, especially
Eastern man, will not forgo his quest for God, a quest that
cannot be satisfied by prosperity. If we, the citizens of the
free world, the self-proclaimed champions of spiritual values,
should fail to live what we preach, we may still witness horrors
worse than any the world has known—for mystical longing,
unfulfilled, may turn against life itself. The East expects of us
neither emotional revivalism nor even ideologies, but a formu-
lation that can be taught in schools all over the world. For
the East is at least our equal in the creation of ideals, but
inferior in its capacity to incorporate them into a workable
system of life. Such a system, opposing the Marxistic doctrine,
would have to be based on the nature of man as belonging
not only to the world of matter, but also to the world of the
spirit.

We may scoff at the very concept of spirit, but the fact remains that we cannot do without it; for one pillar of our being
is so firmly anchored in the spiritual that no single process of
human thinking is possible without it. This is a truth which
can be readily demonstrated by countless facts in human psychology, as has been done by Carl Jung and his associates.
Paradoxically, however, modern man, while he proves through
many of his *actions* that he firmly reckons with a world of the
spirit, has come to deny this world by the ways of his *reasoning*.

The Communists, for example, pride themselves on their
materialistic philosophy; but no less a personality than Marshal
Zhukov, then a powerful figure in the Soviet hierarchy, boasted
to President Eisenhower that the Communists had proved far
more idealistic than their Western allies. Did Mr. Zhukov ever

ask himself what an ideal is, if not spirit? True, people may misunderstand or distort ideals, but the mere fact that they are willing to die for them gives the lie to their materialistic claims. For if they truly believed in what they preach, why should they sacrifice their all-important lives for ideals which lose their reality with death?

And what about the Western world with its overemphasis on material values and its love for life? The vast majority of its citizens has accepted and calmly approved the stand of their governments, which hold that total destruction is to be preferred to abandonment of the ideals of religion and freedom. Does this not imply that a spiritual reality exists, independent of man's physical existence? If not, how could the one be weighed against the other?

Man himself is the bridge between two worlds, and would cease to be human if he were anchored in only one of them. His tragedy, however, lies in the fact that his consciousness is not advanced enough to throw light on the whole span of his psychological being.

Today modern consciousness is well founded in the world of intellect and of the senses, but it is fast losing all support on the far side of existence. Sensing the danger but not recognizing its cause, modern man tries frantically to strengthen still further the pylon within his reach. In addition to what our intellectual culture is able to give by itself, many of the values salvaged from religious tradition are being used to fortify the structure of modern society. But the span of a bridge supported from one bank only cannot carry its burden for long. It certainly will not survive the storms of this age unless man succeeds also in fortifying the other pillar, and making it equally secure. How can this be done?

The gradual change in consciousness, the repeatedly mentioned shift in values, appears to have occurred independently of man's own decisions, and must therefore be considered part of an involuntary evolution. The tremendous intuitive capacity of our ancestors, which gave birth to all our religions, arts, and sciences, cannot be attributed to a conscious training on the part of primitive man. It simply existed or developed as a part of human nature. The same holds true of the development of modern intellect. Its attainment was neither willed nor desired by man, at least not consciously. On the contrary, the most powerful institutions of the transition period, church and state, tried vigorously but vainly to stem the tide of intellectual development. It is for this reason that we can call both intuition and intellect the results of involuntary evolution.

Yet the fact that intuition began to wane when intellect started to flourish should not make us believe that the former has irrevocably died in man. If it had, we could not live, fight, and die for ideals which to analytical thinking have lost their reality. Just as a builder may board off an already finished part of a structure so that more energy and strength can flow into the parts still to be erected, the forces of evolution appear to have put to sleep certain primordial faculties of man so that the bright light of consciousness could stream fully into new areas of his unfolding being. But in view of the scientific, military, and social revolutions of this century, we cannot help believing that the phase of involuntary development has now ended, to be succeeded by a new state of conscious evolution, wherein responsibility rests entirely on man himself. The mere fact that the fate of the whole race lies for the first time in his own hands seems to indicate that destiny has abandoned her reins to man. Thus he has come of age, and the task before him is Herculean. To succeed in it he will need command over all the faculties hidden in his being.

The wheel of history cannot be turned back; modern man neither can nor should give up the high degree of analytical intelligence he has gained in the course of centuries, nor need he lose interest in his great achievements in the material world. But he can match these gifts of destiny by a conscious effort to restrengthen his dormant intuitive powers.

Man needs religion, but religion as it is today has neither protected the world's most devout nations from atheism nor stemmed the tide of crimes, insanity, and suicides. The fault lies not with religion itself, but with the sterile soil into which it has been transplanted. Once reset in its own ground, religion could have a tremendous effect on modern man. But neither coercion nor persuasion, nor the stirring of religious hysteria among the masses, will help to achieve this goal. The first step toward a revival of spiritual forces is a clear recognition of their existence and the expansion of scientific thinking to the point where it can comprehend man as a unique being, and not as the product of accidental molecular and biological processes. Only such thinking can successfully foster the development of objective inner perception, to match the outer perception which has received so much scientific training and support.

Let us assume that a student endowed with rather indifferent faculties is to be educated for scientific observation and interpretation of complicated facts. At first he is likely to perceive and register incorrectly a phenomenon which passes before him. It is for this reason that as a rule scientific education requires the student to acquire theoretical knowledge before proceeding to experimentation and observation. Once the process underlying a phenomenon is known to the student, his mind will automatically start to rectify his sense perceptions. Moreover, an instructor will check on his observations and inform him as to whether or not they conform with reality.

We know from experience that such training methods have developed an enhanced degree of dependability in the sense perceptions of a large number of rather ungifted students. This in itself would hardly be worth mentioning, were it not for the fact that, through persistent training of such kind, the student's perceptive organs become capable of conveying increasingly correct messages also on objects and events of which he had no foreknowledge. In other words, training can refashion man's perceptive organism in the image of reality. This is an evolutionary process entirely disregarded in our mechanistic theories, which liken our nerve functions to mechanical processes. But no machine, no artificial brain, can ever spontaneously undergo evolution by intrinsic efforts of its own. Actually, it is the world around us which is constantly working on our perceptive organs, to make them true channels for its reality, a fact which Goethe expressed when he said that the eye is made by the light which it perceives.

The lower down we go in the kingdoms of nature, the more clearly we find one single reality expressed in the forms and reactions of her creatures, for nature forces her own reality on all creatures but man. A complete change of climatic conditions, for example, may promote in animals and plants mutations of their perceptive and reactive abilities. Mating instincts coincide with seasons propitious to procreation. Other biological requirements have resulted in the urge for migration, and have endowed animals with mysterious talents for navigation. But in man there is a force capable of resisting the dictates of nature. If, however, his strength as individual has become too weak, nature may repossess his biological organism and make him part and parcel of her kingdom. In the sphere of pathology we can observe many such processes. One of them is the phenomenon of sleepwalking with its relationship to the moon phases and the unerring precision with which the nerves and limbs of the afflicted adapt themselves to their physical environment.

In the sphere of morality a human mind, overwhelmed by the forces of nature, will not be able to resist them through the power of reflection, but will simply obey. Hunger and thirst will lead to rapacity, libido to rape, fear to panic or violence. In other words, the "Great Mother"—who devours what she creates and who favors the strong against the weak—will reshape the human organism in her own image.

If, on the other hand, man withdraws too *far* into the reality of a nonmaterial world, his sense perception may become unreliable and vague. Not only will such an attitude estrange him from the world; it will likewise lead to illnesses which may start with emotional misinterpretations of sense impressions and end in illusions, delusions, and hallucinations.

But man can also make full use of his unique position and balance the reality of the outer world with the truth of the inner. He can train his intellect and his senses until they reflect the laws of nature; he can train his intuition until it reflects the laws of divine purpose. Then and only then a third reality will be born in his soul: the reality of love, understanding, and compassion. Some people, born with an instinctive sense for physical reality, are the great masters of science. The average student, less privileged, must constantly check his own thoughts and observations against the superior wisdom of these teachers, that he may acquire by training what they received by grace.

The same is true in the sphere of intuition, except that the genius in this field has become almost extinct and modern man must look back into the past to find an appropriate starting point for the reawakening of his own intuitive cognition and creativeness. Among the great personalities who still knew how to train their intuitive vision in the image of ancient wisdom, was Abraham Lincoln. His main objective in self-education was the development of faculties which would permit him to differentiate clearly between right and wrong. One of his favorite methods to this end was the persistent study of Euclid's geometry. He startled many of his friends by holding forth on Euclid and on the great benefits a lawyer could derive from an intimate study of that ancient mathematician. As history shows, Lincoln's method was highly successful, for it reflected a deep understanding of the art of intuitive training. The great lawyer and statesman was well aware that Euclid's teachings had been surpassed by later scientists and that his *Elements* did not provide the final word in mathematical knowledge. But he understood that intimate contact with the workings of an ingenious mind is prone to create faculties which, born of truth, are capable of experiencing truth in whatever form it may appear.

Lincoln's idea of self-education, from which his intense interest in Euclid sprang, could help greatly to solve one of the controversies which have split the ranks of our educators into warring factions. One of these factions sees in the Humanities a principal element of higher education as well as an important character builder of youth. The other, besides stressing the significance of early occupational training, argues that practical experience has offered little if any evidence of the validity of its adversary's claims. But, if it were clearly understood that study of the Humanities can do much more than convey information, that its true mission is a reawakening of lost abilities, the controversy would soon be settled.

Of course, this does not mean that modern man should accept all the opinions of ancient scholars, but that he should follow their peculiar ways of thought and thus add to his modern consciousness the powers of the past.

Man no doubt is in dire need of discovering and tapping the wellsprings of creativeness which once flowed in his cultural ancestry. But these springs lie in layers far deeper than those which modern interpretation of history has unveiled. Our understanding of the past has been blocked by our reluctance to accept the qualitative changes continuously occurring in human consciousness. One of these changes is the trend to externalization. The modern scientist, artist, and even theologian shuns all mystery, and endeavors to express all his messages in intellectual terms and sensually perceptible forms. His ancient and early medieval counterparts were more inclined to consider any form of intelligible expression as a mere façade to an inner sanctum in which the inexpressible could be experienced. A worshiper at one of the great temples of antiquity had to pass through endless rows of columns, figures of gods and beasts, guides and guardians, all of which played a definite part in preparing him to meet his deity. And the complexity of Hebrew law and ritual, the elaborate courts and buildings of the Jewish temple, all centered around an empty and dark cell in which the High Priest's intuitive communion with Yahweh took place.

Today we have lost the key to most ancient rituals. The giant geometrical figures running for miles through the desert areas of the Southwest and the barren mountains of Peru are of relatively recent origin. But to our consciousness they present an unsolvable mystery. And still people widely separated, and none of them even able to perceive the whole pattern, must have understood their message. Today we are still marveling at the magnificence of pyramidical structures, but what do we know about the meaning they had for Egyptians and Mayans alike? Yet somehow all the clues to this long-forgotten language must still lie hidden in our racial consciousness. We have to find them again if we are not to lose contact with the creative impulse which is the cohesive element in human evolution. Once, when man's outer world was small, his inner resources were inexhaustible. Today we are rapidly losing touch with these life-giving forces by applying all our potentialities to the outer world.

Our mental outlook has rapidly expanded with the growth of our physical knowledge and may soon become overexpanded, when the future opens the immeasurable reaches of outer space. However, by learning to understand his own past, modern man may tap the ancient sources of consciousness again; and this he must do, for unless he learns to balance his outward course into the future with an inward quest into his past, his self-consciousness may disintegrate while his machines conquer outer space.

There are errors and superstitions in ancient teachings, just as there are in our own: but, in order to become capable of differentiating between timeless messages and the embellishments of merely cultural and aesthetic significance, we must first try to understand the mental processes of those whose wisdom we want to evaluate. If we read modern concepts into ancient messages or try to reduce them to the level of our own limited insight, we shall never find the clue to their deeper meaning. It is our capacity for understanding which has to be broadened until it is capable of grasping the expressions of a state of consciousness different from ours. Only when we fully recognize that virtually all forms of expression hold different meanings for people of different epochs, meanings which we must seek by adjusting ourselves to a different consciousness, can we ever hope to lift the veil from the past. Only then may the door of symbolism open so that we can actually share in experiences which have changed the course of history.

In a deeper and subtler way such experiences can do for our inner perception what the exposure to outer reality does for our perceptive faculties in the sensory world. Yet as various methods of training are necessary to keep our physical senses alert, different ways have been used since time immemorial to strengthen the capacity for intuitive experience. These have usually consisted of carefully controlled efforts to loosen man's consciousness from its earth-bound intellect in order to free it temporarily from its preoccupation with the world of the senses. Such methods have differed in various epochs, and for different races and states of evolution. But their universal existence and purpose cannot be denied. The Indian Yoga, the ritual dances prevalent among primitive tribes, the strictly prescribed chants and rhythms in certain religious rites, are but a few of many methods, still employed, to loosen the inner from the outer. Their purpose is to silence the clamor of the physical senses and to awaken and exercise the intuitive faculties of man.

Modern scholars have relegated religious ceremonies to the category of mere symbols. If we accept their verdict, the question must arise: what are symbols? They can hardly be intellectually conceived artifacts. To assure ourselves of this fact we may select at random just one of the more revered symbols of many religions: the dove, representing divine wisdom as well as peace. Anyone who has observed pigeons knows well that these birds are neither exceedingly wise nor particularly peace-loving! Is it not more likely that archetypal pictures arose in the souls of our forefathers who were still capable of such perceptions? These "primordial images," to use Jung's terminology, have their counterparts in the world of the senses. Just why the dove denotes peace and supreme wisdom in most civilizations we do not know. Yet on the physical plane that bird represents one of the characters of a universal intuitive language which, although lost to man for millenniums, has left its imprints not only in religion, myths, and legends but even in traditional figures of speech.

The stage of evolution during which this once living language faded into mere symbolism is recalled in the Bible and widely dispersed legends, in the story of the Tower of Babel. But the universal language is not entirely lost, at least not yet; it can and must be reawakened if an understanding between man and his Creator, and between man and man, is ever to bring peace to this world. Its script cannot be learned by a mere effort of will, nor by speculation. Yet, if intellect were applied to serve man rather than to dominate him, it could point the way to where the inner word, the Logos, could still be found and heard; and once again that word might enter into man's consciousness. That we have not found that way as yet, is by no means the fault of science and intellect, but of scientific and intellectual prejudice. No serious student of history can deny that in some ancient teachings, religions, and art a power must have been active which transcended all modern soul forces.

Today these forces are externalized and appear in the technological achievements of the atomic age. Since they are under the rule of modern intellect they are analytical rather than creative. Their elemental nature is revealed, however, in their almost apocalyptic potentialities of world-wide destruction. At a time when man was more intuitive than he is today, when his innate powers had not yet been fully translated into technology, his abilities were predominantly creative, and bore resemblance to the ultimate creative principle itself, which the Greeks called Logos.

Recognition of these facts and investigation into their historical transitions could take modern man to the very threshold of an inner rejuvenation, a threshold beyond which lies an intuitive rather than an intellectual quest. After a proper, down-to-earth preparation, such a quest is feasible, for in the depth of man's being, the consciousness of his ancestors still exists and can be awakened from its living death. Eventually it will die, however, unless the gates are unlocked and light is permitted to enter. The guides to those gates are the words of the ancient teachers although they were designed to fit their world rather than ours.

Man's fascination with history springs from a longing more profound than mere scientific curiosity. It stems from his hope to find meaning and purpose in life, the lost roots of his own selfhood. For deep in our hearts we all sense that as we go back in time we also dig down into the sub- and unconscious reaches of our own being. As a matter of fact, man's future may well depend on the degree to which he will learn to understand his past.

But such comprehension is not easily attained, since it requires an intellectual as well as an intuitive effort. Without intellectual striving and the painstaking acquisition of factual knowledge, miscomprehensions and illusions are inevitable; and without intuitive submersion into the soul and spirit of a remote era, the knowledge we gain of it must remain lifeless and bare of meaning. Who has not experienced the glow of anticipation and wonder at the mere description of a new archaeological discovery, only to suffer the sense of disappointment and frustration that follows upon its modern "interpretations"? The reason why historical research has failed to give man assurance as to his evolutionary possibilities may be found in the conceited and condescending attitude of intellectualism. This attitude prevents the modern historian from comprehending what he unearths with so much labor and pains.

We must not idealize the past foolishly, for the prevalence of intuitive consciousness did not exclude the co-existence of barbarism, cruelty, and ignorance. Yet in a few uniquely inspired personalities intuitive wisdom reached heights which have never been matched since. It seems as if the contrast between light and shadow was greater in ancient cultures than it is today: while the masses may have lived in relative darkness, the light radiating from a few was of overwhelming strength and untainted purity.

Today our great civilizations are steeped in the uniform gray of a new dawn. Average man has attained a degree of understanding and respect for his fellow creatures, and has become more aware than his ancestors of his own moral responsibilities. On the other hand, the stars have paled that once shone brightly on the dark firmament of earlier ages, and spiritual leadership has almost disappeared from the earth. Thus man turns instinctively to the torchbearers of the past in his longing to find the meaning of life, and the strength to master it. But by intellect alone he can no more grasp their message than a chemist could appreciate the "Sistine Madonna" by analyzing the paint on its canvas. Modern man does not see this, and consequently either reduces ancient wisdom to humanitarianism or censors it as the manifestation of childish superstition. If the former attitude is pathetic, the latter is nothing less than stupid—for common sense should tell us that the ancient scientists, artists, and teachers who brought forth unequaled miracles of wisdom, art, and skill were by no means superstitious children. For instance, is it really possible to believe that the Egyptians—with their advanced knowledge of medicine, anatomy, and natural sciences—expected their dead to make use of wooden ships, earthly food, and metal coins on their journey to Amenti? No, originally at least, hierarchal arts and rituals had nothing whatever to do with superstition. They were simply the visible images of a world of inner experiences. Certainly there was no belief that the wooden ship would carry the dead to his new existence. In many ancient creeds, however, water signified the world of the spirit—and a ship, the support the still earth-bound consciousness of the departed needed in order to find its new bearings. It was also believed that a priest's training and ordination enabled him to imbue a physical symbol with powerful thoughts which those who had shed their bodies could perceive, just as the living could perceive physical objects. To ancient thinking, death was the gradual process of a soul's detachment from the body it had inhabited. In the course of this process the memory of sense perceptions and intellectual concepts would, by degrees, give way to a perception of "Ideas" —creative thoughts—behind the world of appearance. In most ancient religions it was feared that the dead might be unwilling to part with the earth-bound consciousness, and attach himself to the minds of living beings. On the other hand, his soul might detach itself too quickly, lose awareness of the individual identity he had gained through his incarnation, and become a wanderer lost in the boundless reaches of Amenti.

To assure a harmonious transition, familiar objects, especially such of known symbolic meaning, were endowed as it were by priests with thoughts that would become perceptible signposts to the dead on his journey. Accustomed to still his hunger with bread and quench his thirst with wine, the departed was expected to turn to the offerings of grain, bread, and wine, and thus find the spiritual food which prayers and rituals had bestowed on them. The world he had to face would at first appear fluid and all-engulfing to him, like an ocean stretching into infinity; and, frightened, he would look for a vessel to carry him across the surging waves. Particularly in Egypt it was, therefore, considered beneficial to enclose in burial chambers a ship serving as tangible symbol of rituals that were thought to protect the individuality from losing itself in the infinite.

One could add many more examples of ancient thinking, which held the world of Matter and the world of Ideas merely facets of a twofold reality. Whether or not we believe in such ideas is beside the point. What matters is that, were historical and archaeological explorations undertaken with a less condescending attitude toward ancient cultures, they could reawaken our intuitive faculties, which lie buried under the debris of the ages. Modern consciousness is in danger of excessive overexpansion. It reaches from the smallest to the largest, from the world of nuclear physics to the physical universe. It must weather the shock of terrific acceleration, and soon may have to maintain itself in outer space, when time will seem to cease. And the farther we expand our consciousness, the more urgently we need the subterranean springs whence, through the course of history, it used to receive its strength.

Since time immemorial civilizations have followed a certain pattern. Their beginning is often lost in the twilight which engulfs the early history of a little-known tribe or nation. Within such a community an impulse may arise in the form of a religious or ideological revelation which kindles a flame in the hearts of a few specially gifted individuals. As schools and temples spring up under their guidance, the new cultural stream comes down to earth. This stream branches out to give rise to novel skills and sciences which, in turn, bring prosperity and power. Pride and the desire for conquest follow, and the more victorious the young nation is in the ensuing wars, the more quickly it will descend into materialism and spiritual decadence. A nation preoccupied with the countless tasks of maintaining its military power and the fruits of its victories has little chance to preserve intuitive consciousness. Thus it can no longer comprehend the original impulse to which it owes its ascent. The rituals and images which had once been passwords to religious experience are now revered as if they were divine in their own right. This is the origin of superstition, which is not a sign of racial childhood but of materialistic decadence. Eventually the iconoclasts rise—the "progressives," ever ready to fight tradition—but instead of filling the precious, though empty, vessels of their waning culture with new content, they merely destroy what they are unable to understand. This phase of a cultural cycle usually coincides with a political decline, for the forces which made the nation great have all been spent on material gains.

Now a second opportunity opens. Not only can a nation learn from the distant past, but it can also learn from its errors and patiently turn the fruits of its experiences into real progress. To do so a people must take stock of itself; it must rediscover the spiritual values on which it was founded and try to bring them into existence without repeating the errors of its past. Only then can there begin a new phase of evolution, stemming from the free will of men and not from gifts of the gods. There are some examples of such renewals to be found in history. One took place in ancient Egypt under Amenophis IV; although seemingly a failure, it brought a new spark of life to an already dying civilization. One succeeded in China under Confucius. In modern times the most successful rejuvenation of the Occidental impulses of freedom and democracy occurred with the founding of the United States. If, however, a people refuses to learn, if it clings to the memory of its glorious past and to the broken symbols of its faded power, it declines into the dotage of old age.

Modern historians consider primitive peoples aborigines, children in the family of nations. Culturally, however, they are the ancient ones. They are decadent rather than immature, and their rites and legends tell of a long-forgotten past of wisdom and greatness. Their civilizations have died, but there have always been other nations ready to start an ascent where their forerunners failed. Thus, in spite of failure, evolution has proceeded on its forward path, across sunlit peaks and dark canyons.

Today the problem is different. We too are in a declining phase of culture, but we must not let our civilization die, for its dying convulsions might destroy the earth. Our civilization is not dispensable, as were others before our time. And who can save it? Neither dictators nor mass movements, if its aim of

freedom and individuality is ever to be reached. The redeemer
of our culture is the individual, and on the average he seems
willing enough to undertake this task, provided his intellect
can lead the way. For this he needs neither a religious upheaval
nor a social revolution, but merely a more realistic and less
biased form of education.

An essential part of such education could come from a fresh
outlook on the history of consciousness. Today most of our professional interpreters of history are still following—either
voluntarily or unwittingly—the party lines of liberalism or
fundamentalism. The liberal is ever ready to interpret facts to
fit modern views. The fundamentalist has a deep respect for tradition, but he usually fails to realize that a term changes its
meaning in the course of time. For example, we use "love" and
"hate" almost constantly in our daily speech, and in the most
trivial sense: we love our food, we hate to go out in bad
weather, and so on. In the early Middle Ages, however, these
terms signified emotions of elemental force. Nor does the Greek
agape (Latin: *caritas*), which we accept as the basic principle
of Christianity, fully correspond either to our "love" or to our
"charity."

Another concept, hell, originally designated the place where
those who had died of sickness, rather than of violence, dwelt
after death. What has this word, adopted from Germanic mythology, to do with the horrible medieval concepts of eternal
torture or the psychological abstractions of modern times?

Yet fundamentalists are right in this: not one word of the
available genuine texts should be changed lightly, for religious
reality lies in the impulses engendered in the souls of those
to whom the words were originally directed. A growing awareness of this fact can be sensed in our present-day enthusiasm
for historical novels with religious overtones, an enthusiasm
which indicates that the public is beginning to recognize the
need for a more vivid and complete experience of history in the
making. It also reflects the longing for actual inner experience
rather than dogma and dry exegesis. Yet the artistic freedom
of the novelist might easily prove dangerous when he injects
thoughts into the minds of the great historical personalities,

creating entirely fictitious characters and events to support such presumptions. Nobody demands that the artist present a photographic reproduction of his subject, but it is essential that he transmit the inner reality with absolute faithfulness. Where the most sacred realities are concerned, perhaps the only adequate forms of art are either the highest or else the least sophisticated.

Art is only one way, and yet a very important one, toward intuitive participation in the experience of those who were present at the birth of a new religious impulse. As a matter of fact, the true artist is in himself a living proof that great events can be intuitively re-experienced and freshly expressed in forms which, though they vary to suit the immediate historical and geographical environment, still reveal their timeless significance. In the Middle Ages it was the works of great musicians, painters, and sculptors which helped the masses to achieve at least a partial experience of those spiritual realities already much dimmed by the changing state of consciousness. Today we need painstaking intellectual research to prepare the way for a deeper understanding of religion. A few examples may suffice to illustrate what we have in mind.

One of the great events in the history of human evolution was the mission of Moses and his flock. Moses laid the foundation for the form of monotheism which was to give Occidental culture its direction for millenniums to come. But we can hardly hope to understand the secret of a power which, against tremendous odds, was capable of changing the course of history, unless we pay close attention to the spirit of its era. Moses accomplished his mission at a time when astromancy (star divination) was a universally accepted science. It was in the second millennium B.C. For many centuries the sun in spring had risen in the constellation of Taurus, which consequently was considered the regent of heaven and as such revered by most peoples as the genius of the age. The symbol of Taurus, the figure of a bull or a calf, was raised in many temples, to help worshipers lift their souls toward the cosmic forces which were thought to reign over heaven and earth. It was therefore not childish superstition that prompted the Jews to worship a

golden calf. Had it been, the stern punishment inflicted by
Moses would have been cruel and incomprehensible, as well as
entirely out of keeping with the paternal love he had always
shown them before.

Far from being naïve and superstitious, the Jews of that
epoch were ahead of their time, and for this very reason were
judged severely. They were the chosen leaders on the path
toward a new phase of consciousness. Before Moses, men had
been members of a flock rather than individuals, and consequently not readily inclined to conceive of an individual deity.
The highest forces perceived were those manifested in the laws
of heredity, in the wisdom of instincts, and in the miracles of
nature and the cosmos, forces which to the imaginative consciousness of the epoch often appeared in the shape of animal
deities.

The Jews were the chosen people because they were among
the first to look beyond the powers working in nature to the
higher aspect of God as pure spirit. They were told: "Thou
shalt not make unto thee any graven image or any likeness of
any thing . . . ," for they had to find *within* what cannot be
expressed by any symbol taken from nature. They were chosen
to lift their hearts to lonely heights where, far beyond nature,
God speaks to the inner being of man himself. The whole
mission of the Jews was at stake when in distress they reverted
for help to the forces familiar to the age, forces they could
worship in companionship with all the races and nations sur-
rounding them. Thus they rebelled against their mission, a
mission which would set them apart from other men, a mission
which seemed to them bearable only so long as there was among
them one whose inner light was strong enough to communicate
with that stern, invisible God, whom they themselves had to
obey blindly. When the Jews thought that Moses would not
return, they turned back to the power of nature which the
common man could understand.

Moses was not the first monotheist. Before him, Ikhnaton,
King of Egypt, sang of Aton: "O sole God whose power no
other possesseth, Thou didst create the earth according to Thy
heart while Thou wast alone. . . ." The Jews themselves had a

long monotheistic tradition, but it was Moses whose words and deeds ignited in their hearts a pyre which was to fire the soul of the human race. His mission came at the very moment when the soil of human consciousness was ready to receive a new seed. In the course of historical evolution, the words of the great seer—and even the Ten Commandments he brought to the world—may have lost some of their power. But if we succeed in reviving the inner and outer conditions of the era in which they arose, and if we let them ring again in the borrowed consciousness of Biblical times, their magic will reveal itself even to modern man.

Before the time of Moses a clear concept of good and evil hardly existed. Man's inner vision extended merely to the experience of racial or tribal deities: good was what served—and bad, what interfered with—the biological advantages of the family, tribe, or nation. But Moses' moral laws, coinciding with the new awareness of the personal and still universal God within, the God of whom there could be no likeness either in the world of nature or of art, implanted in the human soul the seeds of moral freedom. Such freedom can develop only when man has the choice of obeying or disobeying a supreme law.

The growing awareness that somewhere beyond the sphere of nature an objective criterion of good and evil exists, found its most profound religious expression in the Ten Commandments. But that advance in consciousness was not restricted to the Jews. In different ways it manifested itself in other cultural streams, as for example in the discovery of "conscience" by the Greeks and in the groping of the Romans for the principles of justice. Once it had dawned on mankind that an absolute good exists, man felt his own inadequacy as sin, as a separation from God, which after death might mean unspeakable suffering. And with this fear arose a fervent longing for a divine mediator and redeemer.

Modern man knows all this intellectually, but such knowledge becomes impotent unless it is time and again revived as an intuitive experience. It is not merely to repeat well-known theological facts that these religious events are pointed out; rather, it is to awaken an understanding and feeling for the dwindling of our moral heritage, a heritage which we are still considering the motivating force of our culture.

Christianity itself cannot be comprehended unless the state of consciousness into which it was born is experienced. But lack of comprehension breeds misunderstandings, and the history of Christianity is full of them. They have resulted not only in spiritual confusion but also in political errors which today threaten the very survival of Western civilization.

What have theological problems to do with politics? More than we in the West realize. Neither Alexander nor Cortez could have conquered empires had they not been aided by religious undercurrents. Today the part played by religion in politics is less conspicuous but not less real than it was in the past. Naturally, power plays its role too, since human evolution has not yet reached the state at which the authority of strength can be entirely abandoned. But history shows that the use of power—whether aggressive, defensive, or purely protective— is accepted by others only when it is congruous to the ideology of the nation applying that power. Especially to the Oriental mind, ruthlessness and force are in themselves not so repulsive as Western armchair-diplomats believe, inasmuch as a successful conqueror is considered to be the tool of destiny and hence the servant of a powerful deity. Thus the Moslem leaders who conquered with fire and sword were not only victorious: they were also profoundly respected by the majority of their victims. For Islam leaves the attainment of saintliness to its saints and does not claim to be a religion of peace and humility.

In the area in which religion and politics meet the Christian nations have failed. Being merely human, neither better nor worse than others, they too have used power politics throughout their history. For this they would have been forgiven by the world, had they not claimed that as Christians they were bound to the moral code pronounced in the Sermon on the Mount. While fighting and killing, they preached nonresistance to evil and the turning of the other cheek. While their missionaries taught the Sermon on the Mount, their governments engaged in military conquest, colonialism, and violence. Is it surprising,

then, that some of the most devout native converts turned into
the bitterest enemies of Christianity?

So great has the distrust of Christian pretenses grown that
even Russia, once it abrogated Christianity and embraced the
new creed of communism, became acceptable to such countries as India and China. From a religious point of view the
Soviets appear less hypocritical than the Western Powers to the
non-Christian world. For their creed is candid enough. Its aim
is the establishment of an earthly paradise, a heaven for human
ants and robot men. To achieve this end all means are permissible, since according to the Soviet creed no absolute moral
values exist. The liturgy of that creed is dialectical sophism.
Therefore if the Communists are aggressive, ruthless, and
treacherous in the pursuit of their aims, they are nevertheless
faithful to their creed. In the eyes of the Oriental, it is we who
through history have betrayed our own ideals and have thus
become guilty of the most despicable of all disloyalties, the dis-
loyalty to our God.

There can be no doubt that the Christian nations have failed
at least as much as others in moral achievement. This does not
mean that they have actually broken faith with their religion,
but rather that they themselves have been the victims of theological misunderstandings. Christ, like the founders of other
great religious movements, made different demands of people
in different stages of development. He refused to explain his
parables to the crowds, lest too much knowledge burden average men with too great responsibility. The evangelists took
pains to indicate to whom specific admonitions were directed,
as in reporting the following inquiry by Peter: "Lord, speakest
thou this parable unto us, or even to all?" (Luke 12:41).

Had Christ actually demanded that all men should reject
force unconditionally, his command to obey Caesar in matters
pertaining to this world would have been meaningless.

With this problem in mind, let us have another look at the
Sermon on the Mount. To whom was it given? "And seeing the
multitudes, he went up into a mountain: and when he was set,
his disciples came unto him: and he opened his mouth, and

taught them, saying: . . ." (Matt. 5:1). "And he lifted up his eyes on his disciples, and said . . ." (Luke 6:20).

. . . that the Sermon on the Mount is directed *not to the people but to the disciples* . . . is the key to understanding it. . . . the Gospel says that it was intended as instruction for the disciples . . . . He [Christ] sees the people as the flock which has no shepherd. Because humanity has no leader, he begins to make his disciples into apostles, ambassadors and priests. The Sermon on the Mount is the first great Christian instruction given to priests.[5]

Thus the Sermon on the Mount is not a mandate upon all men, who, as history shows, could not fulfill it. The priest should refrain from violence under all circumstances. But if all true Christians were to do so, they would merely encourage crime and world domination by antireligious powers. Surely this was not intended. And still, in a subtler form, the Sermon concerns all Christians for—if meditated upon—it can give them the strength to defend themselves and their countries without hatred and vengefulness.

Intellectual research into the words and the structure used in ancient scripture is indispensable. But, as we have said before, such efforts take us no further than to the doorstep of religion. The gate itself opens only to intuition. Neither the Bible nor any other sacred writing leaves any doubt about it. Scientifically, there is but scant historical proof that Christ even lived. According to some scholars, the recent discovery of the Dead Sea Scrolls threatens to shake still further the spiritual foundations of Christianity.

"The historian cannot control the details of Jesus' birth and resurrection, and thus has no right to pass judgment on their historicity."[6] Christ's life and his message had unleashed forces that were soon to change the course of history. But they left scant imprints on the minds and works of the intellectuals of his time. Could there be a better example of the essence of creative impulses, of their intuitive rather than their intellectual origin?

Why is it that the early Christian authors were so vague about historical facts? And why is it that the evangelists, who certainly knew of one another, wrote somewhat different versions of Jesus' life? Because their apparent contradictions do not concern the physical plane at all: the Gospels are the stories of two worlds. In a manner characteristic of an even more ancient form of consciousness, physical facts are treated merely as take-off points for the flight of the spirit which reaches different altitudes and permits different vistas according to the intuitive strength of the writer. All the great epics of old are written this way, among them the *Iliad* and *Odyssey* as well as the myths and legends of still more ancient origin. The Romans had introduced into the world a form of historic recording hardly less intellectual and down-to-earth than our own. But the evangelists reverted to the more ancient form of writing since they had to describe an event inexplicable by outer factors alone.

The Bible itself makes quite clear that Christianity owes its acceptance neither to the physical appearance of Jesus nor to his visible deeds. Not even the disciples accepted the divinity of Christ on the strength of his personality or his miracles. At a time when the human organism must have been less brittle than it is now, when man was much more inclined to live intuitively than intellectually, the power of faith, the power of mind over body, must have been stronger than it is today. Ancient literature leaves no doubt that, two thousand years ago, almost everyone believed in miracles. One even expected prophets, priests, and magicians to be endowed with supernatural powers without, however, considering the performer of miracles a god.

Thus Christ's deeds alone could never have accounted for his being accepted as a divine being. That he was, is entirely due to intuitive experiences such as Peter's during and after the Transfiguration.

Physical miracles appeal chiefly to the materialistic and intellectual sides of human nature, and suppress rather than strengthen man's inner vision. Thus it is not surprising that Christ shunned publicity for his deeds, and scoffed at those who believed in him on the strength of outer signs. Historically, the victory of Christianity cannot be attributed to the multitudes who worshiped Jesus for his miracles on one day and demanded his crucifixion on the other, but to those who understood him intuitively. Christianity is a creed based entirely on inner experience and cannot survive on the evidence provided by intellect alone. At its cradle stand the stories of the Annunciation, of the kings and shepherds; it reached adulthood with John the Baptist's vision on the bank of the Jordan; it began to enter human consciousness in the disciples' experiences leading from Easter to Pentecost.

Not only the planting and emergence of the new seed depended on intuitive experience, but also its growth. It was Paul's vision at Damascus which changed him from an enemy into one of the great champions of Christianity. It was this vision which gave him a conviction powerful enough to bring about one of the most singular miracles in history: the conversion of the Greeks. In them Paul did not find a people yearning for, and believing in, the coming of a Messiah, but the most worldly, sophisticated, and philosophically trained nation of the age. The Greeks believed in the existence of an "Unknown God," a supreme deity so exalted and transcendental that even their immortal art could devise no symbol nor likeness for his empty temple—and then they were asked to believe that the creator of heaven and earth had lived in the body of a Jewish carpenter!

The early spread of Christianity in the Hellenic world has defied all attempts at intellectual explanation; it was a miracle of intuition. None knew this better than Paul: "But the natural man receiveth not the things of the Spirit of God: . . . neither can he know them, because they are spiritually discerned" (I Cor. 2:14).

Jesus himself made no attempt to give an answer to Pilate's question: "What is truth?" For there is no definition of truth that can satisfy the intellectual mind. Yet once before he had answered it for people less intellectual and more intuitive than the sophisticated Roman, when he said: "I am the truth." A statement such as this is the strongest possible appeal to pure intuition, since it transcends the faculties of logic, which within its own limits has not even the possibility of accepting or rejecting it. Nothing less than inner perception could be expected to experience truth as a living spiritual reality, and to discern its presence or absence in the soul of another being. And therein lies the secret of qualitative cognition. Ideal realities such as love, freedom, goodness, and truth exist nowhere but in the world of intuitive experience.

But has not the tale of error, heartbreak, and bloodshed which, from the beginning, has marked man's quest for truth, shown that ideals are mere dreams and illusions of men seeking escape from the toil of the world? No, discord and error no more disprove the reality of spiritual truth than controversial explanations of a natural phenomenon disprove the reality of the phenomenon itself. Absolute proof does not exist anywhere for the human mind. Our physical senses and our intellect can delude us as effectively as can our inner perception; and therein lies the greatest of all freedoms, the freedom to err. Could it not be that the very meaning of earthly existence lies in the fact that discernment of reality does not come as a gift, but must be attained by a never-ending quest?

Our sense perceptions can be made more reliable through persistent exposure to physical phenomena. Through such training, our senses become continuations of the outside world as it were, and thus its faithful messengers. Eventually, a state develops in which the scientifically trained can discern a basic natural law even where it appears in an entirely novel and startling form.

Similarly, our insight into intangible realities needs training. The torches from which our own candles must be lit are the great creeds and arts of humanity. And the more our perceptive organism becomes an extension of spiritual reality itself, the more it will enable us to perceive and recognize truth in whatever form it may manifest itself in an ever-changing world.

CHAPTER V

NATURAL PHENOMENA
IN THE MIRROR OF
THE HUMAN MIND

Countless attempts have been made to find clear definitions for philosophico-psychological principles. Although fruitful in an academic way, these attempts have contributed little to a real understanding of man; for the disadvantage of all definitions is their rigidity, which leaves no space for the free play of creative imagination. And without imagination no one can hope to comprehend human nature, least of all one's own. Thus in our endeavor to clarify such terms as "intellect" and "intuition," we shall seek examples of their meaning rather than strict definitions.

There is one philosopher whose concepts of intuition and intellect come close to our own use of these terms: Bergson. To him, intuition is a primary gift of man, a gift that enables him to penetrate into the core of phenomena, while intellect merely interprets what intuition apprehends, defining from without what it cannot comprehend from within. Bergson believes that intellect is not a primary gift of man, but one that he has acquired in dealing with the intricacies of life, and therefore a relatively recent product of civilization.

The contemporary philosopher who has probably contributed most to a renewed understanding of intuition is Robert Ulich. In his classic on "self-transcendence" he states:

First, though intuition is not the mere extension, it is by no means the negation of critical intelligence and of the laws of logic. . . . Second, intuition, though appearing like a "gift" and beyond the reach of mere effort, is nevertheless the result of *preparation,* which may be of intellectual character or of other forms of self-discipline. . . . Paradoxically though it may seem to speak of "trained" intuition, it is the only form which deserves its name. All other claims are on behalf of quackery. . . . True intuition is dedication, false intuition is intellectual self-indulgence. The profoundest man's expressive power depends on his language and the culture within which he speaks. The proof of his wisdom is whether successive generations return to it as to an ever-fresh revelation.[1]

Analytical intellect requires highly developed brain substance as its instrument, while intuitive faculties—such as instincts— prevail at the lowest level of evolution. Analytical intellect is chiefly concerned with breaking down complex phenomena into ever smaller components in order to observe and classify them, and give them practical application, while intuition, wittingly or unwittingly, seeks the *oneness* of purpose and meaning behind the multitude of phenomena. But this is not all, for intuition, being akin to the creative spirit itself, is man's instrument for creativeness as well as for comprehension. In lower animals, where intuition is not opposed by a strong intellect, instinctive comprehension is at once expressed in action; and some of these actions are proof of a wisdom well exceeding human capacities. Growing intellect opposes instinctive wisdom, and blocks its immediate translation into action. Thus the perceptive inlet of intuition becomes separated from its creative outlet, and the gap between them is filled by conscious reflection. In the state of evolution prevailing in ancient times, man was wide open to spiritual realities which flowed through him and emerged on the physical plane as prophecies, miracles, and sacred art.

Ancient man's immature individuality was powerless against these overwhelming forces which he attributed to the irresistible power of the gods. His freedom was restricted to mental reflection, which at first found expression in philosophical acceptance of destiny and later in intellectual rebellion against it. It was analytical intellect, the noncreative earth-bound faculty of the human brain, which changed man from the pawn of the gods into a Promethean rebel against divine leadership, and thus gave him the dangerous gift of freedom.

Intuitive perception and creativeness waned in the course of time, while analytical intellect increased in strength. In no other creature has intellect become as formidable an adversary of intuition as in man. Thanks to this, modern man is endowed with the least wisdom and the greatest freedom of any creature on earth. His lack of wisdom is obvious: even a lowly earthworm carries out its task more efficiently than he does. Yet the freedom for which man has paid such a high price has not been fully secured; for instead of merely restraining the power of intuition to the point where it no longer compels, analytical intellect has repressed it to the point where it becomes paralyzed. This alone can explain man's doubts in the existence of his Creator, and in a higher purpose and meaning in life. For as long as it remains healthy, intuition, itself a part of the creative spirit, must at least sense God's existence and purpose. Without such intuitive perception of the divine, a person with purely intellectual consciousness is as impervious to the nature of a spiritual world as a congenitally blind man is to colors. Or, as Herbert Dingle, professor of history and philosophy of science, puts it in his conclusion to a symposium of seventeen British scientists: "*All* observable physical knowledge now appears to be statistical, so that the 'real' causal world lying behind it turns out to be completely unknown. Secondly it is not only unknown, but unknowable."[2]

Had this been admitted from the beginning, many misinterpretations of scientific research could have been avoided; for materialism and communism are built on misunderstood scientific facts. Lack of self-criticism on the part of some scientists and blind acceptance of their speculations by the public have injected into our era the belief that all ancient wisdom has been thoroughly repudiated on the strength of recent discoveries and facts. We are told that to seek meaning and purpose in evolution is merely an anthropomorphism, an attempt to project human concepts into a soulless universe. Life is said to turn into consciousness, and consciousness into self-awareness, all by itself. If this were true—and we have no proof of it —how did life arise in the first place? Here too we are given answers, but these answers, while pronounced with high scientific authority, are strongly influenced by personal and, therefore, emotional undercurrents. Let us for a moment put aside our habitual science worship and look at some authoritative statements as if they were made by mere mortals. In them, as in almost all human utterances, we shall often find a laboriously built edifice of impressive facts based on no stronger a foundation than subjective opinion.

True, there is an occasional "probable" to indicate the speculative character of an author's premises, but how many readers will really notice such inconspicuous warning? Actually, one would have to make a study of an author's psychology before one could evaluate his far-reaching conclusions. In his influential work *Life's Beginning on Earth,* Professor R. Beutner makes the following statement: ". . . how did life originate on the earth? . . . There was probably some sort of development, perhaps extending over millions of years, before life appeared. We may *assume* that the first primitive forms of life *must* have arisen from non-living matter . . ." (italics mine). And later: ". . . Oparin draws the same conclusions which this writer tentatively developed in 1933, namely that 'life is just one of the countless properties of the compounds of carbon.' "[3]

We believe that Beutner's work is brilliant and sincere but we cannot help feeling that its conclusions are unwittingly determined by the author's personal philosophy as expressed on the last page of his book: "Our thirst for knowledge shows us the road to the pursuit of human happiness . . . ; it gives us power . . . so that we may hope to enjoy a long life which is as near to immortality as we can possibly expect."[4]

A view hardly less subjective, but more objectively formulated, is offered by Lincoln Barnett in *Life* magazine's fifth series of "The World We Live In," called "The Pageant of Life":

As to how life itself was first created science can only speculate. It is theoretically possible that on some distant day at the very dawn of time, when the earth's rocks were still soft and oceans and air seethed with chemical turbulence, certain organic compounds in the hot sea were synthesized by solar radiation, by lightning discharge or by unknown catalytic agents into a complex molecule, structurally akin to the protein molecules that form the building blocks of all life, and capable of generating units like itself. In time these primordial molecules may have combined into clusters to form an organism analogous perhaps to a bacterium. Then, somehow, more complex entities evolved and acquired the art of photosynthesis—of utilizing the energy of the sun. They may have been the blue-green algae whose limy deposits have been found in the oldest of pre-Cambrian rocks. They were probably the first authentic members of the plant world.

Yet both bacteria and blue-green algae represented revolutionary blind alleys. The creature generally regarded as the common ancestor of all other living things is a microscopic glob of transparent jelly, half plant, half animal, called the flagellate.[5]

Many similar statements could be added; some of which evade the issue altogether and claim that life was carried down to earth by spores traveling through cosmic space. As if a problem could be clarified by shifting it farther back in time and space! In general, however, the tenor of most theories is: since life did arise during the evolution of the earth, it had to spring from forces inherent in matter. All such statements are unsatisfactory since the question is not whether or not life arose on the earth, but whether it can be comprehended. That it "must" have originated from matter is based on nothing more scientific than personal disinclination to admit the possibility of a nonmaterial source.

This much about personal opinions accepted by the public as if they were proved facts. Actually there can be little doubt that the conditions under which life did emerge on earth will soon be known, and re-enacted in our laboratories. Recent attempts at synthesizing ribonucleic acid, a vital component of all living cells, have met with success, and Dr. Harlow Shapley, defining life as "self-perpetuation of certain macro-molecules," stated that its origin on earth became quite "clear and devoid of any mystery" from the moment when Urey and Miller, at his suggestion, succeeded in synthesizing all twenty-one amino acids, or traces thereof, through continuous electric discharges into an atmosphere of methane, ammonia, hydrogen, and water vapor.[6]

These and similar reports issued in perfect scientific sincerity are of greatest significance, but they could also become harmful to human consciousness if inaccurately interpreted. The important point is that, while we are close to bringing about circumstances favorable for life to enter into matter, we shall not, even then, have solved the mystery of life. Since time immemorial man has been able to establish conditions incompatible with life but, because of this, he has made no claim of "creating" death nor even of understanding it. Similarly, we shall not "create" life in our crucibles by synthesizing amino acids or by building proteinoids; we shall merely invite it in, just as we let light into our rooms by cutting windows into our walls. The utmost modern science has the right to say is this: the basic element for evolution is matter. Its very existence is beyond intellectual explanation and must be attributed to a causal factor transcending the scope of "all observable knowledge." Its manifestations, from the exquisite form of a snowflake to the grandeur of the starry heavens, are the prototypes of all that is truly artistic in the endeavors of man, and might therefore be attributed to the creative genius of a superhuman artificer.

The concept of God as the great invisible artist who had left His work unfinished as a challenge and stimulus to the creative genius in man, has played an important part in ancient and medieval thought life. The Church, considering herself the legitimate guardian of God's affairs on earth, felt, therefore, duty-bound to control and supervise human art and science lest they deviate too far from divine intention. Only during these last centuries has science in its struggle for freedom from religious tutelage banished such concepts from its sphere of cognition. As in every revolution, however, the pendulum of human sentiment has swung too far. The spirit of inquiry had to be freed from influences which wanted to impose spiritual limitations on man's intellectual search. Yet there is no need to ban all the qualitative aspects of cognition. For without creative imagination knowledge itself degenerates into a mere shell of truth.

With this idea in mind, let us look at the problem of evolution and see if the findings of science are really incompatible with the intuitive wisdom of ancient times. Naturally, faith in tradition must not be allowed to distort facts or to become frozen dogma. But science will always remain "one-eyed and color-blind" unless it gives intuition its proper share in cognition. And intuition can never become reliable unless it is constantly practiced, and tested against scientific facts. Modern consciousness demands an intellectual foundation—for instance, a fair knowledge of botany and biology—before an intuitive approach to the mystery of life can be of value. If we compare the functioning of the human mind with a clock, cognition of truth is the result of the pendulum's oscillation between knowledge and comprehension. Thus every student of science will reach a point where his mind becomes saturated with scientific facts, and longs for an understanding of their deeper meaning. Since this longing meets with scant sympathy from teachers, many students lose all interest in their studies and seek fulfillment elsewhere—or, in resignation, become professors themselves, their minds filled with too much knowledge to have room left for wisdom.

But what can a teacher say to a pupil who has reached intellectual saturation? Maybe the following: we are compelled to admit that to analytical intellect and sensory observation "the causal world is not only unknown but unknowable."[7] Although generally disregarded in our schools, this recognition is well known to the great scientists themselves. Actually it is causing an upheaval in the minds of a few even now, while the popular scientist and average teacher continue to live blissfully in the concepts of earlier centuries. "We have the strange situation that the man in the street has begun to believe thoroughly in science, while the man in the laboratory has begun to lose his faith in his science."[8]

Thus, since modern research has failed to find in matter and energy the explanation for their existence, we have every right to surmise a causal factor of an extramaterial nature. What name we give it does not matter. Being individuals ourselves, we are entitled to assume that it also encompasses the qualities of supreme individuality. We can thus speak of an archetypal individuality who has made man in His image, and endowed him with a creative genius akin to His own. If this assumption is permissible—and there is no valid logical objection to it— man should be able to seek in his own impulses and motives clues to an understanding of his Creator.

The ancient healer who was usually either priest or philosopher knew well that the process of healing could be enhanced by contemplation of divine nature. Today most intellectuals abhor anthropomorphism; but he who believes that he was made in the image of God should also believe that his innate longings insofar as they are pure, are also reflections of a higher reality. If, with this thought in mind, he contemplates the Creator all alone in a universe bound to His will, he could easily imagine that such a Supreme Being would long for creatures who could be His friends rather than His slaves. Such creatures would have to be free, for friendship and love are meaningful only if they can be voluntarily given or withheld.

But the first step toward freedom is separation from the source of origin. A creative idea is no more than an aspect of an artist's ingenuity, until it is given a separate existence in a medium which, though it may be of its creator's making, is not of his nature. For the sake of exercising our imaginative faculties, let us conceive of a sculptor ingenious enough to devise and create his own material, a material which is lifeless, heavy, and immobile. He then works on it, carving out parts of its substance until the dead stone seems to come alive, its heavy weight to soar, and its opaque substance to become translucent for an invisible source of light. Miracles of this kind take place in the workshops of all great artists. Is not nature also such a workshop, even if the artist is not immediately visible? Yet there is a way to perceive the working of this artist. It is a way open to those who search for truth with their hearts as well as with their brains. While we are taught in school how to use our physical senses on the surface of existence, there are dormant powers of perception capable of looking *into* it. The Romans called this kind of vision *intuitio,* the inward glance. Such inner perception has faded in modern man; but it can and must be reawakened if man is to remain human.

No less a personality than Goethe pleaded with the founders of a new scientific era for moral and artistic training of their students, to balance the effects of a purely experimental and intellectual knowledge. He was not heard, possibly owing to his aggressive ways, but had he been heeded, history might have taken a happier turn.

Goethe's scientific publications, which startled his era and aroused indignation among some professional scientists, were not intended to add another laurel wreath to the shining glory of the great poet, philosopher, and statesman. Goethe merely wanted to show that the spirit of inquiry which he proposed, could stand the test of reality. Thus when he proved, contrary to all medical opinions of his time, that the human skeleton possesses an intermaxillary bone, his discovery, although certainly not world-shaking, provided sufficient evidence that trained intuition can contribute greatly to scientific research. To Goethe, inner perception was an absolute reality—a reality, however, which had to be supplemented by an exact training of the physical senses and by logical thinking. When he turned to the problem of life where it appears in its purest form— in botany—he was satisfied neither with natural science alone nor with the purely intuitive grasp of life as it is revealed in the ancient myths he knew so well. While he studied the dry botanical system of Linné with greatest interest, Goethe was capable of meeting the bewildering multitude of separate facts with the unifying power of his intuitive genius; and before his inner eye appeared the "archetypal plant," the prototype of life on earth.

The archetypal plant does not exist in the world of senses, but to the genius still endowed with intuitive vision, it is a perceptible reality. When Goethe describes this reality to Schiller, he does not at first meet with full understanding. ". . . when I had ended, he shook his head, saying, 'That is not an empiric experience, it is an idea.' . . . Controlling myself, I replied: 'How splendid that I have ideas without knowing it, and can see them before my very eyes.' "[9]

Only when Goethe realizes that to Schiller an idea is no less real than an experience is to himself, does he consider a closer acquaintance desirable. "Yet if he termed an idea what I called an experience, then there must certainly be something negotiable, something in common between us."[10]

As an invaluable contribution to science, Goethe brought an artist's mind and heart to the contemplation of the ever-present metamorphoses in nature. To this way of thinking the lower trunk of a tree may still appear suggestive of the dead rock from which it emerges; but higher up, where the stem reaches skyward, splitting into smaller branches, it expresses the victory of life over matter and its mechanical laws. And eventually, as we gaze upon the crown's foliage and blossoms, we may experience within us the triumph of light and air and color over gravity and darkness; and so we shall have gained a little understanding of the nature of life. Actually, life is known to science only by its phenomena, i.e., by its effects on matter. The characteristics of matter are modified by it and, strangely enough, these modifications are mistaken for the cause of life instead of being recognized for what they are: its effects.

We know that every living cell in our body contains certain chemical elements such as sulphur, carbon, oxygen, hydrogen, and nitrogen. We also know that some of these elements show a very great affinity to one another wherever they exist in close proximity. Sulphur will readily join with hydrogen to form H_2S, nitrogen will combine with hydrogen to make ammonia, et cetera. As long as the cell is alive and healthy, all such chemical processes will be held in abeyance; as soon as the organism dies, however, they return to their normal laws, starting some of the well-known symptoms of decay. In other words, life does not appear to carry the material forces on to a stronger manifestation of their own inclination; but, on the contrary, subdues and metamorphosizes their inherent laws. We could attain an intuitive comprehension of the essence of life and of its victory over earth-bound matter were we to contemplate a plant growing skyward in defiance of the laws of gravity, a young animal struggling on its weak legs against the weight of its body, and, above all, a child miraculously standing upright for the first time.

On occasion an animal dies without physical interference, let us say from fright—an occurrence well known to hunters of rabbits and even of black bears and other easily frightened animals. At such a time death of the individual may be instantaneous while the ensuing reversion of biochemical into ordinary chemical processes—the death of the individual cells —follows at a pace that is gradual and relatively slow. Would it not be more realistic to let phenomena speak their own language, and consider first things first, rather than make frantic attempts to assert that even in such cases nothing has happened but a rearrangement of physical and chemical processes? True, emotions exert their influences on cell chemistry, resulting in changes of adrenaline, histamine, and choline metabolism, et cetera—but these changes are obviously secondary. For whatever materially demonstrable influences emotions may exert on the nervous or any other system, emotions themselves cannot be found in a test tube or under a microscope. Naturally, a living organism may also be killed by injuries of a strictly physical nature—but we are not questioning the fact that life needs certain physical or chemical conditions in order to gain or to maintain its hold on matter. When these conditions are destroyed, life must recede, even as water leaves a leaky bowl. Yet the leak does not destroy the water any more than the undamaged vessel creates it.

Let us consider the problem of life from still another angle. The theory widely promulgated today is that somehow in the course of millions of years atomic and molecular changes of matter stumbled on life by mere chance. By the survival of the fittest through persistent struggle, by the competition between species, by mutations and similar processes, higher forms are said to have gradually emerged and established a pattern of life as it is today. The far distant past is an easy subject for hypotheses. But what about the present? How does life perpetuate itself today? What regulates the forces of heredity, adaptation, and mutation? True, there are chromosomes and genes which determine certain hereditary characteristics and their variations. But they are no more than building stones containing the basic characteristics of the whole, the specific components of an entity taken apart. Does this make them the creators of such entity? Just as it is impossible to find in matter the causal factor for its own physical existence, so is it unrealistic to search for the secret of life in chemistry and biology.

There is nothing mechanical in the world of biology. The seed does not contain the plant in miniature, and thus the "preformation theory" was abandoned long ago. Many plants can be reproduced from shoots or even individual leaves without recourse to seeds. Heredity is known to follow strict patterns, yet it may suddenly change through inexplicable mutations. Age-old designs may or may not adapt themselves to varying conditions of climate, atmosphere, or soil. All these and countless other facts indicate that there is a regulation principle which sustains and controls the manifestations of life, a principle much more closely related to the world of thought than to the forces of physics and biochemistry, which it rules.

Biology speaks a clear enough language, a language which is misunderstood only because we have grown afraid of facing an intangible reality outside the emotional shelter of a church. Considerable experience in modern science should have taught us once and for all that, while experimentation, physical observation, and intellectual analysis are indispensable for the study of the means used by the causal factor of life, they cannot comprehend it.

We may be able to attain a clearer understanding of our world when we visualize the four kingdoms of nature as products of a dynamic polarity rather than of a single evolutionary stream. Such polarity exists between creation and penetration.

Matter must be considered as a passive object of creation since it cannot be credited with conscious and self-evolving powers. Those who give it such credit violate the definition of material substance and energy by adding to it attributes of a nonmaterial nature.

Life and consciousness emerge where the creative penetrates

its own creation. Characteristically, this penetration does not occur at the higher levels of the mineral kingdom, but at its lowest; dirt and slime being closer to life than pure metals and precious stones. Consequently, the living cell can hardly be considered a higher manifestation of self-evolving matter, but appears to be the fruit of a new impulse which enters it at its lowest form of evolution. Just as a sculptor searching for a higher form of self-expression will prefer a malleable material to a highly finished one, nature breathes life into dirt rather than into solid gold. We can, with a stretch of imagination, see in physiochemical forces nature's work on the surface of existence, in biochemistry her work from within. Scientists of a future age that will have outgrown the superstition of materialism, will be able to interpret the enigmas of life and death, of mutation, adaptation, and heredity in the light of this polarity.

The animal kingdom is the cradle of consciousness on earth. In it the invisible artist has penetrated still further into his creation, and again his material is taken from the lowest rather than the highest levels of earlier forms of evolution. Were the champions of emergent evolution right, the border line between the animal and vegetable kingdoms should be found in a beautiful rose or a perfect tree rather than in the lowliest of all creatures: the protozoa and bacteria.

Both plants and animals have sense organs, but while in the former, perceptions are entirely turned into activity, in the latter they are partly transmuted into conscious experience. Moreover, we may even say that the single polarity of life and death as it exists in plant life, is split into a biological and a conscious aspect in animals. In other words, a metamorphosis frees some of nature's life-giving forces from their purely vegetative existence and lifts them onto the higher level of instinctive awareness. The animal is just as much under the sway of biological forces as the plant but contrary to the latter, it is aware of it. This awareness we call instinct. Yet the problem of evolution through penetration and metamorphosis becomes even more complex when we consider the influence of mineral substances on an animal's consciousness; for they too reach a level of awareness in the physical structure of its brain.

Matter, far from being an inert solid substance, is recognized now as a cauldron seething with energies of its own. It has its own dynamic laws, which, however, are opposite to those of life.

Just as life enters the sphere of consciousness in instincts, the dynamics of matter play an important role in the development of individuality and intellect. After all, it is matter that separates one being from the other, and the more mineral substances are built into the central nervous system, the more individualistic its mental processes become. A great deal could be said about the influence of inorganic substances on the emergence of individual intellect and the manifestations of this influence in the electrical, chemical, and mineral conditions of the brain. But since such a study would lead far beyond the scope of this book we merely want to call the reader's attention to the new science of cybernetics, which has found so many similarities between the laws of lifeless matter and the functions of the brain.

An animal, whose instinct far exceeds its individual power of reasoning, is less intelligent but at the same time wiser than man. It is capable of navigating over thousands of miles, anticipating meteorological changes; it knows how to find healing plants, and how to practice its amazing skills without benefit of compass, weather forecasts, and intellectual analysis. All these abilities and many others are largely independent of the gray matter of the animal's brain. Far more than by the instrument of its individual intellect, the animal is governed by desires through which the wisdom of the whole species holds sway.

The question must arise: where is the center of all this instinctive wisdom which is capable of co-ordinating, for instance, the actions of countless warrior ants in an unforeseeable situation, or directing the flight maneuvers of thousands of wild geese on their long journeys? Since the reactions of animals are very often co-ordinated, and yet individually different, we cannot possibly ascribe them to an individual brain —nor to any material substance at all, inasmuch as no physical link exists between the individual animal entities. Actually,

animal instincts can be explained only by the assumption of
a nonmaterial force working from within a group organism,
of which the individual animal is only a member or a cell. We
can say that in the animal kingdom the forces of creation have
already become separated from the ocean of universal will, but
no more than a drop of water may be separated from the whole
by a thin layer of dust.

Man is the product of the most powerful impulse of spiritual
penetration, an impulse that may be called the sap within
the tree of evolution. Humanity may be likened to the vertical
stem and top of this tree, and the lower kingdoms to its
horizontal branches. The most advanced animal species have
sprung from the highest part of the trunk and are therefore
possessed of almost all biological characteristics which the tree
could produce during its own growth. Thus it is not surprising that apes resemble us so closely. But the anthropoid
is no more man's ancestor than the topmost branch of a tree
is the ancestor of the highest reach of the trunk itself. In man,
and in man only, the forces of life and death have reached
the highest degree of metamorphosis known on earth today.

In the biological organism of man life battles with death in
growth and decline, in health and disease. In his subconscious
mind the instincts of self-preservation are poised against those
of self-destruction. In the higher spheres of his consciousness
the comprehending and the creative aspects of intuition are
confronted with the analytical gifts of intellectualism. Thus the
creative meets the created head-on in human nature. In the no
man's land between their opposing forces a divine spark lives,
capable of self-awareness and free choice. In all times the divine,
imprisoned in the confines of matter and instinct, has been de-
picted in the legends of the sacrificed god, his dismemberment,
and eventual resurrection through the redemption of man.

When we pursue thoughts of this kind, a divination of the
purpose of existence may stir in us. In spite of their inadequacies such thoughts may gradually lead us to the core of our self,
which is of divine origin, but has become separated from its
universal source for the sake of freedom. It is imprisoned in
a cage whose walls are made of the very forces which are the

builders and wreckers of the universe. Man can reject his mission, he can break out of his confines into the dream world of addiction or into suicide. He can relinquish the freedom for which he was made, to the will of others or to his own subhuman instincts. But if he decides to remake his own world in the image of a divine prototype, he will eventually achieve the true goal of his existence, kinship with God.

CHAPTER VI

THE HUMAN SELF
BETWEEN THE CREATIVE
AND THE CREATED

Modern man has come to a growing awareness that his mental health and moral freedom depend largely on the degree to which he knows himself. Thus he is deeply interested in all forms of psychology, especially in psychoanalysis. Yet this interest will avail him little so long as his mind remains closed to the fact that man is a spiritual *and* biological being. Some people see in the human being primarily a product of physical, biological, and environmental influences, while others resent all psychological materialism and try to explain the human psyche by entirely spiritual concepts. Although both schools of thought have recently been forced to make concessions, they have not really changed their basic views. Yet, regardless of how dear our idealistic or materialistic concepts may be to us, we shall never understand man, i.e., ourselves, unless we realize that our soul life is subject to the influence of two equally strong forces. This, of course, does not mean that in a suprahuman reality the created could ever be a match to the creative, but in man they meet as equals. If they did not, the stronger of the two would inevitably remodel human thinking in its own image. Thus in the course of time man's mind would reflect either the world of ideas or of matter, but not both. It would be a captive of the gods or of the beasts, and incapable of free choice.

Modern psychology knows that biological urges and appetites fail to explain man as a whole, but this knowledge has hardly been shared by the layman. What has entered into the consciousness of the masses is the fact that an abundance of physical and biological factors do influence human psychology, and this recognition has found traditional religion unprepared. Thus it is often the children of deeply devout parents who turn violently against religion, once they have come into contact with modern science. For earlier or later they will encounter facts which to the unprepared mind may well appear irreconcilable with a spiritual concept of man. To give a concrete example, it may be permissible to refer to a personal experience:

Many years ago a friendly discussion on religion took place among the staff members of a hospital. The conversation remained on an impersonal level until a brilliant young scientist rose to deliver a tirade against all forms of religion. He openly admitted that he had joined an authoritarian movement for the sole purpose of defeating those who "build their power on religious lies." His speech was charged with so much hatred and bitterness that contradiction seemed useless. Not until years later, when his obsession had ruined his life, did we learn the story that lay back of his hate. The only child of extremely devout parents, he had been led to an unquestioning faith in man's full moral responsibility not only for his conduct and deeds but even for his emotions. From childhood on he had loved God more fervently than anything life had to offer and, unknown even to his parents, had solemnly dedicated himself to the achievement of inner purity and perfection. All through adolescence and the early years of his adult life he had fought and won countless battles with himself, trying to lead the life of a saint. To help others he had chosen the medical profession, and had succeeded in upholding his ideals all through the junior years of medical school.

But his world collapsed shortly after he had entered a hospital as student resident, where one of his first experiences was an assignment to help a patient suffering from inexplicable character changes. The man, a minister, had been revered by a

large congregation for his unusual kindness and self-effacement. Then a change had gradually taken place in him, a
change which did not seem to affect his reasoning power, but
reversed his character traits to such a degree that he became
prone to choleric outbursts and, ultimately, to physical violence. All efforts to treat him by psychotherapy failed.

Eventually, however, the cause of his condition was discovered: a deficiency of his parathyroid glands. After the diagnosis was made, and the proper medical treatment given, the
patient's personality was restored: again he became an ami-
able, modest man. And it was this experience which threw the
young medical student into a turmoil of doubts. His whole
belief in the spiritual nature of man was undermined by having
witnessed a character changed by illness—and restored after
the administration of a few injections. When, in the further
course of his studies, he realized that an untold number of
physical influences could affect the soul qualities of man, he felt
he had been cheated by parents and teachers. He found that
the human consciousness could be decidedly modified by
changes in the brain structure and in glandular function, by
the composition of the air we breathe, administration of certain
drugs—in short, by an almost limitless number of physical
factors. Where, then, was the soul of man, where his moral
responsibility, if influences of an undeniably material nature
could determine or change his moral sense and even his soul?

The reaction of the young doctor, who was possessed of an
almost medieval personality, might not be considered of general
significance, were it not for the large number of physicians and
scientists who have lost their faith as a result of similar experiences. For who could remain unmoved by the decline of an
intelligent and often highly sensitive person into a subhuman
state, merely owing to a thyroid deficiency; who would not
wonder at the re-emergence of the former individuality under
the influence of nothing more than a few grains of thyroid?

Yet the materialist who is convinced that the extract of thyroid made a sensible being of a cretin is wrong; for the physical
substance of the drug contains in itself nothing akin to intelligence. It was not taken from a sage among animals; nor could

it increase the intelligence of a person whose own thyroid gland functions well. It merely serves to mend the instrument on which the invisible artist strives to play the melody of his life. But while the unquestionable influence of matter on the human mind fails to prove a materialistic concept of man, its significance must not be overlooked. For we are not here concerned with supersensible beings, but with humans on earth: citizens of two worlds, sustained by and dependent upon both.

We do not even have to turn to pathological conditions to see how deeply the forces of the outer world can penetrate the human—and animal—organism. Our eye contains an optical system very similar to the design of a photographic camera, and light impulses behave in cornea, lens, and vitreous body as they do in the inorganic world. The otolith organs in our inner ear, together with the semicircular canals, make use of the mechanical forces of gravity and motion to contribute to our sense of equilibrium and to our muscular tonus. Certain crabs even introduce small stones into their skull structure to sustain their sense of balance.

As we pointed out earlier, there can be no doubt that our consciousness, our thinking, our emotions, and even our actions are influenced by mechanical and chemical processes flowing in from the outer world. In other words, whatever enters our organism, be it through the gateway of our senses or even by way of absorption and digestion, gains access to all layers of our physical and mental life.

Most materialistic, naturalistic, and organicistic schools will agree with us on this point. They are aware of the metamorphoses of forces taking place in the kingdoms of nature. But, while modern thinking excels in knowledge of facts, it is seriously hampered by biased notions on the part of its individual interpreters. Thus it is not science itself but the unscientific overtones, the wrong emphases put on facts, which have brought so much confusion into the thought life of our time. Modern theoreticians see in energy and matter a self-evolving principle and, in man, a kind of generator or, as Professors Kelly and Rasey put it succinctly, "a unit of energy seeking to spend itself."[1] However, such thinking threatens to distort our world concept into a caricature. It could be likened to the following reasoning: The energy of fuel fed into a machine is transformed into heat, heat into mechanical energy which in turn exerts its power on some material to change it into a refined piece of merchandise. Thus a process of evolution has taken place in which the energy of cheap fuel has created a valuable product. This indeed would be magic, but the materialist—even taking investment and labor into consideration—forgets one vital factor. The force which starts in the depths and moves upward could not function on its own. It is guided by something else, something that adds purpose to the blind energies of matter: the creative thought of the inventor.

It was necessary to make this point in order to draw the rather delicate line between our attempt to describe one current of man's nature, and the mechanistic and naturalistic concepts prevailing today. Although, admittedly, outer impulses do penetrate and influence us, they reach in their progress into and through our organization a point where all mechanical and chemical processes lose their primary significance. In regard to sense stimulations this point is clearly marked by the emergence of a mental image. The mental image cannot, by any stretch of imagination, be classified as a physical or chemical phenomenon, so long as we do not confuse the percept itself with the chemical or electrical occurrences which, within every living organism, precede, accompany, and follow mental processes.

Unfortunately, the frequent use of such terms as electronic "brains," "thinking machines," and their like has created serious misconceptions as to the nature of psychological processes. With further progress in electronics, the inclination of modern man to consider himself a living machine is rapidly becoming a grave danger to his mental balance. One proposed device, called the "Perceptron," is said to be capable of learning and forming concepts. To evaluate this claim we must first consider for a moment the meaning of percept and perception.

The word "percept" as used in this book denotes the mental image of a perceived object. A "perception" can be (a) sensual, i.e., an apprehension of a sense object, or (b) intuitive, i.e., an apprehension of qualitative phenomena regardless whether such phenomena pertain to a sense object or a metaphysical reality. (In parentheses we want to reiterate here our belief that both sensual and intuitive perceptions, while subject to errors, are potentially capable of reflecting truth.)

The materialist sees the "percept" in the biophysical re-action of the sense and nervous system; his opponent in the act of association (with its undertones of experience and memory), which is certainly not of material nature but of the character of thought. A reaction without association lacks essential prop-erties of "perception": the automatic reflex of some plants to heat or touch is not a "percept." Hence the prevailing denial of a percept's metaphysical nature seems to some extent a game of semantics.

This conceptual ambiguity is strikingly illustrated by the recent claim concerning the "Perceptron," which for this reason merits a brief and simplified description. It has been asserted that the proposed device (so far only on paper) is capable of "imitating" an alleged physiological "mechanism" of human memory. For this purpose, the device is to have a great number of random connections between its input and its output sides, so that a certain stimulus (action) A_1 may evoke different reactions (responses) R_1, R_2, R_3, etc., each of them through a multitude of connections (channels).

Originally, the device is not biased in favor of any of the channels. But it has a built-in automation of such function that if, *by mere chance,* the first few "observations" of stimulus A_1 happen to find their way to response R_1 oftener than to R_2, then the cybernetic channels from A_1 to R_1 are automati-cally given more strength than are those to R_2. Thereby, on further repetition of the same stimulus A_1, the machine "learns" gradually to produce response R_1 more and more frequently, and any other response less and less frequently, until the statistical preponderance ultimately increases to outright dom-inance (for which the human operator then will form the mental association!). Almost everything about this proposed device is ingenious, but we can hardly accept the claim that it can form percepts and concepts.[2] Yet we do not have to go as far as the concepts to see that what a machine does is basically different from the process within the human mind. According to the *Oxford Universal Dictionary* (1955), perception is the "action of the mind by which it refers its sensations to an external object as their cause"; and a percept is the "mental product of perceiving."

Unless we are intent on confusing issues by describing entirely different processes by one and the same term, we must always keep in mind that a percept is devoid of all characteristics of physical substance and energy. To clear our mind of general confusion caused by misplaced mechanistic concepts, we may visualize a percept as if it were an object freed from weight, space, and all the other fetters of its material being, and lifted to a higher state of existence.

While we must try to guard against materialistic oversimplification, we must be equally careful to avoid the danger of superidealistic phantasy. To the immaterialist for whom the outer world holds no reality at all, our theory of matter and energy, attaining in man's mind a higher form of existence, must appear absurd. There is only one reply to the immaterialist, the reply already made in a previous chapter: the conduct of life on the part of every human being is based on a persistent tacit assumption of existing outer realities, and our search is for a philosophy that will help us improve our orientation in practical life, not for speculations which disregard the only available basis of cognition: human nature.

However, there is another objection to our view, which is more difficult to refute. It is based on the fact that, as our sense organs pick up and bring to our consciousness an extremely limited percentage of physical aspects of an object under observation, they are incapable of transmitting to us a correct picture of the outer world. The confusion caused in modern cultural life by this argument is tremendous. Yet, while the facts on which it is based are undoubtedly true, the conclusions drawn from them are unrealistic; for they could be correct only if our senses were windows in a wall separating compartments on the same level of existence. Since, however, our sense organism forms a bridge between physical objects and metaphysical percepts, it cannot be evaluated by criteria which are valid only in the world of matter.

An attempt to investigate the true function of our senses must be postponed until we know a little more about the other main current of human nature, as reflected in intuition. Until we have acquired this knowledge we can say only that somewhere between our sense organs and our mind the outer world dies, to be reborn on a different level of existence. The polarity between an outer object and its mental reflection is mirrored in the polarity between the physiology of our brain and the psychology of our mind. The brain itself may well be considered the greatest of all wonders on earth. For its structure bears the most perfect imprint of creative thought on created matter. No wonder that many a scientist mistakes the instrument for the performer, and considers thoughts a product of the brain, as if they were hormones produced by a gland. This is, of course, absurd because a hormone, like every other product of substance, has natural properties such as physical and chemical qualities, of which thoughts are entirely devoid. Thinking is no more a product of the brain than music is a product of a piano. Nevertheless, the physical properties of the instrument will, to a great extent, determine the quality of the music which is played on it.

Contrary to medieval thinking, which was still primarily interested in the inner, the qualitative aspects of life, modern science is the offspring of a quantitative, an external way of cognition. As such, it could have completed man's knowledge of himself, had it not in youthful conceit thrown overboard most of the priceless treasures of ancient intuitive wisdom. Instead of adding its new insight to the old, today's philosophy has merely substituted the half-truth of a strictly earth-bound way of cognition for the mystical half-truth of the Middle Ages. Thus, while the medieval mystic was in danger of losing the solid ground under his feet, the modern materialist may lose all contact with his higher life. This possibility is real and stems from two dangers, the first spiritual, the second physical.

The first lies in modern thinking, which has become so shallow that it is in danger of losing its ability to deal with problems of deeper significance. Since in the course of evolution organs are modified by their activity, the human brain may undergo subtle but far-reaching changes, which can transform it into a true semblance of a calculating machine.

The second is physiological. We know that even minute changes in the electrical potentials, the mineral and chemical composition of the central nervous system, can affect human consciousness. What will the absorption of radioactive strontium and carbon, of DDT and the many other insecticides, do to the consciousness of our generation and especially of those to come? Is it not likely that they will coarsen the delicate structure of the human brain until it becomes unfit to reflect spiritual values? That foreign substances even as "trace elements" may exert an influence on human consciousness has been proved by experiment.

That thoughts, too, have an effect on the human physique is less obvious but still noticeable in the changes of physiognomy which take place in people who devote themselves to scientific, artistic, or religious studies, in contrast to those who lose themselves in pursuits that are merely material. Is it then so far-fetched to suspect that the present increase in some disturbing phenomena—such as excessive growth of limbs, reading handicaps, and neuroses—may be traced to a faulty education?

Fortunate for future generations is the rapid pace at which twentieth-century science is outgrowing the materialistic concepts of yesterday. Yet the time lag between the emergence of scientific discoveries and their actual impact on "popular science" is dangerously long. It is therefore of greatest importance that we, the bewildered denizens of an era that "solves" problems with tranquilizers, learn to recognize the undeniable power of matter over the human mind without succumbing to the fallacies of a materialistic philosophy. Ideas on the origin and evolution of the world, prevalent during a certain era, also determine man's concept of himself. If life is just a property of carbon, and consciousness an offshoot of life, then man's thinking is no more than a function of his physical brain, and his emotions are merely the results of biological instincts and social adjustments.

Owing to the growing knowledge of biological and chemical influences on human psychology, spiritual concepts of the human psyche are now considered unscientific. Nineteenth-century science has contributed to this dangerous development, since many of the then leading scientists were actually convinced that increased knowledge of material laws would lead to an ever more comprehensive intellectual world picture, which in turn could be the foundation of a paradise of peace and happiness on earth. At that time matter still appeared a safe and solid ground on which to base an understanding of all that exists in the world and of man himself. Fortunately, the farther science pushed the borderlines of knowledge, the thinner grew the foundations of a materialistic world picture.

Is matter really a foundation on which a world concept can be built? Is it the safe, solid ground of existence which will eventually "explain" all the secrets of man and of the universe?

To repeat a statement partly quoted before:

There is evidence in recent years of the dawn of a new day in science. The materialism of the nineteenth century has disappeared for the physicist, whose job it is to study matter. Many other people, however, still think in terms of this materialism. We have the strange situation that the man in the street has begun to believe thoroughly in science, while the man in the laboratory has begun to lose faith in his science.

The solid hard matter of the older view has disappeared from the scientist's ken. Its rigid closed system has been burst wide open.[3]

In the course of history, scholars have tried to trace the origin of the world to one of the four elements. Either their own temperaments, or the spirit of their age may have had some influence on the direction of their search. Some found the universe made of water; others traced it to fire or air. Nineteenth-century man, the great "realist," looked at the solid ground of matter for the answers to his question. The splendid results of his research seemed at first to prove him right, until suddenly the firm structure of a mechanical universe gave way to a new world of vacant spaces and new dimensions. The study of matter, instead of yielding a relatively simple solution to secrets of the universe, has opened vistas into a nether world as infinite and incomprehensible as the cosmos above us.

Nor should this come as a surprise, since it seems illogical to seek a common denominator for the phenomena of a creative and a created world anywhere but in man himself. When we try to study outer objects scientifically, we unwittingly disregard the integral part which our own psychology plays in the process of observation; when we trust in pure thoughts, we disregard the physical processes which influence the objectivity of our thinking. Thus the master key to a comprehension of the world should be sought not in fire, water, or air, not in atoms or molecules, but in the psycho-physical principle of human nature. This concept, while not entirely new, has never been applied in the sciences, and least of all in modern psychology. Yet, in our opinion, not only is such application possible, but it will ultimately prove indispensable for the future of science, civilization, and humanity as a whole.

The day is still distant when science will discover that man himself is the cornerstone of creation, and that understanding of the world depends on comprehension of his nature. But the time has already come when the first steps must be taken toward a form of self-recognition which takes into consideration man's unique position within the pulsating currents of universal life. Today we prefer to seek self-knowledge through introspection rather than through expansion of our consciousness. We would find it in a healthier and safer manner were we to strive for an experience of the currents which perpetually enter our psycho-physical organism.

Awareness of such currents can be fostered by a kind of reasoning that deals with universal rather than with personal affairs. Let us envisage two main streams, one representing the course of matter as it pours its substance and energy into us through the gateways of our sensual and absorptive organs; the other, the creative, the unifying stream—these meet in us to evolve and sustain our psychophysical organization. One of these main currents represents material energy and substance, as they enter our organism through its various gateways of sense perception and absorption; the other represents the stream of creative thought which enters our mind through the mysterious channels of intuitive perception. Scientists before and after Darwin concentrated on the former, the Bible and the genealogical legends of old on the latter; together they form the true story of evolution.

The process of evolution is by no means confined to the past, but is working in us at every moment of our life. From the outside world a constant stream of forces pours into our organism, sustaining our physical body and influencing our mental and emotional life. The deeper these forces penetrate, the more do they lose their mechanical and chemical characteristics, to emerge at last in an entirely new form of existence, as mental phenomena. Thus we can say that the material world dies in us, to be reborn on a higher plane.

A sound wave reaches our ear. In the external auditory canal it behaves as though it traveled in outer air. Its impact makes the eardrum vibrate in accordance with mechanical laws. But on its further journey from the middle ear inward, the physical phenomena of acoustics die to be reborn in the experience of sound.

The drama of death and resurrection is re-enacted wherever the outer world enters man or animal, be it through his senses or other gateways of absorption. The food he eats, the air he breathes, and the ether waves that reach him through eyes and skin abandon their own existence to expand the scope of his consciousness. They die as it were, but live on in the imprint they leave on every cell of his organism. Animal species existing in complete darkness do not evolve functioning eyes, for it is the light itself which creates the organs of light. And this is true of ears, digestive systems, lungs—in short, an organism endowed with a higher consciousness lifts the lower kingdoms up toward its own spiritual state, and in exchange receives from them the means for its biological evolution.

Every metal, every mineral is, to its smallest particles, dominated by strict physical laws. A molecule of a crystal, for example, will join another at exactly the relative position necessary for the predetermined shape of its "molecular grid." These and similar correlations exist everywhere in the cosmic order of the universe as well as in the miniature wonder of a snowflake. Inherent in the nature of inorganic matter, they bring an element of structure and separation into the all-pervading jungle of life.

The world sends its emissaries through the various pathways of sensory and digestive absorption into the human being to become part of his physical organism and to find themselves reflected in the magic mirror of his brain. In it the secrets of life and death are brought to consciousness by the very power which created the world, and which for this reason is alone capable of comprehending it.

The psychological importance of thoughts like these may be realized by experiments of the following kind: A true music lover might attempt to put to rest his own artistic feelings and, while listening to the playing of an instrument, concentrate exclusively on its technical characteristics, the physical qualities of sound waves, their pathways, and their mechanical effects on his eardrum. After repeating such an exercise several times a sensation will rise in him somehow akin to the "coldness" of purely mechanistic phenomena in the outer world. When he then strives to revive his own love and reverence for music, he will arrive at an experience of an opposite character, of a flow of forces from within which meet and transfigure what reaches his physical organism from without.

Those who maintain that such an experiment cannot bring any new knowledge to an intelligent person, do not realize the breath-taking gap which separates knowledge from experience. Naturally, the outer world is resurrected in the human soul regardless whether or not a human being pays full attention to this perpetual miracle. But, if taken too casually, self-awareness of man is gradually replaced by a form of consciousness which reduces him to the evolutionary state of the animal: for only if we intentionally heighten the experience of sensual-intellectual currents on the one hand and of intuitive comprehending forces on the other, can we grow aware of the unique element that stands between them, the human self.

Yet we do not have to turn to art to achieve a greater degree of self-awareness. In the food we eat, the world pours her resources into our body. In ages wiser than ours meals were rituals. The origin and preparation of food products were studied with keen interest; while the meal itself was taken in a mood that lifted the human soul to its Creator. It was, therefore, not surprising that for the early Christian the common meal was a ritual of surpassing significance. For accepted in such spirit food does not only rebuild the body, but strengthen man's selfhood.

CHAPTER VII

THE EVOLUTION
OF CONSCIOUSNESS AND ITS
REFLECTION IN LEGENDS

The story of man's evolution is twofold. In the language of science, it deals with the evolvement of a biological organism, capable of holding a spark of divinity. In the language of art and folklore, it tells of the descent of the human spirit into an ever closer relationship with this physical vessel. One of the gifts reserved for man alone is his ability to translate each of these languages into its counterpart.

In this chapter we shall try to find some clues to such a translation in the hope of stimulating the interest of some of our readers in a quest of their own.

The story of man himself, of his spirit, cannot be told in intellectual terms; it requires the universal language of art, which speaks to the heart itself. Intuitive experiences can never be adequately expressed in words. However, the magnificent imagery of legends, myths, and true folklore can arouse in all men—as they have in the past—a divination of the absolute. The Bible itself, rooted in this form of consciousness, begins with the dramatic imagery of Genesis and continues through the record of innumerable experiences to the visions of the Book of Revelation, thus presenting mankind with a clear indication of living religion.

While pagan tradition and the Bible relate the visions of a

few chosen personalities, they also hint at an even earlier epoch of consciousness when a great number of men were capable of a direct comprehension of God, of the world, and of their fellow creatures through the medium of an all-encompassing intuitive consciousness. While pagan legends speak of a Golden Age, the Bible tells us of the Garden of Eden and the prehistoric existence of a universal language that disappeared from the world with man's attempt to build a tower "whose top may reach unto heaven."

For some time past our scholars have considered such legends testimonies of a childish, impressionable age. Funk and Wagnalls' excellent *Standard Dictionary of Folklore,* for instance, makes the following statement: "The story [of the Tower of Babel] may have been inspired in the nomadic people by the ziggurats and the swarming cosmopolitan life of the large Babylonian cities."[1] This assertion, however, is incongruous with the one which follows immediately thereafter and reads: "somewhat similar legends accounting for the diversity of languages are found in Africa, eastern Asia and Mexico."

Not until Jung's teachings became known to the world did it occur to a wider circle of modern intellectuals that a profound wisdom might be hidden behind the childlike language of ancient folklore. Still more recently it has dawned on a growing number of our philosophers and historians that, without renewed contact with its own past, modern consciousness may wither like the crown of a tree severed from its trunk and roots. Or, as put by a modern psychologist, speaking about historic and cultural continuity: "The structure of modern consciousness rests on this integration . . . , and at each period of its development the ego has to absorb essential portions of the cultural past transmitted to it. . . ."[2] By way of his own work, Neumann implies that modern man cannot be satisfied with a merely traditional connection with the past, but needs intellectual awareness of its wisdom.

Jung and his disciples have sought and found many ciphers of a universal language in dreams and anxieties, legends and creeds, and consider them "primordial images of the collective unconscious." But has this language always been part of the unconscious? Could it not be that the unconscious has become its prison and potential grave? For, once "the whole earth was of one language, and of one speech" (Gen. 11:1).

And the legend says that men built a tower to reach heaven, and to attain godlike power. "From it some men shot arrows at the sky and they came back bloodied. When the tower was not quite finished, God sent seventy angels to confuse the tongues of the workmen, and one did not understand the next; they fought; some were transformed into apes and demons."[3]

It is hard to see how anyone can believe that any tower of brick and mortar could have given rise to a world-wide legend of this kind. True, there are several ruins and excavation sites claimed to be the remains of the Tower of Babel. But, even if we disregard the fact that similar myths have existed elsewhere, we must remember that ancient peoples were wont to connect by name and tradition certain historical personalities and events with mythology. This was not because these personalities and events had preceded or inspired the legend, but because they seemed to bear out in spirit and deeds the kind of consciousness to which the myth referred. Even today, in countries where intuitive consciousness has survived—as for instance in Tibet—identification of historical personalities with legendary prototypes or with divine beings is quite common. We shall never understand religion or even folklore, we shall never train our own dormant faculties by their wisdom and enchanting beauty, unless we recognize some rules common to all of them.

First: the topic of the myth is inner, not outer life. Its chief concern is the kind of consciousness which determines the course of history, not history itself.

Second: where outer and inner events actually conform, the legend can be mathematically precise. A striking example of this was given by Schliemann, who saw his fondest dreams come true just because he had the courage to rely on the few indications which the *Iliad* devotes to historical and geographical facts.

Third: the legend gives due notice when it refers to non-material factors by modifying its imagery with descriptive qualities which are nonexistent in the world of the senses. "And the tower was so tall that it took a year to ascend."

Fourth: the ancient artist is perfectly capable of abandoning his highly imaginative language for the sake of physical details when he intends to characterize the kind of civilization to which he refers. "And they said: '. . . let us make brick, and burn them thoroughly. And they had brick for stone, and slime had they for mortar . . . ,' " and then, returning to his true topic, history of consciousness, " '. . . let us build us a city and a tower, whose top may reach unto heaven . . .' " (Gen. 11:3–4).

Here the Bible refers to a profound conflict in the nature of man. His longing to become a master in the world of the senses had prematurely separated him from the paradise of pure intuitive perception, the paradise in which the divine, the Biblical "Kingdom of Heaven," had been open to his soul. He had eaten from the "Tree of Knowledge," and started to grasp the laws and secrets of matter. But his triumph had failed to bring him happiness, and his longing for the Garden of Eden had never died in the depths of his soul. Thus he set out to reach the Paradise he had lost, but the means he used and still uses will never take him there. Physical knowledge and intellect can build magnificent civilizations, they can erect towers which scrape the sky, but they cannot, to use the Biblical language, "reach unto heaven."

Is man to be punished for his error? Contrary to many of its interpretations, the Bible gives us no indication of vengeful wrath, only of divine apprehension at man's boundless ambition. "And this they begin to do: and now nothing will be restrained from them, which they have imagined to do. . . . let us go down, and there confound their language . . ." (Gen. 11:6–7). What kind of language was this that had to be "confounded"? It was the language of intuitive experience which, while it had lost its paradisiacal purity and strength, was still an intrinsic part of ancient consciousness. It may have given men special capacities of communicating with one another in an ecstatic state of mind, which certain drugs can induce even today. Such forms of group consciousness can endow human beings with a collective strength which may account for some of the wonders of antiquity, which have so far defied all attempts at intellectual explanation.

It is easy to imagine what might have happened, had later civilizations retained the elemental power of earlier conscious‑ness. Amoral intellectualism coupled with decadent intuitive forces would surely have destroyed man and his world long before he had reached his present state of maturity. Yes, in spite of our failings, we have come of age. A major part of the world population has at last developed intellectual faculties strong enough to understand the past, and steer the future course of history.

But before we can hope to define our goals for the future, we must pause to reflect on the basic elements of consciousness, and on the part they have played in the past. What, for example, is the role of analytical intellect in the master plan of human evolution? It gives independence to man and provides him with the tools for building a better world. Analytical intellect alone, however, cannot lead to happiness and spiritual fulfillment, for love, peace, joy, and even the thrill of adventure are intuitive experiences. If intuition were allowed to die in man's soul, no outer achievement could give him joy, and no improvement of his living conditions could bring him happiness.

The supreme bliss of flying has been man's dream since earliest time, but what was once a mere symbol has eventually become an end in itself. True, so long as mechanical flight was but a remote ideal, it kindled man's imagination, and thus gave him the joy of a shining goal. When it had been achieved, however, and brought to near perfection, another dream died in the human soul. For the wings of Hermes or of Icarus have as little to do with the flying apparatus of a modern airplane as the enjoyment of a Shakespearean play with the study of the grammar it uses. This is not said to minimize the utilitarian significance of great inventions, but only to show that we must not expect of them what they cannot give. Once man looked up to the starry heaven in unspeakable longing, a longing that brought him closer to God. Today we plan to shoot missiles to the moon, and dream of bestowing the doubtful blessings of our own civilization upon other planets. But should we succeed, the prophesy of the legend will be borne out: ". . . men shot arrows at the sky, and they came back bloodied."

The wisdom contained in the Bible and in other records of even older origin should give the champions of "emergent evolution" some pause for reflection. The human race may have existed on earth for millions of years while the great treasures of its culture may not be older than several millenniums. Still the fact remains that, almost as soon as man's spirit could fully express itself through the medium of his physical organism, its messages reflected memories of a world of supernal greatness and superintellectual wisdom. Were it true that the human spirit is merely a higher form of animal consciousness, its first recorded expressions could not have dealt with the *super*natural. Were it true that human wisdom is solely the fruit of trial and error, of social experience, and established habits of civilization, we—or at least our leaders—should have wisdom far exceeding that of the leaders of mankind at the dawn of its recorded history.

Even today many people, including teachers, believe that Darwin actually claimed that man descended from the ape. This, in the literal sense, is not correct. What Darwin's theory indicated was that man and the apes now living have a common ancestry. Later anthropologists, accepting most of Darwin's views, have searched for the "missing link," the transition form between extinct anthropoids and homo sapiens. Yet, although often announced, the "missing link" has proved surprisingly elusive. Even the Pithecanthropus erectus failed to fulfill the early hopes aroused by his discovery. "Scientists continue to believe that the Pithecanthropi were indeed men; but the evidence on which the supposition was based has been dissipated and his erect stature, like so much information on prehistoric man, is now based only upon an act of faith."[4]

Actually nothing could be further from the truth than the widespread belief that Darwin has solved—in principle at least —the greatest mystery of man's evolution. Surely any solution of this kind would have to concern, above all, the human brain. But was Darwin right about the brain? One of our leading anthropologists, Loren C. Eiseley, quoting Darwin's great contemporary, says: "Finally, Wallace challenged the whole Darwinian position upon man by insisting that artistic, mathematical, and musical abilities could not be explained on the basis of natural selection and the struggle for existence. Something else, he contended, some unknown spiritual element must have been at work in the elaboration of the human brain. Why else should men of simple cultures possess the same basic intellectual powers which the Darwinists maintained could only be elaborated by competitive struggle?" And later the author expresses his own views in these deeply impressive words: "We have been so busy tracing the tangible aspects of evolution in the *forms of animals* that our heads, the little globes which hold the midnight sky and the shining invisible universes of thought, have been taken about as much for granted as the growth of a yellow pumpkin in the fall."[5]

The confusion of our age would be considerably lessened if more scientists were as frank as Steward Easton who, in his *Heritage of the Past,* says: "The truth is that we know very little indeed about prehistoric man, and the unremitting labors of archeologists and anthropologists . . . have only scratched the surface of our almost total ignorance."[6] Even this scratching of the surface is a tremendous triumph of human genius, and in the far future it may well unfold the whole evolutionary story of man's biological organism.

But what about the science of tribal history? Does it not show everywhere the gradual development of animal-like hordes into civilized communities? Not on closer scrutiny. For, although the number of primitive cultures was larger in the past than it is today, many of the earliest civilizations show signs of decadence rather than immaturity, while the cultural refinement of a few is still unsurpassed. Naturally, we must never make the mistake of considering low moral standards as indications of man's origin, especially since the most sinister moral aberrations of early cults are of a kind entirely alien to any creature lower than man. In them, biological and spiritual impulses have undergone highly sophisticated perversions of a kind possible only to the human mind.

Referring now to the corresponding ciphers of intuitive

language, we again find the amazing trustworthiness of ancient tradition which, without ever doubting man's spiritual origin, abounds in dramatic reports on the moral failures and early cultural decadence of the human race: "And it repented the Lord that he had made man on the earth . . ." (Gen. 6:6).

One source of misunderstandings which should be clearly recognized, lies in the fact that the very problem of human evolution is usually presented incorrectly. So long as we discuss the evolution of man's organism, the oldest unmistakably human fossils represent the only scientific proofs for or against certain biological theories. Once, however, we turn to man himself, to his consciousness, we find that *its* earliest known manifestations represent the only scientifically acceptable testimonies of his past. Even if tomorrow the "missing link" should be found, we could say only that Darwin was right about the way in which nature has built man's physiological organism. If we should find an unmistakably human fossil with an apelike brain, we could say only that our research had led us back to a being not yet capable of harboring a human mind, or to a decadent offshoot of the tree representing man's evolution.

The history of man is the history of his consciousness. Its testimony unequivocally contradicts all naturalistic and materialistic theories of his evolution. For if it were true that man's mind had its origin in animal instincts, if it were true that only his desire for self-preservation had led him to invent community life, and eventually justice and love, then the history of his consciousness would have had to be different from what it is. All his dreams and legends—at least those born before the age of recorded history—should reflect veneration for nothing higher than a creature equipped with the strongest teeth and sharpest claws, while the story of a Garden of Eden, the myth of a Golden Age, could at best have emerged at the end of his present phase of evolution. Yet exactly the opposite is true. It is modern civilization which believes that every aspect of human relation must be enforced by law, while its ancient counterpart could still conceive of a society based on voluntary decency and brotherhood. "First was the Golden Age, the age which, needing no avenger nor written law, voluntarily kept faith and virtue. There was no punishment, no fear. . . ."[7]

Was there ever a Golden Age on earth? Who knows? But whether there was or not, one thing is certain: even before the dawn of history it did exist in the consciousness of almost all peoples and races of the world. This very fact bears witness to a homeland in the heights of the spirit, as a golden ray lingering on a mountaintop bears witness to the sun set below the horizon; and not to a homeland in the cruel darkness of a universal struggle for survival.

Would this enchanted realm be less real had it never existed on earth? Jung, when speaking of inner experience, says: "It is an almost ridiculous prejudice to assume that existence can only be physical. As a matter of fact, the only form of existence we know of immediately, is psychic."[8]

The "Krita Yuga" of the Indians, the "prehuman race" of the American Indians, the "Golden Age" of the Greeks, all point to a state of consciousness akin to what the Persians called "Paradise" and the Jews, the "Garden of Eden." In the latter, man lived in perfect harmony with his Creator. Still capable of hearing the inner word, the Logos, he understood the true nature of the creatures around him, and could, as the Bible says, give names to them. Of all the literature in the world, the Biblical stories offer perhaps the most impressive picture of a pure intuitive consciousness; for one cannot "hear" the voice of God with one's physical ear nor "see" the "Garden of Eden" with one's physical eye. In that state man comprehended the world within, but was blind to the world without. On his awakening, his first truly physical experience was, by necessity, awareness of the bare surface of his skin. Could there be a more artistic way of indicating the change in consciousness than the brief statement: "And the eyes of them both were opened, and they knew that they were naked . . ." (Gen. 3:7)?

Many have become alienated from religion because of the tenet of original sin and its seemingly unjust consequences for the whole human race. Some, as children, had loved the beauty of the Biblical story of Paradise, but later came to consider its message not only illogical but incompatible with an adult concept of God. Thus it went the way of many other childhood dreams—but with it crumbled yet another pillar of faith. Consequently, some have come to reject all religion as "opium of the people"; some have clung to it, unaware of the conflict in their own souls; while still others have tried to bridge the gap by reducing religion to mere humanitarianism. But the answer lies elsewhere: it lies where modern man in his intellectual conceit will hardly ever stoop to search. It is the humble fairy tale, scorned today as childish superstition and world-estranged phantasy, which tells the story of the human heart, of the powers which have turned it into stone, and of those who can break the evil spell.

Religion will never come to life in intellectual Bible research, in self-righteous virtue, or humanitarianism. It will come to life only if and when that part of the human soul which alone is capable of intuitive perception is released from its deathlike sleep. No one but "the Sleeping Beauty," the eternal child in man, long since paralyzed by the poisonous sting of materialism and egotism, could see and hear the world of the spirit; but she can be awakened from her sleep only when man's intellect turns into wisdom. For the good prince of the fairy tale is man's mind grown wise through trials and suffering, while the princess represents that part of the human soul which was never truly expelled from the Garden of Eden. And the roses which grow amidst the thicket of thorns around the bewitched castle, the flowers which lead the prince to the enchanted princess, are the myths, legends, and fairy tales whose messages ought to be heard again by modern man.

What is there in the story of man's expulsion from Paradise that made so many once-devout people believe that the Bible is but another example of immature phantasy? It is the concept of a God who forbids man to eat of a tree which He Himself put in the midst of the Garden, and then, when the inevitable occurs, inflicts His punishment not only on the guilty ones but on generation after generation. Who could believe in such a God or, if he does, love Him? Yet, as we have said before, modern man cannot even hope to comprehend the sacred writings of old unless he first learns to share in the kind of consciousness from which they sprang. To achieve this, he must consider at least one peculiarity to be found in all ancient theological and cosmological writings. It is the habit of pairing profound knowledge and lofty ideals with the apparently naïve.

The legend of the Tower of Babel, for example, while quite capable of drawing a precise enough picture of an actual brick building, loses itself into the seemingly, almost childish exaggerations of the Tower's gigantic structure. Just as it must have been obvious to the old Babylonians and Jews that no tower can be so tall as to take years to ascend, just as obvious it must have been to the cultured pagan that gods can neither have love affairs nor enter beauty contests. If we do not credit them with that much intelligence, the fault is ours.

The ancient artist was capable of revealing in a few words what volumes of philosophical writings cannot express. How did he accomplish such feats? By a technique which is not immediately effective for the modern reader but which can be made comprehensible to him by effort and reason. As late as in the Middle Ages man used to read (and listen) in a way entirely different from ours. Instead of trying to extract, at a glance, condensed and abstract meaning from a whole group of words, he dwelt on and lived with individual word pictures. It is well known that many medieval sages spent a lifetime on one or two books, reading and rereading them with great profit. Monks gave meticulous care to every letter and word they wrote. And crowds listened gladly again and again to the same stories told by minstrels and storytellers—a custom still alive in the East today. In certain cultural epochs the mere articulation of a divine name aroused in the souls of the audience an ecstatic experience of such power that its utterance had to be reserved for sacramental use or specific occasions. The mere invocation of a deity aroused feelings of awe and devotion, of fear, hope, love, or even rebellion—none of these responses compatible with a trivial interpretation of the gods' motives or actions. It was, therefore, possible to speak of a god's jealousy, vanity, anger, or personal love without expecting the listener to confuse cosmic trends with human passions.

What is true of pagan deities must apply even more to the Highest, to Him whose very name could not be mentioned except by the High Priest in the Holy of Holies. It is entirely inconceivable that in ancient times legends concerning God Himself were understood in the spirit of human psychology. Only today, when intuitive comprehension has all but vanished, has it become necessary to analyze the legends from an intellectual point of view. It is generally assumed that God expelled man from Paradise as a way of punishing the human race for the sin of disobedience committed by its earliest ancestors. Yet the legend itself speaks neither of "sin" nor "punishment." Actually, Adam and Eve could not commit a sin in the present sense of the word, since they had no "knowledge of good and evil" before they ate of the forbidden fruit (Gen. 2:17). And what was God's reaction to their "disobedience"? "And the Lord God said: Behold, the man is become as one of us, to know good and evil . . ." (Gen. 3:22). Does this sound like the verdict of a wrathful god against a fallen sinner? And even more revealing is the Biblical explanation of the cause for his expulsion: ". . . lest he put forth his hand, and take also of the tree of life. . . . the Lord God sent him forth from the garden of Eden" (Gen. 3:22–23). Again no word of punishment, but an undertone of apprehension as we found it in the story of the Tower of Babel.

Let us try to translate at least some of these gigantic pictures into intellectual concepts. Man was created a potentially free being. Whether or not he would accept this greatest and also most fearsome of all gifts, was the object of his first decision. Endowed with intuitive consciousness in its purest form, he was part of a spiritual harmony called the Garden of Eden. He could remain there as an obedient servant of God. But God Himself had planted in the middle of the Garden a tree whose fruit could open man's eyes to another world, a world that was to be his dominion. The partaking of the fruit of knowledge was man's resolve to awaken in himself forces which we, for lack of better terms, may call analytical intellect and predominantly physical perception. Even as intuition is related to universal will, to supersensible and hence eternal life, to an inner understanding of creation, intellect is related to matter and, therefore, to dissolution and death. Only he who learns the secrets of destruction can distinguish between good and evil. "But of the tree of the knowledge of good and evil, thou shalt not eat . . . : for in the day that thou eatest thereof thou shalt surely die" (Gen. 2:17). At one pole stood submission to the command of God, and the gift of undimmed vision and eternal life; at the other freedom, even from God, which in the artistic language of the Bible was called disobedience to His command. But it was disobedience by a being who did not yet discern good and evil and who, therefore, did not yet know moral choice.

And the expulsion from Paradise? The Bible says *God* drove man from the Garden of Eden, for in religious language all lies in the will of God. But it also makes clear that man expelled himself from a world of perfect inner harmony and from the protection by God, by choosing to find freedom through suffering and evil. If he were to start on his long, weary journey into and beyond evil, the Garden of Eden with its Tree of Life *had* to disappear from his vision—until, at last, he might find his way back to it in freedom.

The legend of man's expulsion from Paradise indicates a decisive change in human consciousness. With the statement that death was unknown in the Garden of Eden, the myth itself clarifies a significant point: it does not refer to an outer civilization whose remains could be found by paleontologists. From the expulsion onward, however, the *outer* aspect of life on earth became of growing interest to man. With this growing interest in the world, factual history emerged while myths and legends started to lose ground. But for millenniums they continued to tell the *inner* story of human evolution, the story of man's psyche and of its changing relationship to the outer and inner aspects of the world.

The folklore of almost all peoples on earth contains memories of a primordial intuitive consciousness of singular strength and purity, a consciousness which was, long before the age of historical monotheism, aware of the one God. But awareness of a supreme deity did not preclude worship of hierarchic beings of a lesser order. As man's vision faded, God disappeared from human consciousness, and His servants took His place in the human soul. Gradually man's selfishness and impurity, together with his growing individualism, distorted the originally pure images of superhuman forces into monsters. And eventually all inner vision faded, and made room for the empty abstraction of the latter part of the Greco-Roman era.

What were those gods who for millenniums determined the course of history, who were given credit for all progress in civilization, who were also the inspirers of arts and crafts? Were they really created by man in his own image? The numerous defenders of this theory must have strange acquaintances if they can see the picture of man in the divine dragon of the Chinese, the totem poles of the Indians, or the bull god of the Cretes. Kelly and Rasey, in their book on education and the nature of man, make the following statement: "When man invented his gods, he needed them to be greater than he, so that he could depend on them for help. So he made them all-knowing, all-powerful and ever-present."[9] This passage is quoted to show how little thought is given by prominent scholars of our time to the most important problems of ancient consciousness. For every college student ought to know that the pagan gods were anything but "all-knowing, all-powerful and ever-present." They were inner images reflecting the wisdom and power behind the various spiritual and natural phenomena of existence. Consequently, the scope of influence and the mission attributed to a deity were strictly limited. Far from being omniscient, a god could be deceived—in contrast to the ultimate power of destiny, which held sway over gods as well as over men.

Priests and philosophers of all not fully decadent cultures saw in gods members of a higher principle, which they could no longer reach. Thinkers like Plato and the greatest of his predecessors never ceased lamenting mankind's loss of intuitive vision, on the wane ever since recorded history began. Just as a man going blind may no longer be able to see beyond the outstretched hands of his guide, the pagan priest could discern of God no more than the "fingers of His hands"; and these he called his "gods." But although he was fully aware that behind them was a central Power, the "Great Spirit" or "Unknown God," he worshiped divine attributes as deities in their own right. This explains why almost all ancient creeds, while crediting their gods with superhuman power, see them bound by laws they could not change.

How, then, if the gods were part of God, can we account for their "evil deeds," "vengefulness," and "injustice"? As the fruit of a plant cannot ripen unless the flower from which it stems dies, the human soul cannot mature without trial and suffering. There is wisdom indeed in the blows of fate. But as the flower, were it able to think, would plead with the elements which destroy it, and consider them cruel, so does man dread and sometimes hate the forces of illness and death. To the pagan the wisdom and power behind grief and adversity had the semblance of an evil, vengeful god. Misled by decadent priests he might try to placate such a god.

The most advanced personalities in antiquity knew that people of different racial, tribal, and personal characteristics were meant to learn different lessons from fate. Thence the variety of cults and creeds guided by the teachers of the so-called mystery schools, the ecclesiastic universities of ancient times, who held their fingers on the pulse of civilization.

In the pre-Hellenic era the wellspring of culture was the Orient. There are many indications that students from the West gathered in the gigantic temple schools of Babylon, Assyria, Asia Minor, and Egypt, and even earlier in Ur, to receive knowledge and instruction for their future tasks as statesmen, scholars, and philosophers. ". . . we have learned how that flower of genius [Greece] drew its sap from Lydians and Hittites, from Phoenicia and Crete . . . but the roots go farther back; behind all these lies Sumer."[10] The wisdom of that epoch was overwhelming but entirely geared to the supernatural, the intuitive. "The temple towers on the ziggurats were observatories as well as shrines. Babylonian priests reckoned the motion of the planet Mercury more accurately than Hipparchus or Ptolemy. Indeed, they succeeded in determining the lunar revolution within four seconds of the figure arrived at by the most elaborate technical means."[11]

How did these priests come to their astonishing knowledge? Lacking astronomical instruments as well as the most elementary knowledge of modern astrophysics, they based their research on an intuitive comprehension rather than on physical observation and analytical intellect; and they could rightly say: the god of the planet has revealed his secrets to me.

Even as the science of the ancient Orient was theological in nature, its social order was hierarchic. Kings and priests were considered semidivine mediators between gods and men and, therefore, above good and evil. Had this state of consciousness endured, a higher degree of individualism, freedom, and moral choice could hardly have developed in average man.

Thus the world needed a change of consciousness. In ritual language: the human soul was to be wedded to the genius of a new era, one which neither scorned nor forgot its heritage. For the sages of antiquity knew that into the pattern of the future must be woven the threads of the past; that the human soul had to be wedded to the spirit of a new era, if it were to give birth to a new phase of evolution. "In the land of Tyre and Sidon, Europa, daughter of King Agenor, was reared in the seclusion of her father's palace. Once, at midnight when mortals are visited by fanciful dreams which have a clear core of truth, Heaven sent her a curious vision. It seemed to her that two continents—Asia and that which lies opposite—were fighting to possess her."[12] The next day, when the princess was gathering flowers on the meadow near the sea, Zeus appeared in the shape of a bull, enticed her to climb on his back, and carried her across the ocean to Crete. When she bemoaned her fate, Aphrodite herself consoled her: 'Be comforted, Europa! You were carried off by a god. You are destined to be the mortal wife of Zeus the Unconquerable. And your name shall be immortal, for from this time on the continent which received you shall be called Europa!' "[13]

Let us try to translate the pictorial language of the legend into modern intellectual concepts. Zeus was the father of the

Olympian gods. According to the myth, he was born in Crete, whose youths protected him from his child-eating father Chronos, the Greek word for time. With his reign a new age emerged, an age of light, an age in which great deeds and thoughts would be *recorded* and no longer left to oblivion, or extinguished by the forgetfulness of time. His also was the age in which Oriental mysticism gave way to Occidental reason. And the princess with whom he fell in love was not merely the daughter of a king but represented, as the legend itself implies, the soul of Asia.* The genius of the new era transplants the human soul from the hothouse atmosphere of the Oriental Mysteries into the fresh air and bright sun of the Occidental world.

Yet the unfailing wisdom of mythology tells us more. Zeus carried Europa to the island of Crete, where later a temple was built in her honor and where she received semidivine worship. And indeed, the main cultural impulse of the time, striving from Asia and Egypt toward Greece, had its stepping-stone in Crete.

When, approximately, was the dawn of the Cretan-Mycenaean epoch? Mythology gives us an answer to this question, pointing to one of the great numerals on its cosmic clock. Probably this world clock was already known to the Chaldeans—who had subdivided the starry heaven into twelve segments, the signs of the zodiac. Far from being primitive, cosmic science in its ancient form was an amazingly accurate discipline possessed of a wisdom hardly fathomed today. It made use of astrophysical laws without knowledge of their mathematical-intellectual premises. It was fully aware of the stars' influence upon the earth without knowledge of cosmic rays, radio-stars, or meteoric showers.

Astronomy brings three cycles into the life of mankind: day, year, and Platonic year, comparable to second hand, minute hand, and hour hand of a clock. During each daily cycle, the sun stays projected against the background of one certain fixed star constellation, and it rises and sets together with this con-

* This book is concerned only with the history of consciousness which led to our Occidental civilization, not with Far Eastern or Oriental cultural currents.

stellation. But the sun's position on the canopy of stars changes gradually in the course of the seasonal cycles: while it now "stands" in the constellation of Aquarius, one month from now it will "stand" in Pisces, another month later, in Aries. Every year the sun travels through all twelve constellations of the zodiac. Its present location on the star background indicates the instant phase of the earth-sun orientation, the present point of the seasonal cycle, the month of the calendar; and the reference point of the calendar is spring equinox, the start of new life, the start of a new year for most old cultures. Hence the constellation in which the sun stands at the time of spring equinox has always been considered of great importance; it "governs" the new year, and does so year after year, for an entire era.

Yet just as the earth-sun orientation changes through the seasonal cycle, so does the orientation of the entire earth-sun system against the background of the fixed stars. Slowly, almost imperceptibly slowly through the centuries, the reference point, the point where the sun stands at equinox (the sun's "spring point"), shifts from constellation to constellation, 26,000 times slower than the sun's seasonal travel (and in the opposite direction).* The old Babylonians saw their spring sun in the constellation of Taurus; the Greeks in Aries; the Crusaders in Pisces. Yet imperceptibly small as the shift is during one human lifetime, the priestly astronomers of ancient cultures proudly indicated their awareness of even these minute changes: the very emphasis on the "governing constellation of the era" was their implication that they had observed the progress even of the world clock's hour hand.

In those days scientific research was not yet exclusively devoted to intellectual curiosity, material greed, and construction of weapons. Its original purpose was a quest for cognition of the divine will. Since his expulsion from Paradise man was no longer within speaking distance of God. Therefore, he had to learn how to read His messages, or rather those of His servants, in all that happened on the physical plane. These divine servants were considered the guiding spirits of an epoch. Naturally,

---

* A phenomenon known as the "Precession of the Equinox."

the ancient astronomer-priest did not seek them in the constellations themselves, but in the power and wisdom that lay
behind the constellations. As he looked up to the heavens,
pictures must have arisen before his inner eye—pictures which
have survived to our day as symbols for the star formation of
the northern sky.

In the fourth millennium B.C., Crete's Early Minoan culture
started to write its chapter of the history of human consciousness, a few centuries after the sun at the vernal equinox had
entered into the sign of Taurus, the bull. Thus, in the fascinating language of mythology, Zeus assumed the shape of a bull
when he carried Europa to Crete, whose whole culture was to
remain faithful to the worship of the bull.

The Minoan epoch ended in the second millennium B.C.,
when the sun left Taurus and entered the constellation of
Aries, the lamb. At about that time the next period began, the
age of Achaean domination in Greece. While in that later era
the relationship between cosmic and human history was no
longer emphasized, its pattern can still be discerned in some
of the more significant Hellenic myths. It was a winged *ram*
on which Phrixus and Helle fled from the persecution of their
stepmother; and the sea in which the girl found her death was
called the Sea of Helle—the Hellespont. When Phrixus arrived
at Colchis, the ram was sacrificed to Zeus; and its golden fleece,
revered as a relic, remained there until Jason and his Argonauts
retrieved it and brought it back to the Occident.

Still earlier myths identify the ram with Zeus himself, the
god of light, from whose forehead sprang Pallas Athena, the
goddess of art, freedom, and reason, the genius of the new
enlightened age of classical Greece. But then came the fateful
decision of Paris, prince of Troy, which threatened to block
the flow of evolution. Paris, when guarding his flock (the
legend's usual word for priestly functions), was visited by
three goddesses who asked him to decide which of them was the
fairest. Man had become the judge of gods! "And Hermes said
to Paris: Do not be afraid! The goddesses have come to you
so that you may judge them."[14] Paris, ensnared by the "magic
belt" and the promises of Aphrodite, chose her in preference

to Hera and Athene. The two rejected goddesses were of genuinely Greek origin, both protectresses of law and human rights. Aphrodite, on the other hand, was an Oriental deity, earlier known as Astarte or Ishtar. Her orgiastic Mysteries belong to the oldest rituals known, and were at that time still related to the ancient fertility cults which were part of a much earlier state of evolution. The Greeks had purified these rituals under the name of Aphrodisia, in an attempt to sublimate the fiercest and most elemental instincts in man. But behind the Grecized form of Aphrodite still lived the terrible Ishtar with her ancient magic (the magic belt of the legend) which the era of classical Greece had to replace with the light of Reason. What was Aphrodite's gift to Paris? As reward for his judgment, she gave him the most beautiful woman on earth, Helena of Sparta.

Who was that woman of whom the old men of Troy say that she was worth all the unspeakable sufferings of a ten-year war? The myth itself gives us the answer: born of Zeus himself, Helena was no mortal woman. Her name indicates her true identity: the soul of Greece.

The struggle for the soul of Greece, which at that time was the soul of Europe itself, lasted for millenniums and may not have ended yet. But the legend gives it to us in one dramatic story centered around a politically insignificant conflict, the Trojan War. No wonder the immortal gods themselves joined in the battle for the human soul! Was she to remain under the magic spell of rituals which no longer suited man's changing consciousness, or to strive toward greater freedom? Powerful as the gods still were at the time of Homer, the decision was not theirs.

The outcome of the Trojan war can be laid neither to . . . Achilles nor to the counsel of oracles and gods. . . . The stories of the *Iliad* . . . already point to the hero, who later on was to conquer Troy, not through his courage or divine might, but through the cunning of his human intellect. . . . And with the cunning demonstrated by Odysseus, the new power, that of the human intellect, heralded the day of the further unfolding of consciousness. The dawn of that day came in Hellas whose bard, seer and builder Homer was.[15]

We have tried to show in a few examples how faithfully myths and legends have fulfilled their part in recording the story of human evolution. We must mention still another problem which cannot be omitted in even the sketchiest study of the history of consciousness. It is the problem of moral choice. According to the Bible, man was not created with the knowledge of good and evil. This knowledge was born when he separated his own will from that of God, when—in Biblical language—he was expelled from Paradise. The past course of history was strongly influenced by a subconscious longing for the actual experience of evil, an experience which man needed if he was to become able to choose the good of his own free will. For this reason the path of historic evolution could not, from the beginning, climb upward, but had to descend into depths while still leading on toward the goal of moral freedom.

Man has always possessed a certain degree of freedom, the freedom to choose the subject of his loyalty. But in earlier historical times even this was restricted, owing to inherited tribal and racial ties, to certain cultural and religious impulses. True, most tribes worshiped more than one deity, or opposite aspects of one and the same, as for instance the all-creating and all-devouring Great Mother, Shivo the creator and Shiva the destroyer. But it would be wrong to assume that the moral problems of paganism were similar to ours. What counted most in early times was that one served a powerful god and served him well. In the light of ancient consciousness decay and destruction were as essential for evolution as were healing and creation. Consequently, a worshiper of Baal offering human sacrifices could feel just as righteous and devout as a disciple of Aesculapius.

Even in the history of the Jews which, from the beginning, took a unique course, morality was a matter of obedience rather than of individual choice. Thus it never occurred to Abraham that the sacrifice of his own son, demanded by Yahweh, could be immoral. The remarkable fact that the Bible has nothing but praise for Abraham's readiness to bring a human sacrifice, should bring home to us that what may now seem outrageous might have had its proper place in other states of evolution.

On the surface, the pagan enjoyed a greater degree of religious freedom than the ancient Jew. In case of need he could pick from many gods the one he considered most influential and offer him his services and gifts. This, however, had little to do with religion. Where sincere and profound devotion existed, the pagan had no more religious freedom than had the ancient Jew. For, once he had become fully initiated into a specific cult, its rituals created inner experiences so compelling as to leave him little if any moral choice. Residues of such compulsory experiences are still alive in the trance worship of Asian and African tribes as well as in the Dervish rituals of Islam. Jung refers to the difference between ancient and modern religious freedom when he says: "Religion . . . is a dynamic existence or effect, not caused by an arbitrary act of will. On the contrary, it seizes and controls the human subject, which is always rather its victim than its creator." And later: "I want to make clear that by the term 'religion' I do not mean a creed. . . . Creeds are codified and dogmatized forms of original religious experience."[16] In other words, modern man, by exchanging "religion" for "creed," has won freedom from divine compulsion.

Recorded history is actually the story of that emancipation which has led man through all the phases of spiritual life, from ancient dependence on the divine to today's dependence on matter. While modern man (and there were some "modern" men at all times) does not even know if there is anything beyond nature, the ancient prophet or seer was a helpless tool of the supernatural. Between these extremes, eras existed when man experienced himself balanced between the ecstasy of spiritual and the loneliness of material dependence, and these eras are known as the classical periods of history. In them, seeds were planted for the development of that element which stands between Spirit and Nature, the element of human selfhood. Best known to us is the Classical Age of Greece when, in a few individuals at least, there existed a state of balance between intuition and intellect, between temple mystery and natural science, between inner and outer life. The great personalities of that era still acknowledged the superhuman powers which dominated the mysteries of birth and death, and the innumerable enigmas of nature. But they also felt in their own souls a growing strength, an ability to resist the compelling power of the gods still holding sway in the ecstatic rituals of the sibyls and oracles. The gods were beyond good and evil; consequently, the stronger devoured or enslaved the weaker. But within the confines of human selfhood a light began to glow, a moral principle so new that the Greeks had to find a word for it: *syneidesis,* "conscience." We encounter it for the first time in Euripides when Medea speaks to Jason thus: "I cannot . . . understand whether thou thinkest that the gods of old no longer rule, or that fresh decrees are now in vogue amongst mankind, for thy conscience must tell thee that thou hast not kept faith with me."[17]

A profound change had occurred in the history of human consciousness. Man's spirit on its downward path paused for a brief moment at the halfway mark of its journey. The world of inner experience with its powerful gods had released him from its hold; the world of the senses had not yet made him its slave. Thus, at least the greatest of that age felt in themselves a sense of harmony and balance, which gave rise to the ideals of freedom, of perfection, and of the Golden Mean. And deep within the human soul, like a jewel lit up by the ray of a distant sun, Conscience sprang up as a reflection of the "Unknown God." The priest-astronomer looked up to the starry heaven and found that the heavenly clock had struck a new hour. The era of the Ram was drawing to its end and the sun was entering the sign of the Fishes. The dusk of one and the dawn of another era met in the new religion. Two symbols appeared on the walls of the catacombs: the sacrificed lamb and the image of the fish.

CHAPTER VIII

MEDIEVAL ETHICS

Will Durant in his *Story of Our Civilization* calls the Middle Ages "the age of Faith." And indeed faith was needed to convince the sophisticated Greeks and Romans that the Godhead, the creator of the whole universe, was embodied in a crucified Jewish carpenter.

Today those who urge us to regain the faith of early Christianity, or even that of the Middle Ages, seem entirely unaware of what ancient faith really was. They believe that the mere will to accept a doctrine, regardless of its credibility, constitutes faith in the original meaning of the word. Such an attitude tends to split the human personality even further, rather than to endow it with the strength that once wrought miracles. The Bible itself leaves no doubt about the nature of ancient faith. It was an inner experience, an act of grace. The disciples themselves needed the "descent of the Holy Ghost"; Paul was converted by his vision on the road to Damascus; and there are many more records of conversions by the "Spirit." So strong was the conviction that faith depended on an element of grace that, shortly after Christ's death, the belief arose that God Himself showed to some the truth of Christianity by inner proof, even as He withheld that truth from others. "Therefore hath he mercy on whom he will have mercy, and whom he will, he hardeneth" (Rom. 9:18) or "And the Lord added to the church daily such as should be saved" (Acts 2:47). Thus it is hardly surprising that Paul felt the need of defending God against the charge of injustice; and partly on the strength of his and St. Augustine's words, Protestant churchmen preached centuries later the doctrine of predestination. This doctrine asserts that the Creator judges an individual even before he is born, precluding all his hopes for moral freedom. While such concepts have lost their grip on the conscious mind of modern man, they still form powerful undercurrents in his soul, from where they emerge time and again in moments of crises. Nor should this surprise us too much; for all the major impulses of the history of human consciousness are still at work in the psyche of modern man, a fact that explains why contemplation of history can lead to self-knowledge and self-healing.

Today we are all in the grip of inner conflicts, conflicts far more serious than libido and sex; the psychological paradoxon which makes us long for freedom, and the fear which makes us seek God and doubt His existence. We may well get lost in the labyrinth of these conflicts unless we find our way on the map where they are recorded for all to see.

What was the faith of early and medieval Christianity, and how could its effects undermine man's belief in moral freedom? To understand the state of consciousness prevalent during the childhood of Christianity we must go farther back in time.

In the pagan world the new creed had been preceded by the age of the Mysteries; in Hebrew culture by the prophetic era. Faith in the Christian sense of the word did not exist then, since the spiritual world was a perceptible reality to those who had undergone intuitive training in the Mystery schools or had followed the stern commands of Yahweh. But when the pre-Christian epoch drew to an end, the ancient Mysteries had become decadent. Instead of training some exceptional personalities for great tasks, the temple schools admitted anyone wealthy enough to support the priesthood, and yearly turned out thousands of "initiates." In Jewish culture, the era of prophetic wisdom had died; and the classical culture of Greece, with its Golden Mean, had yielded to the materialism of Rome. Then, when Ezekiel's warning that "without vision the people must perish" seemed verified by the decline of the Western world and the Near East, a great resurgence of inner experi-

ence, the vision of the Resurrected Christ, lit up the already
dying hope for the redemption of man. No wonder that those
who had felt it change their whole being, who had witnessed
its power to purify them of intellectual and material desires,
of their "original sin," thought that the doors of Paradise had
opened again. Had not the disciples themselves spoken in
strange tongues, in the universal language which God had confounded ages ago? The signs and portents seemed to announce
the end of man's journey, the impending recall of a part of
humanity into the Garden of Eden. Man's evolutionary path
appeared to have come to a close, except for the task of spreading the new message to all the peoples. Once this was accomplished, God would have "mercy on whom he will have mercy."
Why should the earth continue to exist thereafter, since the
chosen ones would have reached their goal, and the rest have
been doomed for all eternity? Men—at least those who were
to be saved—seemed to have completed the cycle of their
evolution and again to have arrived at the gate from which
they had once been expelled.

Thus it was an attitude of mind, rather than reliance on
some misinterpreted remarks of Jesus, which led early Christians to the belief that the Day of Judgment was close at hand.
Calculations as to the exact time of the event varied; some
expected it within a few years, some a millennium after Christ.
Yet when the year one thousand arrived, the spiritual atmosphere of early Christianity had waned. Where there had been
joyous expectancy, there was now fearful hysteria. Very few
Christians were still willing to give up material existence; very
few found in the new religion the fulfillment of *all* their desires.

Human consciousness had passed the culminating point of
balance between intuition and intellect. During that short
period of harmony a consciousness had prevailed, in a few
highly developed personalities, which became a shining goal
for human striving, but certainly did not mark the end of the
path for humanity at large.

Not only in Palestine and Greece, but also in other parts of
the world, at various times among different cultures, the course
of evolution had led man to a stage of consciousness in which

intellect and intuition were in balance: brief moments in which
the human ego could unfold its wings. Although such phases
did not necessarily signify a peak in moral development among
the majority of men, they were usually the forerunners of a
new religious impulse, as the Classical Age of Greece was a
forerunner of Christianity.

Today we know the early Christians were wrong in expecting the end of the world, and from the superior wisdom of
hindsight we can understand why they had to be wrong; for
Christian monotheism, far from being an end, marked the
beginning of a new phase in the evolution of consciousness, a
phase in which man can in full awareness obtain or reject the
gift of moral freedom. Naturally, this does not mean that only
Christians possess the potentiality for moral freedom; but
Christianity appeared on earth when this potentiality became
a historical necessity. The *virtus Romana,* the national morality
of the Romans, had all but ceased to exist; pagan ethics had
deteriorated into superstition and hypocrisy; the Hebrew law
had become so rigid as to make it nonacceptable to peoples
other than Jews. If mankind was to progress, morality had to
become a matter of individual responsibility; and Christianity
emerged as a guide for Occidental ethics. By what was considered a divine deed, it implanted into mankind the seed
of individual moral choice, thereby relinquishing to man what
had heretofore been a prerogative of God. Yet only a very few
grew into plant, flower, and fruit at once; for the human race
as a whole, the lofty goal of the new religion had to wait until
still dormant qualities would unfold at a later age. The religious experiences of the early Christian seer were different
from those of the more ancient prophet. They appealed not to
intuition alone, but to a part of the human soul which stands
between intuition and intellect, in the no-man's land of freedom.

The ancient prophets were under compulsion; they could
barely resist the spiritual power unleashed in them. How different was the experience of Peter when, according to the legend,
he fled from the Roman prison! In that vision there was no
command, but an appeal to the human faculties of reason and

love, bearing out Christ's words to his disciples: "Henceforth I call you not servants . . . but I have called you friends . . ." (John 15:15).

According to the legend, Peter was in flight from prison when, on the Appian Way, he encountered Christ, carrying his cross once more. And when the disciple asked: "Where are you going, Lord?" (*quo vadis, domine?*), Jesus answered: "I go to Rome to be crucified again, since you have forsaken me." Then Peter turned back and gave himself up to his persecutors.

Although this event is historically not verified, it lived so strongly on in the consciousness of the time that centuries later a chapel was built to commemorate it. Today it is still called the "Quo Vadis Chapel" and is believed to stand on the very spot where Peter's vision took place.

The impact of Christianity seems to have rekindled the already receding intuitive faculties of antiquity. All through the Middle Ages there were saints and martyrs, sages and priests, who openly professed their contact with a spiritual world; but, as we have said before, their experiences arose in an already heightened state of individuality. Thus the medieval seer was not like the ancient prophet, a helpless tool in the hands of his god: he was capable of accepting or rejecting his inner experiences. These experiences were of a more intimate character, indicating a change whose beginning we can trace back into the pre-Christian era. It was again the Greeks who in their amazing spiritual sensitivity noticed and described this experience in their myths and dramas. One example may suffice:

Originally, a man who had obeyed a god's command expected protection against the consequences of his deeds and a reward for his obedience. Whether the command was moral or immoral was not for humans to decide, but left to divine discretion. Later this attitude changed. Although the individual had still to submit to the rules of his tribal deity, judgment was passed on him by beings other than his gods. Strange apparitions appeared before his inner eye, the dreaded Daughters of Night, known also as Furies or Erinyes. More powerful than the Olympians, they challenged the gods' jurisdiction over the soul of man. The punishment which the gods were thought to inflict on disobedient humans was predominantly in the nature of misfortune, illness, and premature death. The penalties exacted by the Erinyes were of a more psychological nature, taking the form of madness, obsession, and fear.

In other words, a new chapter had been opened in the history of human consciousness, a chapter in which the simplicity of obedience gave way to the torment of moral conflicts. The gods still ruled supreme in the spheres of heredity and fertility, were the guardians of tribal customs such as the sacred practice of blood feuds, but could no longer fully control the spiritual life of man. The twilight of the gods was drawing near. It found its artistic reflection in the great pageants and tragedies of the time, as for example in the story of Orestes, the son of Agamemnon. Agamemnon was murdered by his adulterous wife Clytemnestra and her lover Aegisthus. When Orestes came of age, he had no choice but to fulfill the sacred laws of blood revenge on the murderers of his father. But the Erinyes haunted him for this deed, allowed him no rest by day or by night, deprived him of his reason, and drove him, a madman, across the face of the earth. At last he pleaded for help with Apollo himself, but even the god of light could not protect him from the wrath of the Furies. And then an event took place that was most significant in the history of human consciousness: the Delphian Oracle, the divine court on matters spiritual in the Hellenic world, relinquished its power of jurisdiction and sent Orestes to a court of mere mortals, the Areopagus in Athens. There he was acquitted in an agreement between men and gods, an agreement approved by the Erinyes themselves. From then on they, the dreaded Daughters of Night, became the Eumenides, man's benevolent guides to voluntary atonement.

Ancient wisdom knows so many of the answers which modern psychology has sought in vain. We have chosen the myth of Orestes to recall a change in consciousness which took place millenniums ago. But apart from its historical value, the story contains a message which has lost none of its meaning today. Orestes was a denizen of a changing world, and so is modern man. He, too, lives in the twilight between two eras, not knowing his goal. Whatever he does, wherever he turns, he seems to fail. Should he appease those who would destroy the freedom of the world, or should he fight and thus destroy it himself? Should he harden himself against the hunger and misery of untold millions of his fellow men, or should he feed and rid them of disease until an exploding world population will bring about its own destruction?

Those, of course, are only the outer manifestations of the conflicts which are raging in the unconscious mind of modern man. So severe are his conflicts and so great is his secret sense of guilt that he has all but doomed himself to self-destruction. Yet, a sense of guilt can be turned into will for action, provided man will shake off his mental inertia and seek the meaning of the age in which he lives. Human reason, when it aligns itself with the purpose of evolution, frees man from guilt, by channeling its pent-up forces into creative action.

In the language of the myth the Areopagus represented human reason; for that court was indeed composed of the wisest men of Athens. But, to become wisdom, reason must take into account the divine masterplan of evolution, it must reach agreement with the genius of the time. The era of Orestes fell approximately into the eleventh century B.C. It was the time when the barbaric customs of ancient fertility cults had to be overthrown to lift religion onto the higher level of enlightenment and art. Orestes, the innocently guilty, the man between two eras, had, by keeping faith with the laws of old, sinned against the promise of a better future. The twelve judges of the Areopagus were evenly divided: six found him guilty, six voted for acquittal. The deadlock was broken by Athena herself; the goddess of Hellas, who drew her lot with those who found the accused free of individual guilt.

The deed of atonement imposed on Orestes leaves no doubt as to the mission of his age. He was sent to Taurus to rescue the image of Artemis from her barbaric priesthood, which still offered human sacrifices at her altar.

With the dawn of the Classical Age, the Olympian gods and the Eumenides faded from the dimming light of intuitive perception. In their place, in the innermost sanctuary of the human soul itself, a spark was kindled: *syneidesis,* "conscience." So long as man had been a predominantly intuitive being, he had been dominated by spiritual powers too strong for him to resist. In the future his intellectual curiosity, his "original sin," would make him a slave of his physical senses, free from the gods but a servant to his physical nature. But in the Classical Age his consciousness had reached a transitory equilibrium between intuition on the wane and intellectualism on the rise. The most precious fruits of their harmonious interplay were conscience and the ideal of freedom.

With their emergence the ground was laid for a new impulse, the impulse of Christianity. The vision of the gods and Erinyes had long since faded, releasing human consciousness from the powerful grip of intuitive experience. From now on it was up to man whether he would open or close his heart to the creative word, the Logos; Christ's deep respect for the principles of freedom and individual conscience shine through all his words and deeds. He neither compelled nor commanded obedience, but humbly pleaded for acceptance of his gifts. An apocryphal Bible story tells of the new responsibility imposed on man by the age of freedom.

On a Sabbath morning a disciple approached Jesus to tell him of a farmer whom he had just caught tilling his land. What, he asked, will be the punishment for that terrible sin? For a long time Jesus seemed lost in thought. Eventually he lifted his head and said: "If that man acts in ignorance, his punishment will be stern indeed; if he knows what he does, he is one of the blessed."

The Golden Era of early Christianity did not last long. Its seed had been planted into the soil of human consciousness but had come as a gift of evolution rather than as a fruit of conscious and voluntary effort. It flowered briefly, then withered and all but disappeared. Yet it did not die, but sent its roots down into the hidden streams which flow beneath the surface-consciousness of man. At the time of Christ's Incarnation only a few souls truly wanted what Christianity had to give: the way back to the lost Garden of Eden. The vast majority still longed for man's promised goal, the undisputed mastery of the material world. Not until now has this goal come within our reach. With the intellectual and material conquest of matter achieved, man might at last be ready to head for a spiritual goal.

Two thousand years ago the living force of Christianity could not survive for long in the hearts of its followers; a Constantine became its champion, Christians fought Christians in bloody wars over abstract theological differences, and in the Middle Ages Spanish *conquistadores* almost matched in cruelty and fanaticism the pagans whom they had set out to save. Intuition had ceased to be an instrument of religious experience. Suppressed and distorted, it became the source of pseudo-religion and witch-hunts.

Thus it was intellect which at last had to rescue religion from demoniacal perversion. Intellectually controlled creeds had to emerge to save, at least, the sacred traditions, protecting man from distorted experiences. Or, as Jung puts it:

> What is usually called "religion" is to such an amazing degree a substitute that I ask myself seriously whether this kind of "religion" which I prefer to call a creed, has not an important function in human society. The substitution has the obvious purpose of replacing immediate experience.[1]

What became of the magic power of Christianity with its immediate experiences that purified ordinary people to a degree unheard of in history? Why did it not halt man's decline into a state of consciousness in which a still immature intellect had to protect the human being against his own intuitive-creative forces? It is again the Biblical legend which provides an answer, for although its historical accuracy may well be questioned, as an interpreter of human consciousness it has no peer.

According to Genesis, man was created in the Garden of Eden, in the midst of which stood two trees: the tree of life, and the tree of knowledge and death. Man's choice started him on a journey which led his consciousness away from the creative, life-giving forces to the other pole of existence where the powers of total destruction lie hidden. The path also took him into

growing awareness of the world of matter. His first experience
"when his eyes were opened" was cognizance of his own physique, of his body representing the borderline between the
world within and the world without. From that moment on
he neither could nor would stop his course until he had
reached its farthest limit: the gate where solid matter ends
and another world begins.

Not long ago, a little earlier on this course, the concept of
nature as a chance product of mechanical energies would have
seemed utter absurdity to man. All through the ages he had
sensed the power and wisdom of divine forces behind the elements, and not until a few centuries ago did nature lose its
enchantment.

Kepler, one of the fathers of modern astronomy, still saw
in the universe a living being. The alchemists, who laid the
foundations for modern chemistry, seriously discussed salaman-
ders, undines, sylphs, and gnomes. Paracelsus, the lifelong
crusader against superstitions and often called the first modern
physician, believed that the effect of medicines was caused by
their "spirits"—*spiritus arcanorum.*

Not until his intuition had become almost extinct could
man conceive of an empty universe, of a vast clockwork created,
wound, and set by accidental forces. But then, as had been
promised when he ate of the tree of knowledge, he took possession of this no-man's land as if he were a god.

Moral issues change with the epoch; yet at no time in history
has man himself wielded the godlike power he has today, a
power strong enough to terminate all life on earth. It is,
therefore, only today that he has come to the crossroads of
ultimate moral decision. He has gained, or is in the process
of gaining, all the prerogatives he may want: in the outer world
he rules supreme; his intellectual faculties are tremendous;
his intuition can be reawakened and freed from its prison in
the underground channels of his being. But, having set out on
the daring journey toward freedom, he had to travel it to the
end. Only then, with the power to remake or destroy the world
and himself, could he determine his further course; and the
time for this fateful decision is now at hand.

What man will do with his godlike might will depend on the goal he sets for himself. During the span of his earthly life he is both a spiritual and a physical being. His freedom is so great that he can reshape himself either in the image of the spirit, or in the image of the beast or robot. Modern pedagogy and psychology strongly lean toward the latter. The pedagogue who sees in the child an animal to be tamed and conditioned, unwittingly strengthens the animal instincts in his pupil. And equally at fault is the philosopher who announces to all the world his own neomaterialistic theories as if they were based on proved facts. Under the name of emergent evolution, powerful doctrines have come forth which see not only in man but even in God a product of matter and chance.

This nature begins as a four-dimensional matrix in which it is the moving principle. Materiality, secondary qualities, life, mentality are all emergent manifestations of proto-space-time. . . . Alexander conceives the deity as the next highest level to be emerged out of any given level. . . . For men deity has not yet emerged, but there is a *nism* toward its emergence.[2]

Had Nimrod, the legendary builder of the Tower of Babel, known modern English, could he have expressed his own philosophy in more adequate terms? No, man has not ascended from an ape, but he may very well become one if he so chooses. Or, as the legend of the Tower of Babel said: ". . . some were transformed into apes and demons."[3]

The Middle Ages approached the problem of moral evolution in two basic ways, neither of them fully understood today. One was purely religious and mystical, the other scientific in the medieval sense of the word.

The first was withdrawal into an inner world. Unlike his pagan predecessor, the introvert mystic of the Middle Ages was not interested in the problem of cosmology, the intrinsic nature of all beings; nor was he much concerned with the acquisition of scientific knowledge. It was the enigma of good and evil which he sought to solve. Gathering all the remnants of an intuitive consciousness left to men of his age, the medieval mystic struggled to perceive the principles of good and evil with the eyes of his soul. And before his inner vision two images arose. One was of unearthly beauty, clad in white, the color of purity, with wings capable of a flight that could carry him upward: the guardian angel. The other had the sly expression of soulless intellect, twisted wings that had lost the capacity of soaring to the heights and, as token of an unredeemed bestiality, hoof, horn, and tail: this was the devil.

It was not so much the desire of the flesh which the medieval sage considered evil, nor did he revere all that claimed to be spiritual. But to him absolute good was the purification of man's intuitive faculties until they became angelic to his inner gaze. And absolute evil was the subservience of man's higher faculties, of his Moral Phantasy, to the dictates of matter and flesh. The wings were man's divine heritage. Whether he used them for upward or downward flight, would decide the fate of his soul.

Without this knowledge, we shall never understand the leniency which the medieval Church displayed toward crimes and vices perpetrated on the physical plane, as opposed to her fanatical zeal against deviations in the state of dreams and phantasy. The relentless persecution conducted by Catholics and Protestants alike against those suspected of witchcraft may serve as an example. After all, the Witch Sabbath was not a physical but a supersensible orgy, the delivery of the human soul to "the Beast."

Today we contemplate with horror the cruel superstitions of the Dark Ages, and rightly despise the means applied by Church and Inquisition. But we should also look for the kernel of truth present in every historical impulse. For to some degree history has borne out the fears of the Middle Ages, repulsive as some medieval concepts and methods must appear to later generations. We have entered into a stage of consciousness in which our higher intuitive faculties are so thoroughly wedded to our instinctive, subconscious soul life, that even the greatest of modern psychologists, Jung, finds scant difference between religious experience, neurosis, and libido. Such an attitude, however, is rapidly carrying the human race to a point where moral choice becomes impossible, and religious experience indistinguishable from hallucination.

The other way in which the genius of the Middle Ages tried to solve the moral question was a way of action. Its starting point was the philosophic-theological concept which assumed that God had left His creation unfinished as an incentive to man's innate power of comprehension and creativeness. As a tool for the completion of this task, He had given intellect to the human race. One of the disciplines by which the task could be accomplished was called alchemy, which in its true form was less concerned with the making of gold than with the art of perfecting the not yet perfected.

The alchemists knew well enough that intellect, knowledge, and experimentation were needed; and they accepted material gain as a desirable by-product of scientific research. Their main concern, however, was the age to come, the age that would give man mastery over nature. Could this scientific era be prepared in such a way as to keep man's whole being, rather than his intellect alone, at the task of refashioning the earth? This was the problem of the truly great alchemists, the fathers of modern science and the men possessed of a scientific divination which our age has barely started to comprehend. Yet, why was their terminology so childlike? Because there is only one language sufficiently imaginative to do justice to the principles active in all chemical, physical, and biological processes, and this language takes its diction from myths and fairy tales.

The medieval scholar felt that he needed inner vision to experience principles just as much as he needed experimentation and intellect to evaluate their physical manifestation. To him, only a man who entered his laboratory in a mood of reverence could comprehend and control the intangible forces hidden in all material phenomena. Research without meditation was a way to destruction rather than to progress in the eyes of the adept, who considered science an attempt to recognize the original creative intent in nature, and to complete the uncompleted. One of the main points of alchemist philosophy was the assumption that God Himself had sacrificed a part of His Being to the lower kingdoms of the earth, to be redeemed by the compassion and wisdom of man.

For the alchemist the one primarily in need of redemption is not man, but the deity who is lost and sleeping in matter. . . . He may approach the work as one in need of salvation, but he knows that his salvation depends on the success of the work, on whether he can free the divine soul—it is not man but matter that must be redeemed. . . . the *opus* is no longer a ritualistic *officium,* but the same work of redemption which God Himself accomplished upon mankind through the example of Christ.[4]

It is obviously difficult for modern man to accept or even to understand all the strange ways of mysticism and alchemy. But, in regard to moral choice, he has much to learn from the Middle Ages, for the medieval philosopher knew at least the alternatives of that choice of which our enlightened age is so piteously ignorant. And so, to summarize:

One of the medieval paths leading to the crossroads of moral freedom was the purely religious one. Through the meticulous meditations used in medieval worship, man's intuitive perception could be reawakened. This reawakened and fully purified intuitive vision was called "the star in man, his celestial or supercelestial body."[5] In the light of this star, man could remodel his soul in the image of one of the two prototypes ever present in the medieval mind: the angel and the devil.

The second path was the way of scientific action. It was the path for all who longed for knowledge and deeds. As the Middle Ages drew to an end, the trend to action gradually replaced the contemplative mood of mystical introversion. The human mind became increasingly preoccupied with the outer world, and the material fruits of research and exploration soon overshadowed the spiritual aims of medieval science. Once roused, intellectual curiosity knew no bounds. The Church was at a loss. How could science be contained within the boundaries of religious ethics and kept from damaging God's creation, and consequently the human soul?

The great alchemist saw this problem in a different light. He knew man's irrepressible curiosity too well to believe in the effect of punitive and repressive action. But he felt that the scientist's heart and mind had to be properly prepared if his work was to serve God and mankind. Thus his pupils had to undergo a strict apprenticeship during which they were not only trained in elementary science, but induced to develop *amor perfectissimus,* a perfect love for the work which might be characterized in the following words:

If you enter your laboratory as you enter a Church, if you conduct your experiments as a priest celebrates Mass, if your search for knowledge is motivated by love and compassion even for the lowliest creatures of God, you will grow spiritually; you will gain wisdom and even, should you so choose, material benefits. If you consider nature a mere tool to serve man, science will become an instrument of destruction and thus a hazard to the future of man and his world. To the medieval sage science was religion, and its deeper purpose was to serve God in nature.

Neither man's control of physical forces nor his passionate longing for knowledge would reap for him the coveted fruits of science. For "this thing for which you have sought so long is not to be acquired by force or passion. It is only to be won by patience and humility and a determined and most perfect love."[6]

CHAPTER IX

MORAL IMAGINATION

Is it possible to translate the medieval visions of good and evil into modern concepts of ethics? We believe it is, but before attempting to do so we must once more return to the polarity between intuition and intellect on which man's moral freedom on earth depends. Perhaps history's best-known example for the use of a purely intuitive state of consciousness can be found in ancient oracles like the Delphian. Here the priestess was exposed to drugs that paralyzed certain parts of her brain: the pictures which then arose in her mind were entirely devoid of intellectual reasoning. On the other hand, an example of intellectual analysis in its purest form can be found in the calculations of an "artificial brain," as registered but not yet evaluated by its human operator.

Neither of these two extremes by itself can be called truly human. The first is an abandonment of self-awareness and free will to powers far stronger than the conscious mind of man, powers whose sources of origin were once called gods and whose sphere of action is now called evolution. The second is the reflection of the laws of energy and lifeless matter in the mirror of the human brain. In the first, man closes his eyes, as it were, to return to the prenatal state of the Garden of Eden; in the second, he comes close to yielding to the forces of death.

There is another trend of thought which can deepen our understanding of the all-important polarity betwen comprehensive intuition and analytical intellect. Intuition may be seen as a spiritual process in which creative forces become aware of themselves within the human soul. They share their secrets with man, making him potentially capable of comprehending the nature and purpose of all things created by them.

Thoughts like these were favorite subjects for meditation of the philosophers of the early Christian era, especially the Neoplatonists. Even today such thoughts can awaken an inner experience, an experience which throws light on some of the secrets of human nature. In admittedly inadequate terms they may be expressed thus: A stream of creative forces on its way down into matter, pauses in the consciousness of man to endow him with intuitive faculties. A counterstream, matter returning toward the source of its origin, reveals its nature in the human intellect. Thanks to his intuition, man can participate in the continuous act of creation; through his intellect, he observes the laws of death.

The godhead is at work in the living, not in the dead; it is present in everything in the process of development and transformation, not in what has already taken shape and rigidified. Thus, reason in its strivings toward the divine, is concerned with growth and life, whereas understanding is concerned with putting to use what has already developed and grown torpid.[1]

This is what Engard correctly calls "the kernel of Goethe's philosophy." Unfortunately, however, there is some difficulty in the English adaptation of the German term *Verstand*. *Verstand*, especially in the Goethean sense, corresponds to "intellect" rather than to "understanding." *Vernunft*, on the other hand, should be translated as "intuitive comprehension," or as "reason" in the sense of the just-mentioned quotation, since Goethe himself once said that it is the quality needed to comprehend ideas.

Therefore, it may be permissible to substitute the German originals for Engard's translations of these terms, when continuing with the quotation:

Verstand [intellect] is . . . thought according to schematized categories, of value only in relation to experience; *Vernunft*, on the other hand, is distinct from *Verstand* in that it apprehends in one immediate act the entire system, . . . and is therefore supersensuous. The latter, of course, leads to the archetype, the Urphenomenon.[2]

In other words a faculty exists in man capable of comprehending the world. It does not matter if, with Kant and Goethe, we call it *Vernunft*—with Emerson, imagination or reason—or, with Bergson and many others, intuition. The Bible in its deceptively simple language expresses man's original understanding of creation in the following words: "And out of the ground the Lord God formed every beast . . . and brought them unto Adam to see what he would call them; and whatsoever Adam called every living creature, that *was* the name thereof" (Gen.2:7, 19).

It is one of the most far-reaching mistakes of present-day thinking to assume that comprehension is a result of *intellectual* effort. Intellect is descriptive and differentiating; it classifies and orders; it informs us of the mechanics of natural and even spiritual processes, but it does not help us comprehend their true nature.

Of course, intellect is needed for cognition. For, thanks to its analytical power, it is capable of splitting complex phenomena into their integral parts which must be studied as individual entities. But, if unchecked by the synthesizing faculty of intuition, analysis will continue until the unifying principle is lost in a maze of incomprehensible facts.

To illustrate the need of an intuitive as well as analytical approach to cognition, Russell W. Davenport uses the following example:

Let us turn to the proverbial man from Mars. We have taken a watch to pieces and have put the parts, mixed up, in a pile. We present the man from Mars with the pile and ask him what it is. He will say that it is a lot of curiously shaped little objects. There is no possible way that he can induce from them the idea that they are parts of an instrument to measure time. In order to reach this conclusion he must first have a general idea.[3]

Let us now modify Davenport's simile to make still another

point. Let us assume that an entirely foreign but intelligent being, having no advance knowledge of conditions specific to our physical universe, discovers a clock intact. If his mental inclination is a predominantly analytical one, he might open the case and carefully dismount the work to study its basic individual parts, as well as their mode of function. In doing so he pursues a correct and essential course of analytical action. However, once he reaches the level of purposeful entities, his intuition, if reliable, will give him due warning. This is the moment when intellectual analysis must stop, and a process of imaginative re-creation must begin; for only by an act of creative imagination can the observer hope to reinvent the clock. In putting his idea to the test, he will make use of the material knowledge gained by observation and analysis, and reassemble the mechanism of the clock or even improve on it.

If, however, the stranger's analytical curiosity happens to be more strongly developed than his intuitive faculties, he will not know where to stop. He will continue with his analysis until the wheels, spring, and dial of the clock will have disintegrated into their metallurgic, chemical, magnetic, and electrical properties. Thus our visitor, fascinated by the tremendous wealth of information, will go on until the slightest chance of intuitive resynthesis is gone. Even his descendants will never reach the end of this search. In the tiny residues of what was once a clock they might discover the molecule and atom and eventually the inexhaustible mysteries of nuclear forces. Perhaps millenniums after the stranger's death a scientist of his world would make the following statement: "Research on the object under observation has yielded undreamed-of results. We are now in a position to state (and to prove) that it was made of molecules and atoms. Accidental nuclear changes have resulted in a phenomenon which to our naïve ancestor appeared purposeful. There are indeed old legends born of superstition and phantasy claiming that it once moved. But, from the very first, laboratory tests have failed to support these claims. The scientists who have examined it state emphatically that it never really moved, in spite of their efforts to rearrange its particles and to remove all superfluous parts."

This is exactly the attitude which modern "metascience"[4] has assumed toward the problem of cognition. Its errors lie in the fact that we can no more hope to understand a clock, much less a plant, from the structure of its minutest building stones than we can expect to understand man's living personality by dissecting his body.

Man enters the world as the physical manifestation of a divine thought; he leaves it owing to disintegration of his body into its molecular and chemical particles. The latter are tokens of decomposition; they tell us nothing of his origin.

Yet we do not need to look at man; entities far less complex than he, such as plants, minerals, or even simple tools, defy comprehension through analysis alone. The reality of all that exists lies midway between two qualitatively different principles. One is the creative idea to which an object owes its origin, the other its tangible structure made of a multitude of building stones.

In ancient times the human mind was incapable of fully appreciating physical reality because it was too strongly attracted by the idea behind or within it. Not that ancient man himself was morally better or less destructive than his modern descendant, but he was closer to the childhood state of the world, and therefore more capable of discovering and mastering the forces of creation than those of dissolution. Thus even his inventive genius was more effective in the ways of building than in those of destruction. Regardless of how hard he tried, his war machines were insignificant as compared with his discoveries in the world of agriculture, art, and the sciences. In short, he improved rather than endangered the chances for survival of the human race.

Now the opposite is true. Although more concerned with the preservation of life and much more afraid of death than his ancestors, modern man constantly stumbles onto discoveries which are more destructive than constructive. In cognition as well as in inventiveness, he has overstepped the line of balance and is now in danger of sliding into the valley of death.

This charge may sound absurd when applied to a generation which labors incessantly to probe life in order to maintain and increase the earth's population; and one to which the very word "death" is becoming unmentionable. Yet just as the young and vital person is readier to give his life than the old and sick, so intuitive and creative eras know less fear of death than predominantly intellectual civilizations.

Modern science has been very successful in prolonging the life span of man, with the result that an exploding world population endangers the very survival of the human race. Years ago, long before the Communists seized power in his country, a prominent Chinese physician traveled through Europe on a good-will tour. He used every occasion to convey to the public his government's "heartfelt assurances of gratitude"—a phrase he seemed to cherish.

However, at one occasion—it was during a small dinner party—our guest spoke in a different vein. He pointed out that many centuries ago, when the West was still ruled by "illiterate savages," the Chinese were already the world's greatest experts in the sciences of government and administration. "Do you really think," he asked, "that we, the oldest and wisest people on this earth, needed *you*, to administer our country? True, epidemics, hunger, droughts, and floods have ravaged China; child mortality was high and life expectancy low. But all her misery, heartbreaking as it was, is a minor evil as compared to the catastrophes to come, catastrophes *you* have conjured by your arrogant and stupid interference. Our leaders have known for ages that the life forces of a country must rise and ebb according to higher laws. In this age they let nature take her toll of China's population. Why? For the same reason that gardeners prune and cover a precious tree before a long cold winter, so that it may blossom more beautifully and bear better fruit in the year to come. But you interfered and thus endangered our great mission for the future, which our scholars have foretold for many centuries. First you compelled us to import opium, and all but destroyed the soul of China. Now you remove the safeguards which nature built to keep the size of our population in check. The dam is broken, the disaster can no longer be averted. Not we, but you shall suffer most! For, when the earth will have become too small for its growing population, *you* will reap the harvest of death, whose seeds you are now sowing."

The impassioned speech of the Chinese made an unforgettable impression on all those present. It was then that it dawned on some of us how little we know of the meaning of life. True, our experimental knowledge and our intellectual training have given us insight into life's effect on matter, but only the power of intuition can give us comprehension of its intangible nature.

Nor are our mistakes confined to the sphere of international relations. Our education tends to shorten the truly vital life span of childhood by making intellectuals of babes in arms. Perhaps this is why they spend their later years being childish, in a pathetic attempt to make up for what they have missed.

Even in medicine we believe to serve the cause of life, whereas often we are merely prolonging the process of dying. For we must not forget that every powerful chemical introduced into the human organism must needs have a deadening effect on the vitality of our consciousness, mechanizing it to a greater or lesser degree. Whenever we calm grief by the anesthetizing effect of a sedative, we suppress not only the manifestations of suffering, but also the personality of our patient. As in fighting a blazing fire with a chemical extinguisher, we may control a conflagration in the soul of a human being through modern medicine. But unless we learn to strengthen the intuitive, creative qualities in the coming generation, the flame of humanity itself may yet be extinguished along with its illnesses, conflicts, and rebellions. Just as we use tranquilizers to deaden our emotions, we use stimulants to create a semblance of spiritual animation. Actually, however, living to the full is experience of grief and joy, is courage to live, and willingness to die. It would be a victory of death should we succeed in prolonging the processes of human vegetation beyond the scope of useful existence.

All this is not said as a criticism of modern medicine itself; nor as a warning against the use of drugs, but merely as an attempt to evaluate the price we must pay for the benefits which they bring. Only when we learn to know what this price actually is, can we pay it without impoverishing our inner life; and our scholars themselves are in worst need of such knowledge, for a man entrusted with the tremendous power and responsibility of science requires more than intellect to bring true blessings to the world.

This truth was understood in that short period of harmony, the Classical Age. In the state of consciousness belonging to that time, which granted man a fleeting glimpse of what he could be, it was recognized that the student of science had to become wise and good as well as clever and well informed before he could call himself a scholar. Although most of their ideals failed to materialize in practical life, it has been the light of those ideals, and that light alone, which has restrained scientific curiosity up to now from breaking all moral laws.

A human being in possession of all his faculties, whose intuitive, creative powers have been trained to become as strong as his analytical abilities, will automatically see the world in a different light. Unless consciously evil, he will no more search for means to destroy the earth than an anatomist would propose to dissect a living human being. That scientists of the highest moral standards have often been the first to chance upon the most destructive discoveries, shows that the dangerous trend in our civilization is not caused by evil intentions. It is owing to the fact that modern man does not think, act, or feel as a whole human being, but is awake only in regard to one faculty. "At present, man applies to nature but half his forces. . . . He lives in it and masters it by a penny-wisdom; and he that works most in it is but a half-man. . . ."[5]

A "half-man" will hardly be able to see more than half-truths, unless he recognizes and fills the gap in his mentality. Modern man's lopsided views on cognition—and not his inevitable fate—make him stumble on discoveries whose destructive potentialities are greater than their constructive ones. The analytical intellect, unless checked by intuition, is irresistibly drawn to the processes of dissolution. How well is modern science versed in these processes—all the way down to nuclear fission! But why does it know so little of synthesis, of the forces which build the embryo in its mother's womb and bring about the growth of plants and animals? Because cognition and use of the forces of *becoming* require an intuitive element far too little developed in modern scientists.

Thus modern technology, even in its peaceful version, has become an instrument of dissolution. For the power it uses stems from the transformation of one form of dynamics into another with appreciable loss of usable energy to the household of nature. Instead of trading with nature, we are constantly exploiting her, and thus we may eventually exhaust her resources. Yes, aside from all practical considerations, man's evolution is inseparably connected with the fate of all living and conscious creatures on earth. The true alchemists knew this, and made their primary goal the redemption of nature rather than material gain for man.

Genesis, without moralizing, indicates the great debt which man owes to the lower kingdoms. For it was his expulsion from the Garden of Eden which brought strife, fear, and suffering not only to him but also to the world of innocent nature. According to the legend, it was man and only man who could "give names" to the beings around him, since he alone was creative as well as created. It was his mission to be mediator between God and the world. So long as his intuition permitted him to comprehend divine purpose, the world itself reflected the peace and harmony of original creation. When he set out on his journey he broke the link between creator and created. As promised by the serpent, he became "as a god" himself, and thus took upon himself tremendous responsibilities. Yet even today he is an intuitive being, potentially capable of comprehending the meaning of creation; and at the same time he is an intellectual being, capable of knowing and mastering the forces of nature. But between supersensuous intuitive comprehension and sense-bound, intellectual knowledge, stands his freedom. Owing to this freedom he is still capable of regaining the power of comprehending the needs of his fellow creatures. By strengthening his intellect and actual knowledge, he might still learn to bring them help.

Emerson, who uses the word "imagination" for what we call intuition, says:

Why should not . . . we participate in the invention of nature? This insight, which expresses itself by what is called Imagination, is a very high sort of seeing. . . . there is a great public power on which he [man] can draw, by unlocking . . . his human doors, and suffering the ethereal tides to roll and circulate through him; then he is caught up into the life of the Universe. . . . What noble emotions dilate the mortal as he enters into the councils of creation, and feels by knowledge the privilege to BE![6]

But man can also refuse to help, and can use his intellect for merely selfish aims. Then he is no longer an open gate between creator and created; he has become the guard at a drawbridge which he can raise or lower at will. Thus, between his intuition and his intellect, between his inner and outer perception, lies a sphere in which man is truly godlike. It is here where he dreams his creative thoughts before putting them into action. It is here that the sphere of freedom is found, the innermost sanctuary of the human soul, the seat of man's "moral imagination."[7]

How does moral imagination manifest itself in ordinary life? Let us assume that a surgeon is to take care of a patient critically maimed in an accident. As he conducts his examination, his physical senses will inform him of the extent and character of the damage. Then in response, consciously or unconsciously, an intuitive image must arise in him: an inner picture of that particular person, restored to a state of wholeness. Naturally, the doctor knows quite well that the gap between the two experiences—the outwardly visible and the imaginary—cannot be entirely closed. But he must now summon the image of an altogether new being, such as has never existed either as a spiritual prototype or as a physical creature on earth. Whatever action he takes, the surgeon knows he cannot transform his patient into a person of perfect health. At the same time, obviously, he does not want him to remain in his present condition. His task, therefore, is to create a *new* being. To achieve this, his inner vision, his creative intuition, must engage in profound consultation with his intellectual faculties and his sensory knowledge; for not only must the surgeon adjust his goal to physical limitations, but he must translate his intentions into a multitude of surgical, orthopedic, and medical procedures. This is but one of countless examples of moral imagination in its intimate collaboration between the two polar forces of man's consciousness, which are connected by that most mysterious of all bridges: the human self.

Moral Imagination is not only a manifestation of man's root in the spirit, but also of his freedom. For freedom requires a margin for error and the possibility of evil. Even in our medical case, the actual result will depend greatly on the doctor's compassion, diligence, knowledge, and skill. Similar examples of opportunity and responsibility could be selected from the life of any human being. Thus Moral Imagination, or creative phantasy, plays as decisive a part in a businessman's dream as it does in a sculptor's struggle to fashion from the unyielding substance, however inadequately, the image of an unattainable ideal. Yet in our age it is precisely this most precious of all divine gifts which is in peril. Exposed to an abundance of obvious dangers, modern man is likely to lose sight of the greatest of them: the threat to his humanity. His only chance lies in self-knowledge and in a determined fight for the preservation of his true self.

No philosophical doctrine or abstract treatise can give man real self-knowledge. But resolute and individualized meditation on an example such as the one given above, may make him intuitively aware of the core of his being and thus show him what is his to protect.

The obstacles on the way to moral freedom are manifold. One of them lies in political ideologies. But even there the focus of attention is misplaced. For instance, communism is abhorrent to the Western mind for many reasons; but were some of its most repulsive by-products soft-pedaled, the public would become only too willing to condone its existence. Actually, however, even if terror, forced labor, and political aggressiveness should disappear, the real threat of communism would remain: its attempt to reduce man to a merely biological or pseudo-mechanical being. Few people have seen the crux of this problem as clearly as Russell W. Davenport. "Dialectical man . . . represents the human being in terms that can only seem to us inhuman."[8] "The communist world . . . is engaged in a far-flung processing of mankind to transform flesh-and-blood man into the likeness of the image of Dialectical Man."[9] There lies the ultimate of evil, the trend to pull man into a lower sphere of spiritual existence. And what is most frightening in this thought is that it might succeed.

The full emergence of man's self, of his individuality, is of relatively recent origin. This extremely important fact has been widely recognized. We find awareness of it in many books—such as Fromm's *Escape from Freedom* and Neumann's *History of Consciousness*—as well as in historical sketches. The *Encyclopaedia Britannica* refers to the Egyptian King Ikhnaton in the following words: "We must look back on him today . . . as . . . the world's first *individual*. . . ." Moreover, the chief theme of classical tragedies has to do with the emergence of individualism, of freedom and conscience, and with man's liberation from the tutelage of superhuman forces. Christ spoke of the new phase of evolution in which man should become the friend instead of the servant of God, and his concept of the Son of God and the Son of Man clearly indicates the dawn of a new era of consciousness.

The young ego can exist only in the center of man's being. It must neither be overwhelmed by intuitive experiences nor become dependent on material factors. For it can be overwhelmed and enslaved by encroachment from either side. Unless allowed to become the supreme ruler within, it is incapable of true morality, which is inseparably connected with freedom.

The hermit who closes his eyes to the world, who seeks premature liberation from his physical organism by mortifying his body and treating the world of senses as if it were mere illusion, deserts his fellow creatures. He tries to return to a paradisiacal state, his Nirvana. On a lower level, the same goal is sought by those who unconsciously strive for a renewal of ancient consciousness by drowning their intellectual faculties by the use of narcotics, mescalin, or lyscergic acid.

But the majority of modern men fall victim to the opposite extreme, to the encroachment upon their selfhood by biological and material forces. Their egos become increasingly weakened by materialistic education, by self-abandonment to ceaseless sense impressions, among them advertisements designed to penetrate their defenses and compel them to accept what they do not really want. These and many similar influences pour in on modern man in such rapid succession that he is left no time to comprehend their meaning, nor to accept or reject them on their own merits. Yet the forces of imagination and intuition cannot be entirely silenced; they seek refuge in the subconscious, intuitive life of artificially overstimulated sex impulses. Perhaps the medieval artists were not so naïve after all, when they pictured the devil with a face which expressed nothing but cold intellect, and a body with hoofs and tail. A human organism whose intellect becomes a robot, and whose intuition merges with his animal instincts, has no room left for a human ego. The equilibrium between intuition and intellect is disturbed, and the area of freedom which existed between them becomes overpowered by the analytical, segregating forces of pure intellectualism. Under their influence this area may be split, whereupon it may disintegrate into what we today call a "multiple personality."

The action of a calculating machine bears an admirable resemblance to a part of man's intellectual activities, yet it has nothing in common with the intuitive faculties to which the machine owes its very existence. Only when we lose awareness of this can we liken a machine to a human mind or try to trace the mysteries of man's evolution to mechanical laws. Dissatisfied even with the soulless concept of a purely biological evolution, we are now proceeding to liken man to the lifeless. Speaking on "Information—Theory and Life," Homer Jacobson says: "The message is transmitted around a *feedback* loop (the life cycle). Occasionally noise (mutations) arise in the message. The noise affects the *gain* of the message . . . (fertility of the species). . . . And their maximal gain messages may be vastly more complex than the original message (evolution) . . ."[10] Does such a theory of evolution hold any meaning for a human being of flesh and blood, soul and spirit? Or does it not rather fit a mechanical monster, a Golem or Frankenstein? Being free, man can remake himself in the image which he forms of himself, and the moral choice of our time will be reflected by the likeness this image will assume.

On his quest to gain the knowledge of good and evil, and to become "as a god," man started out from a legendary state of intuitive consciousness. The quest opened his eyes to the world of the senses and led to the development of analytical faculties which made him wise to the ways of death. Once his decision was made, he could no longer check his course, until he reached at last the far border of physical existence, where matter loses itself in the material void of nuclear energy.

During all the stages of his long journey, man has been compelled to make individual decisions between good and evil according to the varying laws and conditions of the epoch. But only today—when the second wing of his being, his intellect, has unfolded—has it become possible for him to make his final moral choice. From now on, his path goes neither forward nor backward, but either up or down. He has gained the power and the potential insight to re-create the world and himself in the image of the Spirit, or in that of Matter.

A growing recognition of this conceivably ultimate crisis in human evolution is dawning on some of our leading scientists, inspiring them to an almost apocalyptical language:

> Since there also seems to be no reason why self-reproducing machines might not be made, the autonomous evolution of mechanisms becomes a distinct possibility. It is perfectly possible that in this way, almost unwittingly, a mechanical model of Satan might be constructed which would in fact satisfy most of the theological requirements of the Anti-Christ.[11]

Yet there is one point in this statement with which we cannot agree. The real cause for dread is not a machine turned human, but a human turned machine. Mortally afraid of the responsibilities of freedom, man may make his last irrevocable choice to re-create himself in the image of a robot. For he has the power to do so: "Neither heavenly nor earthly, neither mortal nor immortal have we created thee, so that thou mightest be free according to thy own will and honor, to be thy own creator and builder."[12] No, not the machine threatening to become human is the ultimate danger, but the madness which might turn man into a machine. Nobody seems to know this better than Norbert Wiener himself, the father of cybernetics.

I have spoken of machines, but not only of machines having brains of brass and thews of iron. When human atoms are knit into an organization in which they are used not in their full right as responsible human beings, but as cogs and levers and rods, it matters little that their raw material is flesh and blood. . . . The hour is very late, and the choice of good and evil knocks at our door.[13]

The terms used by Hutchinson and Wiener are unmistakably modern; their messages, however, differ little from those of a time long past. Thus they have answered the question asked in the opening line of this chapter. It *is* possible to translate the medieval visions of good and evil into modern concepts of ethics.

CHAPTER X

THE HYDRA'S HEAD

Professor Wiener's warning is as timely as that now being brought to us by the growing power of our political and ideological adversaries. His words should remind us that the threat to our civilization cannot be met by outer means alone; for the issue of our time lies in the critical stage into which the age-old struggle between good and evil has entered. Yet all warnings would be useless were man not able to differentiate between good and evil, and were he not capable of free choice.

Man's capacity for moral choice, together with the responsibility engendered by it, has increased with his intellectual and individualistic evolution. Still there are philosophical schools which doubt the very existence of freedom. They point to the multitude of known and unknown factors to whose constant influence man is subject, even though he may believe himself to be a free being. These skeptics are in error, inasmuch as they are looking in the wrong place for the answers to their questions.

Freedom is an idea: as such, it is dependent on intuitive, and not on intellectual laws. True, ordinary life is at times a precise reflection of intangible realities; but it is no more than that. Man's great deeds and sacrifices in the service of freedom are such reflections, but we cannot expect to find proof of freedom in analytical and experimental investigations of the human mind any more than we can hope to find the reflected object within the structure of a mirror.

Freedom is an ideal that has always existed in the intuitive consciousness of man. Intuitive experience is, of course, no less subject to error than sensual perception. Consequently, the true meaning of freedom has been a highly controversial issue throughout the course of history. But, while we may differ on its interpretation, just as we may differ on the nature of a physical fact, we have to deal with it as a reality, whose earthly reflection is more or less distorted owing to our own inadequacies.

While some go as far as to deny the very existence of free choice, others tend to credit it with too wide a scope. Actually, freedom has little in common with the "do-as-you-please" attitude of rugged individualism. Its manifestations, even in present-day consciousness, are few and far between. Furthermore, it permits only one of two possibilities in any given situation; this is not immediately obvious but, once recognized as one of the secrets of freedom, it can be of great psychological help. Seemingly there are always many ways open to choice. Yet a searching self-analysis and a careful evaluation of facts will show that in every critical moment there are two basic directions open, and no more. While this statement cannot be proved, it must nevertheless be asserted so that the reader may be induced to reappraise some of the vital problems of self-recognition.

Freedom and its laws may reveal themselves to us when we relive those rare moments of life during which we have actually held the reins of our destiny. Those moments are usually veiled by pride, fear, self-reproach, or any of the many other emotions which almost inevitably follow and mask a crucial decision; but after enough time has lapsed, objective self-investigation can still emotions until we learn to see ourselves in retrospect as if we were our own dispassionate but understanding judge. A memory aroused in this way tells us a great deal about ourselves. From it, an intuitive experience can arise which, though faint at first, may eventually disclose to us the reality and nature of freedom.

A man once came into a doctor's office and told the following story. Ever since the day he had failed to rescue a stranger from drowning, his hitherto great self-assurance had given way to doubt and a mounting sense of frustration. He had never been a good swimmer, Mr. L. explained. So, one day, when he saw a man jump into a river, his first reaction was to seek help elsewhere. But nobody was in sight. Apparently seized by terror, the victim began a frantic struggle; and for a moment, as Mr. L. recalled later, time seemed to stand still. There was his own life, his family, and his future—all dear to him—to be risked for a stranger who, a few minutes ago, had wanted to die. At first the scales of decision bore down heavily on one side, but soon they became suspended by a sense of compassion that grew until he seemed to feel the drowning man's anguish in his own heart. Personal fear, horror of cold water, even concern about his clothes—all these feelings were there, and yet not quite a part of himself. It was possible to weigh them, to measure them against compassion and the premonition of future self-reproach.

Mr. L. said that never in his life, either before or after, had he felt as lonely but also as free as in the moment when he made his decision to risk his life for the stranger. However, no sooner did he feel the icy water on his skin and the pull of the currents against his limbs, than he became his normal, cautious self. Again he forced himself on but, when he reached the struggler, he drew back in fear. A few minutes later unexpected help came, which could have saved both of them had he held on to the victim for only the briefest span of time. As it was, the stranger drowned. It was long before Mr. L. could forgive himself. Assurances given by the physician were of no avail except for this: the patient began to meditate on the event, and gradually learned that the course of his adventure had been determined by conditions which, at the crucial moment, were beyond the control of his free will. His momentary decision had been completely overruled by upbringing, innate anxieties, neglect of physical training, and lack of any strong desire to help another without reward. These weaknesses restricted the scope of his freedom, so that he could not accomplish the moral deed he had set out to do.

But the incident was by no means futile: it helped Mr. L. to discover himself. In the end he became even grateful for an experience enabling him to understand the limitations of his freedom; and he learned how to work toward the development of a more harmonious personality which at long last would permit a greater degree of moral choice.

Most people are like Mr. L., in that they possess good will, a fair amount of courage, and common sense. Yet—though they may manage their own lives well, and do their duty as good citizens—they find themselves incapable of dealing successfully with such a situation. And just now our whole civilization is facing a radically new situation which demands more than ordinary courage and decency: it requires inner vision and strong capacity for free choice. It is not enough for modern man to oppose evil in its physical manifestations like injustice, open aggression, or threats to liberty. These are merely "the mortal heads of the Hydra" which renew themselves when cut off. Only when its "deathless" head is recognized and destroyed can evil be conquered. But, to accomplish this, we need eyes to see the deathless head. And we need the strength of Hercules, the legendary hero who stood as the symbol of freedom and moral victory for the Greeks.

Dragon fighters have gone out of fashion, but not dragons of a strength and fierceness hardly known before. Who has made their breed so powerful on earth? In the answer to this question lies a deep tragedy of human evolution. For it is not always the evil in the individual which brings evil into the world; oftener it is misled idealism. In a time when true vision has grown dim, it is those whose inner longing is greatest who are prone to satisfy it with distorted ideals. Such people are moral in a subjective way, but their pride and lack of self-knowledge deprive them of moral vision. The political fanatic for whom no personal sacrifice is too great for the attainment of his ideal, is undoubtedly a moral person; but the results of his own morality may demoralize and corrupt millions. Yet being a monomaniac he resents *all* restrictions except those imposed by him.

Communistic leadership is aware of this psychological fact. It uses its monomaniacs in the initial stages, but it endeavors to eliminate them as soon as they have helped it to power. As to the masses, authoritarian governments are wont to use terror as a means of enforcing dogma, however only as a stopgap measure. Their foremost aim is to perpetuate their rule through education appropriate to their ideology.

. . . administrative measures of any kind . . . can only lead to strengthening and even intensifying . . . religious convictions. . . .

. . . the struggle against religious beliefs should be regarded now as an ideological struggle of the scientific, materialist world outlook against an antiscientific, religious world outlook. . . . antireligious propaganda . . . is an integral part of the communist education . . . and has as its aim the dissemination of scientific, materialist knowledge. . . .

Modern scientific discoveries . . . convincingly refute religious dogma.[1]

The child who is casually taught scientific facts so cleverly distorted that they appear as proof of a mechanistic or naturalistic world picture, will require little persuasion to become a foe of religion. Nor will sermons or religious exhortations sway him from this path.

In the East millions and millions of youths have found a creed. Convinced that traditional religion, intoxicating as it may be, is untenable in the light of proved facts, they had no choice but to channel all their intuitive and idealistic longings toward the establishment of a paradise on earth, not so much for their own sake as for the imagined good of future generations.

To these idealists, personal gain has much less appeal than personal sacrifice involving tears, sweat, and labor. Misled by apparently irrefutable facts, they must consider religion and such ideas as freedom, good and evil mere inventions, propaganda to further the Western capitalists' egotistic aims. No wonder that President Eisenhower was hard pressed when Marshal Zhukov blamed America for her materialism, and extolled Russian idealism. Does not most of what we teach in our schools, what we announce to the world as scientific theories, contradict our professed spiritual aims? And what can we hope to achieve with our all too superficial anti-Communistic propaganda? No more than to cut off the mortal heads of the Hydra, with the result that *two* new ones will grow in its place.

Promises of improved economic conditions and of religious and political freedom may be attractive to the older generation. The young Communist cannot be swayed by sermons, nor lured by promises of a better life for himself. History has proved to all but us that deprivations, sacrifices, and even martyrdom inspire the idealist rather than repel him, especially when materialistic indoctrination has left no other outlet for his spiritual longings.

The Soviets do not seem to realize, however, that their clever use of unfulfilled religious longing must encounter at least one great psychological obstacle. They may succeed so long as danger of war exists and serious economic and agricultural difficulties challenge the imagination of their youth. But when their economic goals are achieved, their frustrated intuitive longings will seek new outlets. The first signs of this rebellion already loom on the horizon of Communist society. Juvenile delinquency, youth's revenge on a society depriving it of its hopes for inner fulfillment, is now on the rise in Russia too. Among the adults a maximum in alcohol consumption, coupled with an epidemic of deadly boredom, has been worrying the Soviet leaders for some time. "A vigorous anti-boredom campaign is in full swing in the communist lands."[2] But while anti-boredom campaigns will hardly solve the Communists' psychological troubles, the newly aroused fascination with space travel may benefit them greatly.

The Soviets, who have at times displayed an uncanny insight into folk psychology, must surely be credited with knowing their own people. The Russian is a mystic at heart. His culture has always been marked by a deep nostalgia, a fervent desire to withdraw from physical existence and find refuge in another world. For a time the professed ideals of Soviet religion, the hope of building a paradise on earth, have roused his imagination. But now he threatens to withdraw again. The first signs of such withdrawal appear as a threat to communism, greater possibly than open rebellion. The Soviet leaders have had no choice but to offer new hopes for escape, hopes they believe will keep the mystical longing of their people appeased while holding them mentally and physically bound to earthly chores.

What more expedient scheme could they choose than one which shrewdly substitutes the illusion of escape to another planet for true spiritual flight! Thus the Communists, using these and many other designs of advanced psychology, are still gaining in their bid for world power, while the West has become more and more resigned to a defensive role. What is the cause of this tragic development? The fact that we ourselves do not fully believe in the reality of our ideals. Deep down in our hearts we fear that intuitive perception, should it actually work, might give the lie to all our religious and ideological traditions. Out of this fear come almost hysterical outcries against anyone suggesting that man not only *can* but *must* develop his God-given faculties of intuition if he is to protect his sanity and orientation under the present onslaught of materialistic madness.

Of course, all unnatural attempts at developing these faculties: world estrangement, denial of logic, material science, and sensual reality, are to be rejected, and most of all the present trend toward such vision-inducing drugs as mescalin and its chemical substitutes. But there are ways within the sphere of common sense, suggested by all great religions and by its very laws, ways which *can* lead to a happier and saner future. If the lessons of history are at all valid, we must conclude that all the truly great deeds of humanity were done by those who had the courage to break through the narrow confines of a merely sense-bound consciousness. Their capacity for intuitive perception varied, and so did their teachings; but basically they all agreed that a spiritual reality exists, accessible to those who seek it with all their hearts.

Once this is recognized, our responsibility is clear. It is up to us to prove the reality of our ideals by devising a form of psychology which takes into full consideration the human being as a whole.

True, we must continue to fight on the physical plane, if need be with force of arms. But while liberties can be defended, freedom must be won, and the fight for freedom must take place in a sphere which is *qualitatively* different from the material plane on which the Communists have become the

champions of our disenchanted age. To stress the difference
between spiritual and material battlegrounds, we have brought
together in this chapter such apparently incongruous subjects
as an individual's struggle for inner freedom and the plight of
millions deprived of their liberties.

To the high priests of communism, individual freedom is an
error of biological evolution, an error which must be eradi-
cated if the human species is ever to enjoy peace and social
justice. In order to achieve this goal a small clique of dictators
seeks control over the whole world, principally for one purpose:
the remodeling of the individual through controlled education
into the likeness of a well-conditioned animal or a calculating
machine with built-in reactions. The Soviets have made great
forward strides in their gigantic scheme. Why? First, because
we, being thoroughly materialistic ourselves, have refused to
believe that at least some of our adversaries might be actually
possessed of a dynamic, though misled, idealism. And since we
have failed to understand our enemies, we have been incapable
of combating them. Second, because dictatorship is eminently
expedient for the achievement of imperialistic goals. Third,
because the Soviets, unlike ourselves, have made a clear moral
choice, a negative one to be sure, but one which best serves
their purpose. Soviet statesmanship has entered the power
sphere of what we must call evil, and has learned to draw
strength from it. The Communist leader is no longer hampered
by moral qualms; his decisions can be swift and to the point; he
has decided that good is whatever can serve his cause.

Light is always stronger than darkness, but darkness will
prove more than a match for moral indecision, which is neither
white nor black. This drifting around in an ideological twilight is our greatest danger. We feel clearly enough that
communism is evil, but our vision is so dim that we cannot
decide just where its evil lies. We have sought it in Soviet
Russia's socialistic philosophy and in her deification of auto-
crats; in their quest for world domination, and above all in
their ruthless political methods. But all these are merely the
mortal heads of the Hydra, which may be shed at will. The
Communist social order, for instance, ceased to exist long
ago. Today a considerable number of Russians earn extremely

high wages, up to one hundred thousand dollars a year and more. They pay relatively low taxes and can bequeath their possessions to their families. This is the beginning of capitalism, and the fact that only a small percentage of the population shares in its benefits makes it even less socialistic.

We must realize that present-day Russian imperialism is by no means a communistic innovation, but merely a vigorous continuation of prerevolutionary trends. Autocracy is interchangeable with party dictatorship. Whenever this change occurs there is an excellent reason for it, but not one from which the free world can draw comfort or hope. It simply indicates a new phase on the path toward the old goal. This goal requires three successive stages of leadership.

First comes the fanatical utopian whose power of conviction inspires the masses to violent action: the revolutionary who destroys the old forms of government and establishes the foundation of a new society. He is replaced by the cold, calculating dictator, usually power-drunk and sadistic, who must be ruthless enough to control the aroused masses and eliminate all political foes of the regime. The third stage can follow only when a considerable number of the population are thoroughly indoctrinated and know little of the prerevolutionary ways of life. This stage relies on a party machine or "collective leadership," which can be tried time and again; if and when public unrest reappears, it can be abandoned for a temporary return to the second stage, the individual autocracy. In our opinion collective leadership is more appropriate to the ideology of bolshevism than individual dictatorship and, should it succeed, would mark the beginning of the dreadful form of society which Orwell described in his novel *1984*.

The Gremlins behind the Kremlin know only too well that any individual, regardless of how cruel and depraved he may be, is still human and, as a consequence, changeable. Even the most hardened criminal may undergo a change of heart that will alter his whole being, and therefore only a political machine can be fully trusted to perfect and perpetuate a society of robots.

And what about the methods applied by Russia and her allies? They are but the logical consequence of a philosophy which denies the existence of higher moral criteria and accepts the doctrines of Marx and Engels, who saw in the material, sensuously perceptible world the only reality, and in the human mind the highest product of matter. The Westerner has played with such ideas for almost a century. He has found it possible to adapt his mind to them and make them part of his educational philosophy without, however, giving up his traditional religion and professed spiritual aims.

The Easterner is not so adaptable. Whatever he accepts intellectually, he embraces with his whole being. Once convinced that man is no more than an animal, he will deal with him accordingly. He knows from his experience in husbandry that the strongest members of a species are its natural leaders. In the human community the strongest are those who know how to attain and hold power. So long as they can maintain their position of leadership, their opinions are sacred insofar as they represent to him nature's highest form of mentality at the momentary state of evolution.

Since in the view of Marxist philosophy evolution is an accidental process, it is now up to "the most advanced minds" to prevent mankind from foundering. The only way the Communist brain trust considers itself capable of saving man from his own fallacies and from potential biological regressions, is the unification of all human animals into one gigantic herd. In such a herd the individual would not count beyond the part he plays in the biological improvement of the whole species, a part which in general will appear pitifully small.

Obviously, ideas like these cannot be refuted on materialistic grounds nor defeated by sentimental slogans. Their challenge can be met only by a science of ideas, a science which in the sphere of intuition can be as accurate as physics is in the sphere of the intellect. Above all, we need clarification as to the reality of our own professedly spiritual ideology. Should such a clarification show that Moses and Christ were wrong and such men as Marx and Engels right, then we may as well concede defeat at once, for domesticated animals are better served by supervised methods of conditioning, breeding, and restraint, than by freedom.

But man is more than an animal. Biological processes cannot account for the existence of ideals which often defy the very urge for survival. And without these ideals human history becomes meaningless. Its whole inspiration comes from the innumerable deeds and sacrifices of men who have valued spiritual reality higher than material values, higher than survival itself.

Doubts have arisen as to the spiritual nature of man, because the mirror of his soul has grown dim, while his intellect is still immature. But no single scientific fact exists, no single law of logic, which contradicts a spiritual world conception. The free world, therefore, has no need for an ideological campaign of its own. If it truly believes what it preaches, its children should be brought up to unfold their spiritual as well as their biological nature. No indoctrination is necessary, only a clear distinction between actual scientific facts and hypotheses based on personal inclinations. If we help our children to become harmonious beings, we have nothing to fear from Communist propaganda. Indeed, truth is self-evident for him whose organs of intuitive perception are not closed by a faulty upbringing.

In his present state of evolution, man is neither capable nor in need of knowing the whole truth. But his search for realtiy must not be hampered by indoctrination and bias. If we believe in the objectivity of science, let us, when dealing with children, strictly separate facts from personal interpretations. If we believe—as we claim we do—in the spiritual nature of man, let us train a child's intuitive faculties even as we are encouraging him to be accurate in his sense perceptions and intellectual grasp. If progress in material knowledge were to be balanced by a deepening of inner perception, man's divination of truth, even though still pitifully immature, would become more objective. Only then would one of the greatest dangers to humanity be lessened, the danger caused by the misled idealist playing God.

The Hydra has many heads, but there is only one that counts, the head that represents man's distorted image of himself. Of this image Russell W. Davenport says:

. . . Dialectical Man is a frightening, if not revolting creature . . . he can be no more than a *material* man, because only matter is real, . . . he cannot be . . . an individual. . . . He thus emerges as a kind of social puppet, deprived of individual dignity, exiled from the search for truth, and incompetent to choose between good and evil.[3]

The meaning of words changes in the course of time. Thus even "communism" may assume tomorrow a denotation apparently far less ominous than today's. Do we not already feel complacent about such of its brands today, as for example Titoism? If political friction should ease in the world, the West, always eager to dismiss disquieting thoughts, may then think of statements like Davenport's as outgrowths of unsubstantiated fears and hysterical fancies. Yet, let us not be deceived by the changeability of terms! Whatever it may be called in the future, the impulse known today as communism will remain a dire dread for humanity, unless it is fully recognized and combated with all the ideological means at the disposal of free men.

Communism draws its strength from a powerful impulse which tends to relieve the individual of the fearful responsibility of freedom, and to reshape him in the image of an intellectual animal or a thinking machine. Today the cold war waged against communism is fought predominantly on political and economic grounds. What will happen if Russia, owing to her tremendous resources, should prosper, if China should actually succeed in her economic ambition? Maybe the need of the Communist bloc for internal and external terror would then cease to exist. But will we then have won our crucial fight for survival?

Hardly, for only a *mortal* head of the Hydra would have disappeared, giving rise to others, threatening us where we might least expect them. No, communism is just one manifestation of a greater evil, an evil which we compared with the *immortal* head of the Hydra, not because it cannot die, but because it is concerned with the immortal soul of man.

The many-headed dragon is an ancient symbol representing the eternal challenger of man. Its immortal head has taken various forms in the course of history. Today it appears as the distorted image which man has created of himself.

CHAPTER XI

AN ASPECT OF CRIME

Today political pseudo-religion may well be the main manifestation of organized evil. Its characteristic is the perversion of an era's spiritual longing by a minority of self-styled "saviors" who mistake their own immature concepts of good and evil for moral vision. This minority is too conceited to recognize that moral vision presupposes an intense effort at ethical self-development, just as scientific discernment requires a thorough training in intellectual and sensual faculties. Unfortunately, such utopians attract the most ruthless elements as willing henchmen, and exert a hypnotic influence on present-day society, which is floundering in the moral void of agnosticism.

Another major problem of our time is evil in the guise of moral disease as it afflicts individuals in the form of crime. There has always been crime, but its motivation, its psychology and philosophy, change with time. Understanding its nature is not only essential for the protection of law and order, but also for the realization of the specific trends and countertrends which confront man in ever different forms at various stages of his evolution. Since the human race has not yet outgrown its weaknesses, a too rigorous attempt to suppress them is, in general, unrealistic; it can even lead to disaster, as the experiences of the prohibition era proved. But there are types of aberrations which, if not treated rigorously, can infect and destroy a whole civilization. In eras less sentimental but wiser than ours, certain kinds of crimes were singled out for ruthless punishment in order to forestall such danger. Today more than ever we could learn a great deal about the history of consciousness if, instead of shaking our heads at the "barbaric" laws of other eras or civilizations, we tried to find out why, under specific conditions, a particular form of crime was discouraged by the sternest means available.

In our time the answer to crime is rightly sought in attempts to effect cure and rehabilitation rather than to inflict punishment and fear. But for this very reason we are in special need of a profound psychological comprehension of the criminal mind.

Although there is no room here to discuss the problem thoroughly, it may be permissible to point out a few of its contributory factors; for these might furnish a clue to many causes of delinquency. Contrary to the professed opinions of some criminologists, the criminal tendency has little if anything to do with intellectual deficiency on the part of the potential delinquent. Without a high degree of intelligence, the underworld's ability to keep up a relentless and rather successful fight against all the brains and resources of modern law enforcement would be inexplicable.

From an intellectual point of view we are rather inclined to feel a grudging admiration for the amazing technological, administrative, strategic, and political abilities of organized crime. No, there is nothing wrong with the I.Q. of the successful criminal. But what, then, is wrong with him? Many of our respected citizens merely shrug their shoulders at such a question and maintain that the problem is simple enough: the delinquent has a wicked nature which turns him against law and order. Yet, is this true? We cannot believe the answer is as simple as that. Convicts rarely turn from an appeal for help. A surprising number of them have donated blood, offered skin and even their eyes, to aid a suffering child; and, as most wardens will confirm, the motivation for their offers is often unselfish. Moreover, criminals are frequently willing to subject themselves, without promise of reward, to medical experiments requiring contamination with syphilis and other diseases more abhorrent to the human mind than physical torture. Such often

published facts are time and again confirmed by personal professional experience with the depraved. There seems to be
little doubt that people prone to commit criminal acts may,
under certain circumstances, be capable of surprising kindness
and even of self-sacrifice. Naturally, this does not contradict the
general view that delinquents are, on the average, morally inferior to law-abiding citizens; but it does help us to realize that
moral condemnation alone does not contribute to an understanding of crime nor does it help to solve its enigma.

Where then can we hope to find the clue to crime? It may
be found in records of the history of consciousness, of which
we shall give but one example. At the beginning of the second
millennium A.D., Europe had sunk into new depths of selfishness and cruelty. Not only trade, but even civilization itself,
came nearly to a standstill; for it had become a favorite pas-
time of lords and barons to ambush caravans and to torture
and kill merchants, before robbing them. Utter lawlessness and
incredible cruelty were at their peak when the idea of the
First Crusade emerged. And the most surprising thing happened: some of the most hardened evildoers enthusiastically
took the cross, gave up the possessions for which they had shed
so much blood, and willingly suffered the severest deprivations.
They exposed themselves to suffering and death in order to
"liberate" the tomb of Christ, whose every command they had
previously broken without hesitation. Contrary to modern al-
legations, at least the First Crusade was unselfish and not mer-
cenary. "Lands of great value until now were sold at a vile
price, and everyone bought arms to go to avenge God against
the infidels. Thieves, pirates, various criminals were touched
by grace. . . ."[1]

A whole generation still endowed with a vivid intuitive consciousness had turned criminal in its subconscious rebellion
against the approach of a disenchanted era. Comprising the
most vigorous and powerful elements of the time, it was ready
to drown its civilization in a sea of crime and cruelty, and so
prevent, or at least delay, the emergence of the new age.

Clerical orders provided a haven for those who resisted the
earth-bound trend of consciousness but were averse to lawless-

ness. Many, however, craved an incentive more powerful than contemplative mysticism and the ideals which chivalry could offer. To them, the unworldly task of saving the Holy Land from the infidels was an answer to deepest longings. What did it matter if one were to lose one's life on such a mission? The deadly desert of the Holy Land became a gateway to heaven, and physical suffering a purification from sin. True, not even the ecstasy of the First Crusade could banish the fierceness and brutality from the hearts of the cross-bearers. But he who looks at their mission in scorn and condescension has scant knowledge of medieval man and of his peculiar ways to redemption. Pain and death meant little to him, whether he dealt or received them. It was eternal life that counted, while physical existence was like a cup of wine to be greedily drained and then smashed to the floor. Vicious urges were not the fault of man as much as that of the devil. Save for an act of grace, there were only two ways of purifying them. One was mortification of the flesh, the other dedication to a noble deed. And what nobler deed was there than the liberation of the Savior's tomb?

Thus the crusades performed two invaluable services for medieval Christianity. Men of fiery rebelliousness, who might have felt sure of damnation as their lives drew to a close, were permitted to die at peace with themselves and their God. Moreover, the crusades freed the peace-loving population of Europe from oppression too heavy to bear. Relieved of a hundred thousand unmanageable rebels, Europe could proceed in her progress toward modern consciousness.

Investigation into the mass psychology of the adventurers who turned explorers, and of the delinquents who settled in Australia and New Zealand, could shed a great deal of light on the history of consciousness and its relationship to crime. History offers innumerable examples of antisocial epidemics which acted as monitors for whole civilizations, but a study of those already mentioned can easily show that crime waves indicate crossroads on the path of evolution.

Naturally, individual vice is a manifestation of antisocial and destructive instincts in man. Yet only when these instincts are augmented by a subconscious resistance against prevailing trends of historical evolution do they become a menace to society as a whole. It shows poor judgment in psychology if the causes of such resistance are not recognized and mended before they lead to revolutions or else to loss of freedom. Undoubtedly, improvements in social conditions are beneficial, but not to the degree modern materialists believe. Nazism and communism have tried to give power and relative wealth to the most violent elements among the heretofore underprivileged classes, with the result that they have merely transferred their criminal trends to the sphere of statesmanship.

Regardless of what modern man may think about the crusades, for the Middle Ages they were the answer to an otherwise unsolvable problem of man in rebellion against the coming of a disillusioned age. Today there is some hope that space travel will, in the future, do a similar service to mankind. But is this hope founded on psychological reality? We doubt it, for it was not the lure of distance and adventure alone which kindled the imagination of the young; it was the inner experience which those prepared by suffering and trial could still attain in the Holy Land.

What can man expect to find on the far side of the moon that will give his life a deeper meaning, and still the nostalgia of his soul? Very little indeed. And therefore the exact opposite may happen to what took place in the Middle Ages. Those who have adjusted best to our time will seek adventure in outer space, while all the criminal elements will remain with us. The reason for this sad prediction is that the former are still in search of a better world, while the latter have abandoned faith in life. Unwilling to face a lifetime of inner emptiness, they look for the sort of adventure which even an animal can enjoy, the adventure of destruction. Crime, especially in its juvenile and apparently senseless form, is a result of devious imagination, deprived of a worthy goal by our mechanistic and animalistic concepts of man and his world.

More affected than his fellow men by the creeping paralysis of intuitive faculties, the potential criminal easily falls victim to the ideological fallacies of our time. Owing to unfortunate hereditary and environmental conditions, to lack of opportunity and of affection, he has become even more incapable of joy, compassion, and moral freedom than the rest of us. He, like every human being, searches frantically for happiness. Not finding in himself the capacity for this purely intuitive inner experience, he merely puts to the test what advertisements, movies, and fiction preach daily; namely, the doctrine that happiness is a by-product of material acquisitions. From posters, television screens, and magazine pages glamorous figures appear before him, their faces radiant with joy. And the cause of their bliss? An expensive car, a new house, a big sum paid by an insurance company for the demise of a dear relative. Who has ever told the child that, while earthly goods may rouse joy in those capable of it, the very capacity for happiness is an inner gift which must be acquired first? Not knowing this simple truth, the neophyte in delinquency will find himself eternally disappointed with the results of his exploits. Unaware that he lacks the ability for joy, he will attribute his joylessness to the inadequacy of his spoils or his lack of prestige among his associates. Like a man tormented by an unquenchable thirst, he will seek fulfillment in ever greater gains and ever more power in the underworld, undeterred by warnings that crime does not pay and that eventually his life may end in disaster. What he subconsciously seeks is real happiness, and for a moment of it he is willing to pay any price.

We may call this type of delinquency "motivated crime." Punishment stern enough to prove to the intelligent criminal that his search for happiness is ill-directed is obviously necessary; however, a cure can be achieved only by educational efforts to awaken his intuitive ability for joy, which by its very nature depends on moral pursuits.

More ominous, and unfortunately even more typical of our era, is crime without obvious motivation, a category to which many cases of juvenile delinquency belong. Naturally, there is no distinct line separating these two types of crimes: the latter merely represents a more advanced state of criminality, the incipient disintegration of the human ego itself. Owing to such disintegration, many criminals in this category act in a state of obsession or dimmed consciousness, and are addicts of alcohol

or narcotics. Far oftener than is recognized, they are manifestations of a "multiple personality," of a split in consciousness of
the "Dr. Jekyll and Mr. Hyde" type. Under strict discipline, of
the sort prevailing in a good rehabilitation camp or a well-
managed prison, the delinquent of this type may recover some
of his moral identity. The imposed discipline and routine substitute, as it were, for his own weak will forces, and relieve him
of personal responsibility and the need of making moral decisions. Thus his diseased imagination is given a respite and a
chance of partial recovery. This type of delinquent may turn
out to be a model prisoner and a likely prospect for early
parole. Released, however, he is again compelled to face the
perplexing difficulties of modern life and to suffer from his own
incapacity for love or even contentment. Then his personality
breaks down again, and leaves his organism to the rule of the
most disastrous of all dualities: cold intellect and burning
desire.

Let us consider the problem of juvenile delinquency from
still another angle. A great deal has been done to combat it: increase in police protection, improvement of social and economic
conditions, guided activities, and many other external measures.
But has not the crux of the problem escaped us? Why is it that
juveniles band together in gangs, called by the most imaginative
names such as "white knights," "crusaders," and the like? Why
is it that they direct their most vicious anger against clean
modern houses and centers built for their own good? Why is
it that they often risk life and limb for the protection of a member of their gang?

What every child seeks is an outlet for his phantasy, for his
innate longing for high romance. This longing is the life struggle of his soul in a world of bleak materialism and stupid
pseudo-realism. No wonder that many an adolescent hates the
laws of modern civilization as intensely as a wild animal hates
the bars of its cage. And still, modern youth is capable of a
fanatical loyalty, a loyalty he reserves for those who, like Hitler
and Lenin, offer him an outlet for his phantasy. He hardly
cares how false they are, how high a price they exact, so long
as they promise escape from a world without dreams. Such

leaders need not be political fanatics; they may be cold-blooded, petty thieves.

Modern youth needs adventure, and the only adventure within his reach may be defiance of the law. The gang becomes his Order of Chivalry in his fight against a disappointing world. The boy with the rebellious ego is cut out to be the leader, while the boy of weak personality will, in his desperate need for guidance, obey him unquestioningly. In case of further moral decline, and when left to their own devices, the former will be inclined to "motivated," the latter to "unmotivated," crime. Both could be saved, one with the help of punishment and re-education, the other by strengthening of his selfhood; but neither will accept the "enlightened" and primarily utilitarian approach of today's materialistic psychology and sociology. The juvenile, while he may make use of recreation and sporting facilities provided for him, rebels subconsciously against the worship of material objects. Often he feels compelled to defile and destroy what a few hours ago he had seemed to enjoy. Why? Because, to one who starves for inner fulfillment, modern charity gives stones instead of bread.

Yet man's longing for adventure rather than material reward is not limited to children and adolescents. At one time an English explorer, unable to find participants for his dangerous project, promised poor pay, hardship, no glory, and possible death to all who would join him. The result? A flood of enthusiastic volunteers. Churchill promised his despairing countrymen blood, sweat, and tears, with a response that astonished the world.

It is the fairyland of creative phantasy which man craves, the world which lies between the spheres of intuitive and sensual activity, a domain all his own. Phantasy is an expression of individuality and freedom, it is the most precious seed in the soul of a normal child. But it can easily become corrupted. Too much "freedom," too little knowledge in a child after his seventh year may promote daydreaming to a point where phantasy becomes world-estranged. Such phantasy is not moral since it can hardly lead to compassionate action, and may therefore be called amoral imagination.

When, on the other hand, a child is brought up to be prematurely intellectual, clever, and earth-bound, his phantasy loses its spiritual feeding ground and withdraws into the dark recesses of the subconscious mind. Phantasy is a child of heaven, not of the earth. If it is permitted to draw strength from its native soil, it can stand the bitter reality of existence, and brighten it with creative and enduring youthfulness. Unless infinite care is given to secure imagination its proper place in upbringing, phantasy, instead of supporting life, designs means of destruction. It becomes the immoral imagination of the delinquent mind.

How naïve our modern educators are, when they preach the following: "Enlightened self-interest and selflessness become the same. When the individual acts in full realization of his own need of others he enhances the other in his own behalf."[2] A noble-sounding phrase, but of little help to troubled youths! Enlightened self-interest has rarely ever made a decent man of a delinquent child, though it may have kept him out of jail. What every youngster longs for is a world of wonder somewhere "on the far side of the moon" and yet on earth. This search is easily discouraged by an adult who believes only in what he measures, weighs, and counts. Yet, such discouragement does not make the adolescent trust that selflessness can be attained by enlightened selfishness. Nor does he see much that gives him reason to believe it. If there is nothing real but the world of senses, then he, like everyone, should fight to get his share.

In such climate religion loses its reality; it becomes a mere pretense, to many youths a symbol of adult hypocrisy.

In a soul-searching article, John B. Martin tried to find the underlying psychological causes of a terrible and senseless crime committed by youths of respectable families. His sad conclusion reads: "Stated in simplest terms, this murder occurred because two factors came together—a psychopathic individual and a delinquent society."[3]

Our society is delinquent because it deprives children of their childhood's Garden of Eden. It gives them stones instead of bread, and then is shocked when they grow up with hearts of stones.

Yet the fate of our era will be decided less by crime itself than by the way in which we shall control it. For controlled it will be, being too wasteful for society to bear. The question is, which way will we choose?

Even today medicine has the means to alter the human personality. Psychology has already succeeded in subduing difficult conflicts by removing inhibitions. Some patients become reasonably well under such treatment for, once the ego has ceased to struggle, its conflicts cease. Similar methods, coupled with drugs, hypnotism, and possibly brain surgery, could conceivably do away with crime altogether, and create docile robots incapable of moral choice. Such danger becomes formidable where governments take over medicine. For a government charged with preserving peace and order may well be tempted to prefer medical treatments to imprisonment or expensive rehabilitation. Thus a program may start which, appearing benevolent enough at first, may well end in the complete destruction of freedom.

The remaining alternative is unattractive to modern man. It requires an intense effort in thinking, an effort which alone can lead to the self-knowledge and self-education that form the basis for true leadership. It requires a ceaseless investigation not only into the problems of good and evil, but into man's very nature as it emerges in the course of his historical evolution. Nothing but an education based on such knowledge can lead to a strengthening of man's ego and to a moral evolution of his creative phantasy.

CHAPTER XII

PREREQUISITES OF LOVE

Once upon a time Uranus and Gaea—Heaven and Earth—gave warning to Zeus that the child of Metis, the genius of cosmic wisdom then still in its mother's womb, would lead man away from divine guidance. Heeding the warning, the god swallowed Metis before her time came, and the child sprang from his own forehead. This child, Pallas Athena, was worshiped as the goddess of science and art, the genius of harmony, justice, and freedom.

Here, in its own language, the myth tells us the difference between ancient and modern consciousness. The impulse which created the Classical Age of Greece sprang from the forehead of a god, and not from that of a man. A new force attributed to the forehead—the frontal lobe of the brain—emerged in that period. Although wisdom had existed before, it had been the fruit of an instinctive, purely intuitive insight, an insight which permitted man glimpses into the laws of astronomy, higher mathematics, medicine, and many other sciences without need for analytical deductions or the use of exact instruments. The ancient priest-physician simply knew which herbs had healing qualities, and how they had to be prepared, even as native medicine men have been able to provide modern medicine with invaluable leads. This still earlier instinctive insight was attributed to the function of the occiput, the posterior lobe of the brain, and during the height of Egyptian culture manipulations were still used to lengthen the back of the head by modifying the growth of the skull.

The Classical Age of Greece was the era of the frontal lobe, of man's ability to grasp intellectually what he once knew only by instinct. The statues of that time stressed the Olympian head, not yet the forehead of ordinary man but that of his divine prototype. The gods knew that if Intellect, the child of Metis, were to be born in average man—still morally so immature —it would separate him from all more profound wisdom. It might prove his undoing. Thus, for a while at least, the power of intellect and freedom was protected in the veiled teachings of the temple schools, where it was revered as the gift of Athena. Maturing intellect, the impulse which created the Classical Age, belonged to a divine, not a human, domain. Not until the appearance of a new era which coincided with the birth of Christianity, could intellect be gradually entrusted to man's individual use.

Had the fire of early Christianity been permitted to draw fuel from pagan wisdom, its glow might have endured and given rise to a truly constructive science and a civilization of world-wide brotherhood. Since it did not, religion lost its foundation in earthly life, and science its moral aims. The medieval Church recognizing the dangers but not their cause, felt she had to protect man from his own premature intellectualism, and re-tard the progress of science.

Today the barriers are down and science has emerged as mistress of our age. No power on earth can or will dethrone her, but her reign will become a blessing only when thought is tempered by love. Every great religion has implanted in the soul of humanity a new seed, a seed by no means reserved for its followers alone. The gift Christianity brought to man was a capacity for love greater than had existed before. Whether or not we attribute this gift to Christ himself is a matter of re-ligious conviction. But one fact can actually be proven by historical evidence: the particular kind of love which appeared in man's consciousness almost immediately after Christ's death is an entirely novel factor in human evolution.

Were we to deal with problems of biology, we could talk of a mutation. Since we are concerned with the human spirit, we must say that some new seedling was implanted into the soul of human consciousness, which flourished for a short time, and then became dormant. Therein lies the still hidden significance of the Christian impulse which is a potentiality rather than a fulfillment. To draw that seedling forth into a state of flowering and fruit-bearing is a task for man's free will, and the method of achieving this goal is education in the purest sense of the word. Correct education is a complex problem. It is a necessity for the young, but is of even greater importance for the adult, since the fate of youth lies in his hands. Only wiser and better-balanced parents and teachers can answer the needs of the child.

Such re-education of our adult generation is a painful and difficult process because we are all burdened with the shortcomings and prejudices of our own upbringing. And still we, the present generation, should not put too much blame on our parents and teachers, since their materialistic conceptions were rooted in an immature and therefore overconfident science. Our parents have at least a good excuse for their mistakes, although they are largely responsible for the miserable state of affairs in the world they have left to us.

Today we have *no* excuse for repeating the errors of our elders, inasmuch as twentieth-century science has given the lie to the materialistic world picture which seemed so real a few decades ago. Nothing but mental inertia now prolongs the acceptance of a "scientific" philosophy which is neither scientific nor philosophic. True, the term "materialism" itself is out of fashion, since even its stanchest supporters have never succeeded in explaining on material grounds one single fact of consciousness or of life. But instead of admitting this, they merely change their terminology and arbitrarily attribute divine power to molecular and biogenetic forces. Thus a concept of the world and of man which is not only factually unfounded, but is harmful to the mental life of the growing child, still persists in education. For whatever a teacher may do or say, it is essentially his concept of man in whose image the personalities of his charges are wittingly or unwittingly molded.

What are these concepts of man today? In a book widely accepted as a classic, we find the following statements:

The human organism being composed of atoms, is therefore an embodiment of energy. . . . What he [man] really is, then, is a bulk of space or an embodiment of energy. . . . How may the dynamics of stored energy be controlled and released to the advancement of the organism? These are the questions which confront those who would educate.[1]

How could organisms of this kind ever be free? Such hybrids between power generators and vegetables could merely follow their intrinsic electronic and biological energies without choice of their own. The authors' own premises obviously permit no other logical conclusion, a fact emphasized rather than repudiated by this concession: "The problem . . . is complicated by the fact that the human organism has some control over the expenditure of the energy of which it is constituted."[2] Complicated indeed—almost as complicated as the feat of the famous liar Münchhausen, who once saved himself from drowning by pulling himself out of a swamp by his own hair!

The above-quoted statement by Kelly and Rasey is characteristic of the reasoning of almost all materialistic and naturalistic philosophers, in that it is self-contradictory. For whatever is capable of controlling the expenditure of its own energy must be somehow superior to this energy. Since the latter is material and biological, the controlling agent must be supramaterial and suprabiological, and this is exactly what we call soul and spirit. The interesting but unfortunately neglected circumstance is that materialists and naturalists, while denying its very existence, cannot do without the spirit.

Now let us examine the premises which represent the "essence" of human relationship to our authors.

Man, then, is a social creature, or he is nothing. . . . Others thus become as essential as food or shelter. Since others are essential no man can be unmindful of others. Being mindful of others, seeing that others survive to fulfill one's own social need is the essence of co-operation.[3]

Such purely utilitarian views on human relations may explain why some governments prefer slave labor camps to wholesale elimination of political enemies; but they could never explain nor encourage the spirit of unselfish love and compassion, without which, in the words of Paul, "we become as sounding brass or a tinkling cymbal." And by what mysterious influence would "bulks of space" and "embodiments of energy" be motivated to risk their existence for the sake of ideas since, once extinct, they could hardly fulfill their "social need"?

How many of today's parents are aware of these and similar views in modern educational philosophy? And is it surprising that the children themselves subconsciously resent such concepts, or that they react violently against their teachers and the dreary, soulless existence in which they believe?

Every youth of today, even the least intelligent, is fully aware that his life may soon end in a nuclear war. Why then should he refrain from drawing every ounce of satisfaction and thrill for his own "embodiment of energy" as long as life lasts? Or do our "experts" really believe that a young tough can be induced to self-restraint, kindness, and compassion just because John Dewey found moral deeds "refreshing"? Or because the youth wants to protect his "social needs"? These are well taken care of by the gang or the subversive party to which he belongs, especially when he can outdo his comrades in brutality and crime.

No, we may as well face the fact: whoever sees in children "bulks of space" or "embodiments of energy" or higher animals, is bound to strengthen the subhuman element in them, and no amount of superimposed sentimentality will change this. For nothing but belief in his spiritual nature, and appeal to his nonegotistical, nonbiological potentialities, can awaken in a child love for freedom and moral values.

Yet how can the teacher appeal to something he has never seen or heard? We must admit that to a generation which has lost the faculty of intuitive experience the human spirit is elusive indeed. Since modern man relies predominantly on sense impressions, soul qualities are prone to escape his attention unless revealed in words or deeds. A very young child is obviously incapable of individual self-expression of this kind. It offers instead a great variety of reactions most of which have their source in desires shared by man and animal alike. New-born babies resemble one another almost as much as do individual members of one and the same animal species. A six month old does little which an anthropoid could not do better, and many of a child's actions actually can be attributed to instinctive, biological impulses.

These and many similar facts have encouraged modern psychology to see in the eventual emergence of undeniably higher faculties in the growing child merely a continuation and refinement of his innate instinctive consciousness. In this view lies the whole tragedy of modern upbringing, a tragedy unsolvable by arguments alone. For there is only one answer to it: intuitive experience.

We cannot convince a modern materialist of spiritual realities any more than we can prove the existence of a distant object to a person who insists on keeping his eyes closed. True, materialism as a philosophy is rapidly losing ground in the free world. Its elevation to the status of a government-sponsored creed in the East has induced many Westerners to seek new philosophic terms. Yet this change in terminology has done little for the rank and file of modern intellectuals who seem to cling more than ever to the deceptive security of a purely sense-bound consciousness. Prompted by a deep-seated suspicion of the unfamiliar, they have become fugitives from a reality which they fear and, therefore, resent.

Yet this reality is by no means weird or even mystical. It is perceptible even to the weakened intuitive faculties of our generation in the highly familiar phenomena of babyhood. Naturally, every form of intuitive perception requires in our days an act of will. Without it even a very young child will appear merely as a growing organism endowed with more or less refined animal instincts. Yet with some effort it is possible to sense in a child, before his third year, elements of a nonbiological nature. These elements may, at first, manifest themselves in even usually unnoticed acts of spontaneous self-renunciation, such as his offering to another person a thing which he himself craves. The already half-consumed lollipop landing at an unexpected moment on the nose, in the mouth, or on another sensitive area of a loved adult, will rarely arouse a feeling of gratitude toward the little donor; yet the one possessed of a stoic nature, or the mere bystander, may in such an instance catch a glimpse of another world.

A young child's eyes have not yet turned into the likeness of a photographic lens, and therein lies the reason for their transparency. They do not yet grasp distinctly the optical phenomena of their physical environment; but are open windows through which an inner world shines outward. The adult can close the windows to his inner life until they reflect only the outer world; and the shutter he uses is intellect. The eyes of the child in his preintellectual state lack the protection of blinds. Undoubtedly, most of his expressions stem from such instinctive emotions as hunger, contentment, fear, anger, or shelter-seeking affection; and yet once in a while an expression appears in a child's eyes, which seems to carry a message from a nonmaterial world. The very young child is still closer than the adult to that state of consciousness which the myth calls Garden of Eden, or Paradise. He carries with him a breath from that mythical land, a breath which the adult can feel, thus receiving a fleeting glimpse of a forgotten reality. It may be this reality to which Jesus referred when, speaking of children, he said: "of such is the kingdom of heaven." He certainly did not mean to imply that all children are possessed of an angelic nature!

Nothing but intuitive experience can prove to modern man that he may learn to behold a spiritual world through the eyes of a child. Great artists have had this experience, and succeeded in keeping it alive—as Raphael did, in the child of his "Sistine Madonna."

Average man may lack the artist's gift of communicating his intuitive perceptions to others. But he, too, can find the secrets of the human soul, the keys to self-knowledge in experiences which psychology of today either disregards or treats with sentimentality. The adult can find in the child the clue to his own buried self. And the child needs such recognition if he is to grow up to become a harmonious being. In fact it is the only way in which the adult can make contact with the true personality, the ego of the child, and it is therefore the prerequisite for successful education. For how can we ever hope to meet the real needs of another human being, unless we first make his acquaintance?

Today the physical and intellectual development of most children receives full attention, while their intuitive spirit is allowed to starve—often to death. Parents inclined to cherish in their children "their own flesh and blood," who expect to "live on" in them or to achieve through them what they themselves have failed to accomplish, may never discover their real, independent self.

During the first three years a young individual cannot express his needs in words and intellectual concepts, and therefore depends on an intuitive communion with his environment. Another significant period in a child's development begins with his first question, and lasts approximately to his fourteenth year. The answers a youngster receives to his questions are to his soul what food is to his body. They can strengthen his personality, leave it deficient, or poison it. To understand why strong and happy personalities are so rare today, we have merely to listen to the replies the average adult gives to a child. How much attention have we paid to research in essential foods, and how little do we know of the basic requirements of a growing individuality!

Before attempting an answer to his question we should recall that the child's mind is in many ways superior to ours. His ability to acquire knowledge, his penetration into the essence of things, his memory and power of observation, exceed by far the working capacities of the adult mind. Therefore, all talking down to the child is utterly nonsensical and often responsible for the resentment and contempt against parents and teachers so frequently encountered.

In early childhood a human being is less intellectual but more intelligent than in later life, and by far more intuitive. As was said before, the child of preschool age is still potentially able to enter into a state of consciousness bearing a faint resemblance to the Garden of Eden, the childhood state of the human race. For his whole being, physiological as well as psychological, is in the phase of *becoming*. As the legend would put it, he is still living under the Tree of Life. The small child is not yet wholly separated from the world around him. The sun and moon, and the birds in the sky, seem almost as close to him as his own fingers and toes. He will communicate with the dumb creatures near him; and usually they will understand and therefore accept from him a treatment not tolerated from an adult.

To the child whose consciousness has not been spoiled by clumsy interference, the world reveals its true nature, its intangible life. For this reason he can lavish his love on a doll of rags or the crudest toy. To his intuitive perception, the outwardly imperfect will most readily release its inner beauty: the living soul bestowed on it by the love and understanding of the person who gave or made it. Similarly, the unspoiled youngster will sense intangible realities behind flowers and trees, and experience them in pictures: the pictures of elves, good fairies, and the "little people of the forest" that have appeared for ages in myths and fairy tales.

All this is in opposition to intellectual consciousness, for which all that lives assumes a mask of death and becomes a corpse to be weighed, measured, and dissected, but never understood. The living intuitive consciousness of childhood is a tiny part of the kingdom to which Christ referred. Yet to approach it, an adult need not become a simpleton, nor renounce his intelligence, for the child is neither simpler nor less intelligent than he. What the small child still has and what the grown-up must reawaken in himself is intuitive perception. For this alone can grasp the intangible "Kingdom of God."

In earlier times the consciousness of childhood was intense enough to leave its mark on all later phases of life. Almost all medieval tradition reflects this kind of consciousness which, in its purest form, shone in the life and deeds of St. Francis. In lesser men, and distorted by materialistic impulses, it took the form of medieval superstition, which was rightly rejected by the forerunners of a scientific era. Still, in rare cases, childhood consciousness was allowed to show its true potentialities.

These are apparent in the beauty and warmth of medieval art, in the romanticism of chivalric ideals, and in the communion of some saints with all things dead and alive. Childhood in those days stretched further into adult life and, when molded by life experience and mature intelligence, ripened into the wisdom of old age. Today intellectualism encroaches on childhood, and threatens to make of children caricatures of their elders, while old age has become a manifestation of petrification rather than of the rejuvenating power through which living wisdom can prevent the hardening of the vessels of the brain.

Intellectual progress with its encroachments on youth may have been inevitable up to the present time, but it must not go further and carry us into a future of living death, a future in which most children will become little adults and most adults living mummies.

The modern child does not desire to remain forever in his Garden of Eden—nor should he do so. He, too, longs to partake of the fruits of knowledge, and to become free to choose between good and evil. His questions are therefore chiefly concerned with one problem: How can my innate intuitive world be translated into intellectual concepts, and how can I find my place in the material world of the senses?

But instead of building a bridge firmly anchored in the realm of childhood—a bridge over which the young individual can travel, taking with him all his treasures—we attack his world with all the empty abstractions of our own clever intellectuality. Thus we not only rob the child of his childhood, but we destroy the continuity of his consciousness, dooming him to remain forever a stranger in a world deprived of deeper meaning.

Intellectual analysis and scientific knowledge represent essential parts of the bridge, the parts of the span called adolescence and early maturity. When offered too early, they become harmful to the small child who in our time is already in great danger of losing his rich inner life in the course of his journey.

Let us assume a child asks why a stone falls to the earth. If he receives an answer at all, it will have some bearing on the law of gravity. But what is gravity? Has even the greatest mind ever explained it? What we call the laws of gravity are merely outer manifestations of the intangible force of attraction between two bodies. As a matter of fact, the more intellectual we become, and the more we learn about details and mechanisms, the further we remove ourselves from the comprehension of the whole. The child feels this immediately and counters abstract "explanations" with a most sensible response, an endless series of "Whys?" Usually the conversation ends with mutual resentment or frustration. Yet it is not too difficult to answer the child's question, provided we keep in mind that he is closer than we to a grasp of causality, and merely requests a translation of his intuitive comprehension into intellectual terms. True, he is not versed in physical laws, but the normal child does know affinity to his parents, to his home; separated from them, he has already experienced moments of longing and loneliness. These emotions are self-explanatory to his intuitive consciousness and, therefore, never subjects for his famous "Why?" If he were told, "You see, stones are as heavy and hard as the rocks under your feet; it is there, where they belong, where their home is, where they want to go," and if he were given the stone to hold, so that he could feel by its weight its desire to return to the ground, he would be permitted an inner experience more akin to a true understanding of gravity than any physicist's treatise could convey.

Nature reveals her secrets to those who open their hearts to her. If we are at all willing to see truth in artistic experience, we should seek it also in the universal world of folklore which, since times immemorial, has likened flowers and blossoms to the sun and the stars. The child who asks why a flower grows upwards is usually satisfied when told that the living plant is a child of the sky, to which it wants to return, just as the stone he held in his hand, wanted to return to earth.

In this way the bond that links the heart of every baby to the soul of nature remains unbroken; the flower, the stone, and eventually all creatures become brothers and sisters to the growing child. Yet, what had been instinctive and amoral before now becomes a moral obligation. For, if the power of intellect is not misused to the detriment of intuitive comprehension, it becomes its guide to love. In short, the child who has gained

the power of speech asks his first questions to find out how the
outer world can be related to his inner life. Unconsciously he
craves knowledge about the strange and wonderful world of
the senses, a knowledge that will be acceptable to his still intellectually untrained mind. It is this yearning from which his
endless questions spring. The answers he ordinarily receives
contain no reality; they are mere abstractions which leave him
confused and dissatisfied, even dully resentful. What develops
under their influence is a starved soul, an individual without
ability to love or respect the world around him.

At an early age the child is still capable of reaching the
world intuitively. If this contact is kept alive, factual knowledge and intellectual explanation will carry it to the sphere of
thinking and action. A child who loves the world because he
finds his own emotions reflected in its laws of attraction and
repulsion, cycles and rhythms, will be eager to know more about
it. As a rule, no one is very much interested in the names and
habits of strangers, and will not remember them for long.
Names and habits of friends, however, are important. The child
who knows a flower, who learns to love it and to watch it climb
toward the sun, will have no difficulty in recalling its name and
the details of its life.[4]

CHAPTER XIII

INFORMATION AND EDUCATION

The fate of our civilization may well depend on the answers our children receive to their questions. Mastery of the atomic age requires a strong capacity for imaginative and creative thinking, a capacity whose wellspring is the consciousness of childhood. The channels from this "fountain of youth" must be cleared and guarded so that they may flow into adolescence and adulthood; otherwise future generations will be even less capable than ours of mastering their problems. Possibly due to the materialistic climate into which children are born today, their reservoir of youthfulness is shallow enough. In their questions they ask for help, only to receive answers which dim further the light of their intuitive consciousness and thus deprive them of an irreplaceable source of happiness and future strength. For purely intellectual knowledge, when offered too early, will block the child's intuitive lifeline as effectively as lime will clog the narrow shaft of a well.

In the previous chapter we have tried to show how such damage could be averted. Obviously, the individual child is not wiser than the average adult, but is fully dependent on his guidance and leadership. Yet the consciousness which sustains the child is richer and far closer to reality than the thinking habits of modern intellectualism. Possibly owing to the fact that so few of them were ever granted the blessings of real childhood, the majority of today's parents and teachers know little about the psychology of the normal child. The clue to his consciousness lies in mythology and folklore, which carry in an indelible script an imprint of the childhood of the human race itself. This is not true of fairy tales invented by clever individuals, but of those which, emerging as archetypal images in the consciousness of generations, have been preserved through the ages. In folklore of this sort, figures and images are similar the world over; and in them the last residues of the "One Language" linger, the language which was confounded when man set out on his material conquest of earth and sky. Modern child psychologists make a tragic error when they frown on fairy tales, and blame them for untoward effects which result, actually, from a wrong emotional attitude on the part of the storyteller himself. For centuries, as we all know, generation after generation has grown up under the influence of fairy tales, to become far less neurotic and desperate than modern youth; and many years of caring for problem children have convinced us of the protection from anxiety and criminal urges that folklore affords.

When we tell a fairy tale to a child, we must never forget that it deals primarily with man's inner life, his soul life. Its characters represent psychological qualities rather than people of flesh and blood. Its kingdoms are not of this world; they symbolize the vast, partly hidden realms of the human soul. In these realms, unselfish will and purified emotion must find their union as prince and princess, to rule their domain with the help of reason grown into wisdom. Such wisdom, according to the fairy tale, is to be found in nature. Her animals, forests, rivers, flowers, and stones can become man's teachers on his quest for inner kingship; and yet if his search for knowledge is selfish and overbearing, the power he acquires may become his undoing. For in the fairy tale, as in reality, everyone can grow up to be king in his own soul only if he learns to respect the dignity and sacredness of his fellow creatures. While most branches of modern psychology merely describe and analyze the psyche, the fairy tale reveals the most intimate secrets of the human soul due to a knowledge which is not analytical but creative, and capable of speaking directly to the child's innate understanding.

If critics of folklore would only accept the obvious—namely, that the evil witch and the magician represent greed and cruelty—they would be less shocked by the punishment dealt out to them. For in the crucial struggle within the human soul there is no room for leniency toward evil. When parents and teachers are too sentimental to expose their children to this truth, they may find themselves fully responsible for criminal careers, for lives ruined by lack of self-control or prematurely ended by guilt and despair. Theirs is the kind of sentimentality so often encountered today in "do-gooders," who try to protect the criminal at the expense of his future victims, and thus take upon themselves the spiritual consequences of his crimes.

In the unavoidable struggle between good and evil, it is the fairy tale which can best aid the cause of good—if it is permitted to speak to the child in its own unique language, the one language which goes straight to the heart. Naturally, it will be necessary to choose the right kind of stories for different temperaments and personalities, and it may be permissible to mitigate some of the modes of punishment taken from medieval justice. Otherwise, no changes should be made, for there is intuitive wisdom in mythology and folklore which by far transcends intellectual psychology, a wisdom which prompted the great philosopher and poet Novalis to see in the true fairy tale "a presentation of prophecy, of ideals, and of absolute inner necessity."

Dr. Mary H. B. Wollner, in an article published in the September 1957 issue of *Today's Health,* says:

A miasmic reform has crept upon many of the old fables, fairy tales and nursery lore. Radio and television versions now omit or alter the once satisfyingly drastic punishments meted out to wicked stepmothers or blood-thirsty giants. Jack's Giant . . . no longer meets his death by crashing headlong from the top of the beanstalk . . . but fades out in a huge bubbling giggle. . . . I should think children today might be alarmed by the possibility that such a giant might giggle his way into life again; he obviously isn't quite dead enough.

An inexpensive series of children's books presents further ingenious decontaminations: witches . . . are now delightful, whimsical creatures . . . the Wolf in Red Riding Hood doesn't get to swallow Granny . . . Humpty-Dumpty is carefully mended, and equally absurd liberties are taken with many, many other well-known Mother Goose characters.

* * *

Grimm's too grim for the modern child, we are told. Children don't like violence and cruelty; besides, if all their reading is purged of baseness, they will grow up noble, kind and gentle. In fact, they might turn out to be such lofty citizens, because of lofty literature, that all society would benefit.

* * *

There has, indeed, hovered over us in the last two decades a cloudy theory in child development and educational practices. It is a theory ascribed to psychologists who once warned . . . that indulging children in folk-tales, fairy tales and stories of magic and enchantment, would encourage unhealthy wish-fulfillment fantasies and daydreaming, or cause confusion . . . between the real and the fanciful. . . .

* * *

Now if the psychologists and educators would take a good long look at the adult in these United States . . . , they would see that today he is reading magazine fiction allied to soap operas—that is, written to formula and sparing no pains to arouse false . . . daydreams; that he attends movies, which . . . wallow in suggestiveness and flaunting self-indulgence; that he is filling his literature- and truth-starved mind with blood and thunder and magic and superstition in radio and television and comics.

* * *

. . . Children's psyches are not as naïve as some people think, and . . . their tastes, when not distorted and misguided, lead them to enjoy stories which would be judged great by the standards used in judging all great literature. In other words, the nursery lore, folk tales, fairy stories, myths and legends . . . because they are literary expressions of timeless psychological and sociological truths, as these truths have welled up out of the unconscious cumulative wisdom of the human race—persist in their appeal . . .

and at the same time yield vital and indispensable nourishment for the growth of children.

. . . To study folklore and mythology is to come into possession of almost more than we can assimilate and use about the development of the human soul. To study the child is to appreciate with what astonishing accuracy literature reflects life.

* * *

Fortunately, for every insipid story found in the graded readers, some Aesop's fable, myth or folk tale . . . could be found to offset it. . . . Adults need to read aloud and tell stories much more than they are doing. To revive the fainting, doubting spirits of our apparently apathetic school children, we need to revive the children's classics and to inject powerful emergency doses of enlightenment, enjoyment and effortless understanding into library, schoolroom and nursery.

* * *

. . . We of little faith need to draw upon the wellsprings of faith in the world's literature.[1]

The fairy tale not only offers the child an incentive to be good, but serves as his natural guide to religion. It gives food to his starved intuitive faculties, puts them into their legitimate place, and keeps them from seeking outlets in purely libidinous adventures. Such danger of perverted intuition exists; in the words of the fairy tale, somewhere within the soul lies hidden the cruel sorcerer or the evil witch, waiting to turn human longings into animal instincts and man's heart into unfeeling stone.

The dreariness of our abstract intellectualism, which robs the child of happiness, is responsible for his seeking joy in realms destructive to his mind and body. This futile search will drive him into libido long before he is old enough to purify it through true affection for an individual, or else it will bring him to cruelty and crime as a means of abnormal satisfaction. But the fairy tale, if permitted to bestow its blessing, can deepen and prolong the happiness of childhood, and provide the sense of adventure which the young needs for the preservation of his moral and mental health.

Regularly recurring occasions for joy have been celebrated

for ages as the most powerful healers and protectors of the human soul. But what is a great religious festival, like Christmas, without the magic key of the fairy tale? An expensive nuisance to the donor, and a source of a strange, subconscious resentment to the recipient of gifts. Or is it true that its mystery is a deception, be it concerned with "Santa Claus," the "Christ Child," or any of the heavenly messengers of other creeds? And is it true that these stories must eventually lead to disappointment and mistrust? We do not believe so. For the fruits they bear are real, so real that years later the memory of them has sustained many a person in hours of trial and grief.

However, we could avoid deception and disillusionment altogether, were we only to abstain from sentimental materialism. It is not necessary to tell a child that Christ or Santa Claus has brought the Christmas presents which, after all, he may have seen in a shop window. Would it not be better to say that these gifts have received a special blessing from such beings? This would add to the gifts an unseen treasure, a breath of the invisible for which every normal child longs with all his heart. Would such a statement be a lie? If so, then every prayer, every blessing, and every religious service is also a lie.

The great religious festivals, if celebrated correctly, are the child's safest guides on his dangerous journey into adulthood. It is they which gently lead his inner perception from the world of the fairy tale into the world of adult religion. It is they which bring purely qualitative faculties, such as joy and gratitude, into proper relation with pleasure derived from material gifts. And it is they which weave magic bands of love around a family, and thus prevent the estrangement between parents and children, so often at the root of juvenile delinquency.

But the bridge between childhood and maturity, between the intuitive and intellectual poles of consciousness, does not end at the completion of preschool age, the age in which the fairy tale should reign supreme. The fostering of factual knowledge and the development of acute intellectual powers, together with a preserving and strengthening of intuitive faculties, should be the goal from the day the child enters elementary school to the end of his studies. The two main principles of upbringing are education and information. The very word "educate," derived from the Latin *educere*, means "to lead outward"—while "inform," coming from *in-formare*, indicates a form-giving process. In Latin *e* expresses an outward motion, while the *in* points to something static or inward bound.

Education thus signifies an effort to bring to healthy manifestation what already exists in a human being as the content of his personality. Information denotes an attempt to impose limits on that personality by molding it according to the strict rules of logical and natural laws.

Traditional pedagogy was predominantly concerned with information and discipline. It functioned under the more or less overt assumption that a human being is evil unless remodeled by puritan discipline, and brutish unless enlightened by knowledge. Today the other extreme prevails. Strangely, it is materialism which considers the human being intrinsically good, and therefore seeks the cause of his shortcomings in suppression and inhibition. Both extremes are harmful. The first has often resulted in the development of repressed, inhibited personalities, prone to be overly docile and hypocritical. The other is likely to promote shapeless individualities dominated by their own unrestrained instincts.

What the child and the adolescent needs from his parents and teachers is a deep understanding of his innate longings. He must be permitted, and even encouraged, to express himself. This is *e-ducation* in the strict sense of the word; it requires leniency, love, kindness, intuitive understanding, and self-effacement on the part of teachers and parents. Yet this is not enough. The child asks of the adult not only encouragement of self-expression, but also the limitations needed to shape and mold his character. And the "kindly" pedagogue who fails to see this is either too foolish or too selfish to recognize his true duty toward the young lives placed in his charge.

The two extremes in educational philosophy may be illustrated by a rather commonplace example. In earlier times a child inclined to be noisy was usually ordered to be quiet, and punished when disobedient. Thus a repression occurred which often caused neurotic tendencies in later life. Today the prevailing trend permits the child to make as much noise as he will, with little or no concern for the comfort of innocent bystanders. For this reason the child fails to learn respect for the undeniable rights of others, a failing which in later life tends to make him lonely because it estranges him from society. From both an educational and a disciplinary viewpoint, the problem might be solved by providing a variety of artistic outlets—one of which might be the playing of a musical instrument—but always with due regard for other people's rights.

This example is anything but original, and known to almost every kindergarten teacher. Yet the application of the principle involved should be by far wider and more scientific than it is today. Experience shows that, while very strict parents and teachers are often remembered with warm affection in later years, too lenient ones become more resented as time goes on. This psychological paradox may be explained by the fact that, whereas worthwhile qualities will generally surmount the severest restrictions, the shapelessness of an undisciplined personality cannot be amended later, except through grievous suffering; hence the pampered child's bitter hatred of parents, whose omissions have doomed him to a life of neurosis and frustration.

What has scholastic information to do with discipline? Knowledge serves as a mold for the volcanic content of the growing individual, whose degree of balance depends on it. Knowledge of a large number of confusing and apparently unrelated facts misshapes the personality into a mental and emotional structure both bizarre and discordant. On the other hand, knowledge imparted with the understanding that every item of information is but a piece in the mosaic of an all-encompassing wisdom, creates a harmonious structure promoting a sense of security as well as a feeling of freedom within the framework of purposeful necessity.

Naturally, this does not mean that the modern teacher should preach a creed, or try to show purpose and meaning in facts when he does not see them. But twentieth-century science has already rendered materialism untenable and therefore unscientific. Today every well-trained teacher has the right to say:

Underlying the new ideas, including those of modern physics, is a unifying order, but it is not causality; it is purpose. . . . One might even say, as a general "modern" principle, that the elements (for we no longer really talk of "parts") will be found to arrange themselves so as to serve the purpose of the whole.[2]

If the individual is permitted to see facts as building stones, arranged by a higher wisdom to serve "the purpose of the whole," he himself becomes a harmonious being. It is knowledge which gives shape to the character. If this knowledge is a true reflection of a meaningful universe, our minds will reflect the higher purpose underlying the order of the cosmos.

A child brought up in this way is rather easy to discipline. For it is not true that man wants to obey his selfish desires. He does so only when he despairs of a higher meaning in life. It was the search for such a meaning, rather than desire for a comfortable life, that inspired our most significant discoveries in natural science and technology; for one hoped to find the secrets of creation in matter and energy. Now that we have been disillusioned, it has become difficult to attract an adequate number of young people to the study of the sciences. A certain hopelessness as to cognition of truth has invaded all facets of our civilization, and led us to doubt the very existence of true values, of meaning and purpose in life. Strangely enough, it is the adolescent and even the small child who most keenly, if subconsciously, divine the frustration which haunts our age. The grown-up can find moral support in his work, in the hope he bears for his children, in his obligations, and in the satisfactions and pleasures of his daily life. The child understands little of all this. For him, the main source of joy lies in his phantasy which, contrary to general belief, can never be fully content with sports, material gains, or intellectual achievements. His future as foreshadowed in the life of his elders appears unspeakably dreary to him, and not worth fighting and working for. Only if adults see life through the eyes of a child, can they become the friends and leaders of their charges. Actually, schooling is of little use for the foundation of a secure and happy individuality unless it is a truly joint adventure shared by teacher and pupil alike.

This, however, can hardly be achieved by a kind of education which burdens a child with the responsibilities of initiative and leadership he rightly expects from his elders. What counts is the teacher's awareness that the unspoiled child intuitively knows more about the meaning of life than the most brilliant intellectual. Such awareness opens an adult's mind to the rejuvenating influence of an intuitive consciousness, and his eyes to the individual needs of his pupil. He will see, for instance, that too much information given too early or too quickly may overwhelm the child's inner life, just as logs thrown too quickly into a fire may extinguish the flame they were meant to sustain. This can result in a warped, narrow-minded, unimaginative character. But he will also recognize that lack of discipline and insufficient knowledge may bring forth a world-estranged, shapeless personality.

There is still another angle that deserves attention. Obviously, it is possible to impart a great deal of information to pupils by mnemotechnical methods or through television. But this is not education. A child watching passively may remember much of what he has seen and heard but, unless he is made to struggle with the subject, the information received will remain a foreign body in his mind. For any kind of knowledge is useful only to the extent to which it enhances inner activity. If merely imposed on the mind, it becomes a heavy weight, paralyzing the forces of will.

What, in the last analysis, is human will? It is man's individual share of the power of creation. This share, feeble in our generation, can be aroused by wrestling with the facts and phenomena of nature, the laws of mathematics, and the major events of history. It is weakened, and often extinguished, when knowledge is channeled into a mind reduced to a mere receptacle. This, however, does not mean that everything a child has to memorize should be "explained" to him intellectually. On the contrary, experience has convinced us that a youngster exposed to too much reasoning before the age of twelve to fourteen years is often likely to become overargumentative and neurotic.

There is a great capacity for acquiring and retaining knowledge in the age groups of seven to fourteen years. This capacity should be fully utilized, and not allowed to remain passive: every piece of information transmitted by the teacher should be met by an imaginative-artistic activity on the part of the pupil. Geometric figures ought to be traced in games and motion, historical characters interpreted in improvised plays, botanical and zoological facts brought to life through drawing, painting, and sculpturing.

In this manner, the creative in man responds to the created in nature, and knowledge becomes alive through comprehension. The faculty to comprehend, however, differs in degree only from the power to create; it is the gift of man which once made it possible for him to "give names" to all other creatures.

With the externalization of human consciousness, man's instinctive comprehension of nature has become replaced by a vast knowledge of external facts—and, consequently, his creativeness by technological productivity. Today, to re-establish the balance of consciousness, the process of externalization must be reversed. Such reversal does not require abandonment of scientific progress. It does, however, require the teacher's understanding that every piece of information must be imparted in a way that will challenge the student, and stimulate his creative imagination.

CHAPTER XIV

TRAINING IN INTUITION

People today rarely reach middle age before losing their capacity for original thinking, a fact only too conspicuous in the unimaginative actions of modern statesmen. According to tradition, this was not so in eras less intellectually advanced, when the old were still sought out by the young for counsel and consolation. Perhaps this lack of mature wisdom is not entirely due to a surplus of fat and minerals in the blood vessels of the brain, but also to the fact that most of the knowledge modern man receives today remains a foreign body in his mind.

As was said before, matters are made worse by a strong tendency to impart information in an effortless way through excessive use of educational television and similar methods of passive absorption. This does not mean that our students should learn less. On the contrary! But a civilization based on knowledge acquired in a state of tuned-down self-awareness, not to speak of subliminal experience, presents an ultimate danger to humanity. We cannot be reassured by the fact that our schools are not yet making use of the "hidden persuader." There can be little doubt as to the dangers ahead, when we learn that hypnotism is used to an ever increasing degree for reconditioning human minds; even to the point of fostering the self-confidence of salesmen. Of what use will political freedom be to men whose likes and dislikes, desires and aversions, are dictated by information beyond their conscious knowledge and control? The pressing need for adult re-education is shown in the naïveté with which we, the champions of liberty, undermine our own freedom, and the complacency with which we tolerate the deadliest attacks on our humanity.

The answer to military aggression is armed strength; the answer to false ideologies is truth. But truth, religion, and freedom cannot be perceived by our physical senses; they are real only to immediate experience, to an inner vision which, for lack of a better word, we have called intuitive perception. This gift, long fallen in disuse, must be reawakened today by conscious effort.

How can this be done? Scores of volumes have been written on the subject, and this book would not have been added to their list, had not a need for it been indicated by practical experience of the terrifying fear and hopelessness lurking just below the surface of modern man's mind. It is not a need for new spiritual facts and revelations which we have tried to meet, but a need for waking up to the recognition of already existing truths.

The world of literature is rich enough to contain the answers to all the basic questions of mankind. Yet somehow these answers are regarded as if they were museum pieces, treated with the reverence accorded to a grandfather's clock kept for its dignity and beauty but not for telling the hour of the day.

Mankind has always recognized greatness, instinctively. But it has never fully grasped that the words and deeds of history's great artists contain more than aesthetic values—that they contain, as well, the actual solutions to the problems of their age. Together, they represent one gigantic book composed of many chapters, a book which, were it but read correctly, would bring man closer to the fulfillment for which he has longed since the beginning of time. This universal book consists of three main parts. Two of these parts, religion and art, have long ago reached a high degree of perfection, while the third, analytical intellect, is even today in its childhood stage of trial and error. Paradoxically it is its very immaturity which makes analytical intellect appear so all-important to humanity today, just as the demands of the least mature child may cause parents to neglect their older children.

Once intellect will have reached maturity, it will itself become the rediscoverer of lost values, and form with them an imperishable trinity, the trinity of Wisdom, Art, and Religion. In the meantime, however, humanity is in grave danger. The edifice of its present civilization is precariously balanced on one pillar only, the one of growing—but still immature—intellectualism. The two others still exist, but are buried under the debris of time. They can and must be recovered, but the only guides leading to their hiding place in the human soul are reverence and wonder.

Unfortunately, the very capacity for these feelings has fallen victim to the progressive externalization of human consciousness, and cannot be restored without vigorous and persistent training. To preserve qualitative experience as long as possible, a training of that kind was widely practiced in the theological seminars of antiquity, its recipient being called *mystes* by the Greeks and *initiatus* by the Romans. It was based on the assumption that everything sensually perceptible and intellectually conceivable is merely the garment of a spiritual reality, of a god. To a varying degree many members of ancient or "primitive" societies underwent the so-called initiation rituals, which were supposed to open their intuitive perception to the deeper meaning of their vocations in life.

How important it was to keep the qualitative, the intuitive experience alive, may best be seen by the fact that in Eleusis alone, where both sexes and even slaves were admitted, "more than 30,000 Greeks sought initiation . . . yearly."[1] The disciple of Aesculapius, the student of medicine, underwent a rigorous training in meditation on health and illness, plants and minerals, until the intrinsic relationships between specific diseases and certain substances revealed themselves to him. The Mesopotamian astronomer-priest started with contemplation of the divine powers of the universe, and proceeded from a comprehension of their nature to the exploration of astronomical laws. Factual knowledge was considered the reward of intuitive comprehension and not be dispensed without proper preparation. Thus, when Anaxagoras taught that the moon's light was a reflection of sunlight, he was prosecuted for "betrayal" of "mystery" secrets.

In antiquity, a spirit of inquiry prevailed, diametrically opposed to our primarily intellectual and experimental philosophy of science. It demanded of the student a meditative training that would give him insight into the evolutionary purpose and meaning of a scientific impulse, before entrusting him with the knowledge and skill necessary for its application. Where this insight was totally missing, material knowledge was deemed dangerous, and withheld.

Instead of criticizing this attitude too severely, we might ask ourselves how the earth would look today, had the priest-scientists of old been less cautious with the dispensation of their knowledge. The technological skill of the priesthood of ancient Egypt must have been extraordinary—as revealed in the construction of its temples and pyramids, its unmatched irrigation systems, its apparent knowledge of electricity, and many aspects of science and medicine. But merely a small portion of this power, to which even modern man looks up in wonder, must have been revealed to pharaohs and generals, whose war machinery was kept on a relatively primitive level. For ages the Chinese scholars knew the secrets of explosives and rocketry, but how sparingly was this knowledge used for mass destruction until the coming of Western man!

With the decline of the mysteries and the emancipation of individualism, secrets once kept hermetically sealed penetrated into all walks of cultural life, and especially into philosophy. The great philosophers of antiquity felt that the time had come when wisdom and knowledge would have to be shared by all. But they never failed to stress man's need for a deeper, an intuitive comprehension.

The methods they recommended to their pupils varied.

Initiation into the Pythagorean society required, in addition to purification of the body by abstinence and self-control, a purification of the mind. . . . The new pupil was expected to preserve for five years the "Pythagorean silence." . . . The scholars were accordingly divided into *exoteric* . . . and *esoteric* . . ., who were entitled to the secret wisdom of the Master himself.[2]

Aristotle developed his own methods in accordance with certain rhythms in walking and transport. At his Lyceum in

Athens "he walked, talking, and talked, walking, . . . with the students who . . . were called the *Peripatetics*. The thoughts were really and actively 'walked,' 'stood' and 'under-stood' with limbs, heart and head."[3] He never forgot the ultimate goal his teacher Plato had set for all learning: The highest of the ideas is the Good.

To perceive this . . . Good, to vision the molding ideal of the creative process is the loftiest goal of knowledge. Motion and Creation are not mechanical; they require in the world, as in ourselves, a soul or principle of life as their originative power.[4]

Great efforts were made to carry the pagans' mature experience in qualitative education into Christianity, especially by Plotinus and his pupils, but these efforts, which might have prevented mankind's relapse into the barbarianism of the Middle Ages, were thwarted when the Church, in her attempt to curb analytical intellect, created a split between scientist and cleric. This split might have become irremediable, had not men like Thomas Aquinas, Albertus Magnus, and others built a bridge between scientific intellect and religious intuition.

In more modern times it was Goethe who tried to bring the qualitative aspects of reality into full partnership with their quantitative counterparts; but his work was valued for its artistic form rather than for its philosophical content. In America, Emerson presented a way which was similar to Goethe's; but his message, too, was far more treasured for its aesthetic values than for its intrinsic truth.

In 1861, Rudolf Steiner was born in a small Austrian village. After obtaining his Ph.D. at the University of Rostok, he edited Goethe's works on natural science and became deeply interested in the poet's world conception which he applied to various facets of modern life. Far from losing himself in a world of subjective mysticism, he became one of the great realists of his time. Intuitive cognition was, to him, unreliable unless preceded by a merciless quest for self-knowledge and an intense effort at mental and moral progress.

Although the world at large has, so far, failed to recognize Steiner's stature—possibly due to difficulties in translation, unfamiliar terminology, and mistakes made in his name—a large and ever-growing number of noted educators, scientists artists, and theologians have accepted his views. To give the reader an opportunity of checking for himself the practical results of Steiner's approach to the various fields of cultural life, we have included in our bibliography some of the authors who acknowledge his influence, even when their works had no direct relationship to this book. At this point we want to quote just one of the great artists of our time, Bruno Walter, speaking of Steiner's influence on his life:

. . . I feel compelled to conclude all I have written as a musician with a word of acknowledgment to anthroposophy . . . great is my gratitude for the immeasurable enrichment which it has given to my advanced years. It is wonderful, at my age, to have become a student once more. In my whole being I sense the rejuvenation which strengthens and renews my being and my work in the sphere of music.[5]

Steiner knew that what came readily to a mind like Goethe's, was by no means a common gift of ordinary man. In his view, the genius differs from other people insofar as he is awake in spheres of consciousness in which others are asleep. But he was fully convinced that evolution had at last reached a point where the spark of intuitive perceptiveness and creativeness can be kindled in almost every human being who seeks more in existence than its mere surface.

Steiner's gift to the world was a moral and meditative way to objective vision, a way appropriate to the psychological and physiological constitution of Western man. If accepted in the spirit of humility, altruism, and truthfulness in which it was given, it could bridge the existing cleft between a man's religious conviction and his intellect and will. It could add comprehension to our existing knowledge and thus revive the vision without which our generation will hardly find the solution to its problems.

But the path Steiner suggests can be found only by a thorough study of his own work. All that can be done here is to give a general idea of the attitude modern man will have to take if he is to save his most valuable gifts from obliteration.

Rudolf Steiner's teachings have exerted a strong influence on the author's approach to psychology. Thus full credit had to be given to them before proceeding to suggestions which stem from personal experience during thirty years of medical practice. One thing seems certain: intuitive training has become the prime necessity of our time. Quite apart from its value for cognition, it has proved effective in cases of neuroses, addictions, and criminal instincts which, heretofore, had seemed hopeless. Intuitive self-training is a matter of common sense, and accessible to all who seek it. Its basic rules are indeed so simple as to inspire little belief and enthusiasm in those whose hearts are set on miracle drugs for the spirit.

Yet, while the rules of intuitive training require no more from a human being than that he pay full and undivided attention to the qualitative aspects of life—and this only at freely chosen moments—systematic compliance with their demands is not at all easy. Just as almost every forward step in our time, it requires continued efforts at clearing the underbrush from the path ahead. This effort consists of critical, though by no means negative, evaluation of the conditions which confuse and hinder modern man. We simply must recognize where our difficulties lie, if we are ever to overcome them. Many qualitative aspects of life so essential for the development of man's dormant faculties have been sacrificed at the altar of excessive utilitarianism which, far from bringing security and strength, have made him a stranger in a hostile world. So lonely has he become that he can hardly trust his own family, because he has never learned to reach another being across the separating walls of matter. The boy reared in the belief that all he needs for happiness is a successful career, a satisfactory sex life, and a number of children, will usually marry to secure an inexpensive housekeeper and mistress at a minimum effort and at an early age. When, in spite of all this foresight, happiness does not prevail, he will usually blame his wife. His intuitive faculties were never wakened by self-effacing love, and the fondness he may feel for his wife and children is in reality no more than affection for his own desires. Likewise, the girl brought up to value the external goods of life first and foremost will not even know how to love, although she may be truly in love with her husband's physique, position, and, above all, with marriage itself.

However, it would be wrong to believe that egotism and greed are solely responsible for the utilitarianism of our time. Has not modern man shown that he is capable of a generosity unheard of in earlier epochs? Though by no means greedier than his ancestors, he has lost the ability to appreciate the significance of qualitative values—in his charity as well as in his demands. How can he learn to revive them? Certainly not by paying lip service to such qualitative values as freedom, love, and compassion. But he can learn a great deal by giving heed to certain clues which nature herself offers to those who listen to her language.

Most of nature's children are born helpless, and in need of physical assistance. But while in the animal kingdom the cub, once able to fend for itself, is mercilessly rejected by its parents, the human child is protected far beyond his biological needs. He is thus given a unique chance of perfecting nonbiological qualities such as love and gratitude, in response to the physical help he has received at the time of his biological dependency.

Nature is perfectly capable of producing an offspring which is, from the moment of birth, independent of parental care. As a rule, creatures of this sort—insects and many of the big reptiles, for example—are highly complex organisms, functionally; yet they stand far down on the ladder of consciousness. However, the further evolution progresses toward individualized consciousness, the longer the cub remains with his parents —until, as in the human kingdom, he may, when fully mature, become their protector and guide. A small child is unable to repay parental benefits in kind. Yet nature has given most of her more evolved children a tendency to reciprocate, a trend which comes to fruition in the individual loyalties and antipathies of a tame animal. In wild life these tendencies hardly ever grow beyond strictly biological urges, possibly because of the cub's early experience of rejection by its parents. Nor would it seem beneficial for an animal to develop spiritual qualities, since they might tend to impede rather than to assist it in its ceaseless struggle for survival.

In man, a normal parent-child relationship serves a purpose far beyond the biological, since it activates the child's spiritual potentialities at the right, i.e., the earliest possible moment. Of course, this is true of a normal relationship only, since the parent whose attitude is one of caring for his own "flesh and blood" rather than for a separate individuality, tends to destroy rather than to stimulate the higher qualities in his offspring. But when the child senses that the care given to him is unselfish, his innate tendency to reciprocate begins to unfold at a very early age. So early indeed that an experienced psychologist can get a pretty good idea of the parental attitude from the facial expression and emotional responses of a six-month old. Owing to his physical limitations, the child cannot offer material compensation for the care he receives; but, seeking recourse in the world of qualitative values, he can reward his parents with gratitude and love.

In later life, every human being will be obliged to offer material returns for material services, but from the experience of early childhood he should have learned that only the qualitative can fully repay the quantitative. Every normal child, raised under normal family conditions, has an intuitive knowledge of this fact which seems so elusive to the adult. We just have to listen to the telltale stories of a four-year old to learn how thoroughly free he is of any sense of debt and unfulfilled obligations if he loves his parents, and how in turn their show of joy fully repays him for what he does for them.

Naturally, a child spoiled by bribes will very soon lose his natural esteem for qualitative values and become a mere trader in the superficialities of life. He who expects and demands that his love be repaid by love, that his good deeds be repaid by good deeds, has not learned the meaning of life. He does not know that man's mission is to lift material values to a higher form of existence with the help of his spiritual nature, and vice versa to support what is good and beautiful with the material means at his disposal. Without such understanding, deeds and counterdeeds, giving and receiving, are but empty gestures, a reshuffling of values devoid of all meaning for the cause of evolution.

Fate does not compel, it only shows the way, and the child

is prone to fail in his first faltering steps unless he is guided by
the wisdom of parents and teachers. His early and uncertain
attempts to repay care with love and gratitude need understanding and encouragement. Such feelings need not even be
channeled toward parents and teachers; they may be directed
toward God and nature, the universal prototypes of the paternal
and maternal principles on earth. What matters is that the
child be spared the desolation and emptiness which are the
inevitable results of a casual and irreverent acceptance of life's
gifts. He must not be permitted to take anything for granted, be
it the food he tastes, the care he receives, or the toys with
which he plays. Surprise at every new experience is natural
for a child, but unless the innate sense of wonder is preserved
and fortified with gratitude, it will soon give way to boredom
and frustration. For it is awe and gratitude which are the
wellsprings of all the qualitative capacities of later years, among
them the ability for joy, creativeness, and love of life.

The adult who has been denied the upbringing conducive
to qualities of such kind—and most of us belong to this unhappy
breed—can benefit tremendously by giving it to his children.
For reflected in their eyes he will find proof of a higher reality
which his dulled sense of inner perception is unable to find
elsewhere.

There are other ways open to him, ways which are marked
by patient efforts to revise his attitude toward the three fundamentals of civilization: Wisdom, Art, and Religion. The manifestation of man's search for wisdom is science. Science today
has all but monopolized the ways of cognition in which man
is wont to deal with the world around him, without paying
heed to the qualitative aspects of his relationship to nature.
The effects of this omission are felt everywhere. They are comparable to the results a teacher would achieve if he were to
preach to the children: "You have not only the right but
even the obligation to exploit your parents to the limits of
your God-given smartness and growing physical strength. Never
waste a thought on repaying them with gratitude and love, for
these feelings are impractical and inexpedient." Children thus
taught would hardly become fully human, and neither shall

we, unless we learn to counterbalance the effects of science's predatory attitude toward nature with a determined training in nature appreciation.

But does man still know what love of nature means? Once, millenniums ago, he knew it well. He sought and revered the spirit of creation in the majesty of snow-capped mountains, rocks and forests, oceans and rivers, and even in the twisted shape of a sacred tree. His worship of nature was not utilitarian in the modern sense of the word, but nevertheless reaped countless benefits for his race. Most of his discoveries in basic foods, agriculture and forestry, in the use of herbs, and in many other fields, were made in the sanctuaries of nature.

The Middle Ages were concerned less with nature than with salvation. But among the spiritual leaders of the time there were some who held that the human heart could best reach God through selfless love for His creatures. This was the basic philosophy of Francis of Assisi, the man who is still considered by many the savior of Christianity. At his time the crusades, history's last adventure in high romance, had ended in a sea of blood, treachery, and frustration. The masses who had put all their hopes on the reconquest of the Holy Tomb, had fallen into despair and cynicism; and among the learned, all belief in moral progress had been shattered and replaced by utilitarianism. For the first time in history religious vision seemed to become extinct in the world of Christianity. Francis set out to restore it.

What was his secret? He was a simple man; neither his faith nor his ideals of chastity and compassion were novel to his age. But he was unique in his capacity for purest love, a love which was less concerned with attaining personal salvation than with serving God by helping His defenseless creatures. "His love overflowed from men to animals, to plants, even to inanimate things. . . ."[6] According to legend, this love awakened in him the "One Language" which had once united nature with man and man with God, so that he could preach to the dumb creatures in fields and forests, understand their longings, and be understood by them. "One [legend] told how Francis preached to 'my little sisters the birds' on the road between

Connora and Brevagna, and 'those that were on the trees flew down to hear him and stood still the while St. Francis made an end of his sermon.' "[7]

However that may have been, one thing is certain: St. Francis and his followers brought back to the world a glimpse of intuitive consciousness and thus fulfilled the command he had heard within his heart: "Now go home, Francis, and build up my house, for it is nearly falling down."[8] Modern man whose "house," too, is nearly falling down, might find it salutary to compare his own attitude toward nature with the spirit that flows through words like these:

> . . . Above all Brother Sun,
> who gives the day and lightens us therewith.

> And he is beautiful and radiant with great splendor;
> Of Thee, Most High, he bears similitude.

> Be Thou praised, my Lord, of Sister Moon and the stars;
> in the heaven has Thou formed them, clear and precious
> and comely.

> Be Thou praised, my Lord, of Brother Wind,
> and of the air, and the cloud, and of fair and of all weather,
> by the which Thou givest to Thy creatures sustenance.

> Be Thou praised, my Lord, of Brother Fire,
> by which Thou hast lightened the night,
> and he is beautiful and joyful and robust and strong.

> Be Thou praised, my Lord, of our Sister Mother Earth,
> which sustains and hath us in rule,
> and produces divers fruits with colored flowers and herbs . . .[9]

Man has learned at last that his welfare and his very survival may depend on the preservation and development of natural resources, but he has forgotten that nature is also the temple of God and His workshop of creation. Once the sun was considered the highest manifestation of divine grace in nature. It was worshiped not only for its life-giving power but also for the spiritual strength it gave in the universal struggle of light against darkness. In our day, man's personal relationship to the life center of his solar system is "enlightened" and casual. Basically, it consists of hours of dull-witted exposure to its rays;

small wonder that instead of a sunny disposition he often acquires burns and cancer of the skin.

No doubt there are still people who are truly moved by the
beauty of a sunrise, the song of a bird, or the varying colors
shining even through the smog and pallor of a modern city.
But these sparks of joy, if acknowledged at all, are considered
but minor enhancements of ordinary life. They make fishing
more enjoyable, a picnic tastier, and a date more romantic. But
irreproachable as such an attitude may be, it springs from a
love of nature that is no more profound than a man's affection
for a juicy steak. Nor is it expedient. For if we channel all
the qualitative experiences which nature gives us toward the
enhancement of biological and material ends, we shall exhaust
all the resources from which our ability for enjoyment should
have come.

A normal child is born with a strong capacity for joy and
creative power. Yet, unless it is replenished by conscious efforts, this capacity fades in the course of time until in later
years nothing may remain but boredom, fear, and depression.
The fairy tale knows these dangers well and never ceases to
warn of them. Most of its stories deal with the depredation of
the human soul and the powers which strive to destroy her. Usually, it is love for nature and her creatures which saves the hero
and leads him to his kingdom. But the prince of the fairy tale
is not practical, often he is not even clever. He does not look
at every tree for the fruits it may hold for him; but without
seeking them he finds priceless treasures under the roots of a
hollow tree or at the bottom of a well. And what do these
treasures represent? Intuitive comprehension of the secrets
of life, of the forces which make a tree grow or a well spring
up, of birth, fruition, and death.

Not too long ago thousands spent their lives as recluses to
find spiritual vision in the solitude of nature. Modern man
need not become a hermit to achieve this goal, for it is neither
ecstasy nor world-estranged mysticism his era demands, but
a balance between quantitative and qualitative reality.

Modern man, with his reduced capacity for intuitive perception, is unlikely to benefit from the contemplative life of
a hermit in the wilderness. But what he can do is to give un-

divided attention, at times, to a natural phenomenon, observing it in detail, and recalling all the scientific facts about it he may remember. Gradually, however, he must silence his thoughts and, for moments at least, forget all his personal cares and desires, until nothing remains in his soul but awe for the miracle before him.

Such efforts are like journeys beyond the boundaries of narrow self-love and, although the process of intuitive awakening is laborious and slow, its rewards are noticeable from the very first. If pursued through the course of years, something will begin to stir in the human soul, a sense of kinship with the forces of life and conciousness which rule the world of plants and animals, and with the powers which determine the laws of matter. While analytical intellect may well be called the most precious fruit of the Modern Age, it must not be allowed to rule supreme in matters of cognition. If science is to bring happiness and real progress to the world, it needs the warmth of man's heart just as much as the cold inquisitiveness of his brain.

Nature is the main object of scientific exploration. She may well fall victim to analytical urges gone berserk, unless these urges are balanced by the comprehending wisdom of selfless love to all her kingdoms.

Just as science is concerned with the world at—or below—man's level of evolution, religion seeks to explore a world higher than his own. But just as intellectual knowledge without intuitive comprehension has failed to bring wisdom and happiness into our scientific era, so has religious form without religious experience failed to meet man's longing for spiritual fulfillment.

True, there is a revival of religious interest in our time, but are its motives truly religious? According to Archbishop O'Boyle,

Many people are turning to religion as they would to a benign sedative, to soothe their nerves and to settle their minds. . . . I do not want to be cynical about any man's struggle for religious faith . . . but for me . . . religion is not a thing of mere sentiment or personal escape from fears and dissatisfaction. . . .[10]

All great creeds have permitted man to turn to God for help in his earthly needs, and Archbishop O'Boyle certainly does not intend to deprive him of this inalienable right. But demands and requests alone do not constitute religion. Today we speak of religious revival because people are starting to rediscover the great emotional benefits to be derived from religion, the healing effect of prayer, the social and political advantages of churchgoing, not to speak of church parties, dancing, and bingo. Two thousand years ago the concept of religion was different—so different indeed, that in the gentlest phase of Christianity death was accepted as just punishment for Sapphira and her husband who, claiming to have sold their property for the sake of the church, had concealed part of the price received (Acts 5). For at that time the "all or nothing" law prevailed in religion, and halfhearted dedication was deemed an offense against God worse than rejection. Modern man may not be able to assume this attitude in his everyday life but, unless he does so during moments of devotion, he mistakes spiritual utilitarianism for religion.

What really counts is the direction in which a current of psychological activity flows. In work and play, which fill most of man's waking hours, it is predominantly earth-bound, flooding the world of senses with a dazzling light which, by contrast, throws the sphere of qualitative experience into an ever-growing shadow. Consequently, intuitive perception lacks the light of conscious attention and will eventually cease to exist altogether, unless the flow of man's psychological attention is, at least at times, fully reversed. This, however, occurs only during those moments when we offer our whole being to an intangible reality without claiming any reward for ourselves. This is no simple feat, for modern man is not easily persuaded to spend any time or effort on an unprofitable venture. However, once he does become convinced of the tremendous potentialities of intuitive consciousness, his motives for reawakening it could no longer be called unselfish. All great religions, therefore, have stressed the necessity of moral development preceding or at least accompanying the quest for a higher form of intuitive awareness, to make selfish use of its gifts impossible.

The ways leading to religious experience need not be described here; they are embodied in the rituals and exercises of all great creeds. The spirit which renders them effective, however, is all but lost to modern man; it is the same spirit of compassionate devotion of which we have spoken before. But while it may be easy to find pity in one's heart for any creature living on earth, how can man learn compassion for a god? This problem was well known to ancient theology which thought that divine beings entered animals, to suffer sacrificial death. Was it not conceivable that these beings, separated from the Godhead and chained to a cruel world, suffered more than any creature of flesh and blood? Consequently, epics and dramas, pantomimes and pageants, told of the sufferings of the gods, to arouse compassion for immortals in the hearts of mortal men.

Yet it was in the early era of Christianity that love and compassion for a suffering god reached its height. It was then realized that the ordeal of Christ was far more than the nailing of his earthly body to a cross. Had not thousands suffered the same, and worse? His true agony was his sharing in all the pain of the world. It was for this reason that the Middle Ages rarely pictured Jesus as the triumphant victor, but worshiped him still nailed to the cross.

Originally the strongest motive for Christian charity was compassion for Christ. What one did for the least of men, one did for the Son of God who shared the suffering of all humanity.

The alchemists went a step further. They felt that God had given part of His self not only to living and conscious beings, but to *dead matter* as well. There it lay imprisoned to await deliverance through creative deeds of man. Man, in turn, could regain his lost vision of God only by his compassionate love for the divine in nature. Compassion for the Savior made hundreds of thousands take the cross, gave unearthly beauty to medieval mysticism, and inspired the mysterious legends of the Holy Grail. It found expression in Richard Wagner's *Parsifal* which reveals the message of the Grail in the drama's final words: "Miracle of highest grace: redemption for the Redeemer."

The era of religious romanticism is gone, but its message

is as true today as ever. Neither humanitarianism nor self-centered sentimentality posing as religion can open man's inner eye to the world of the spirit. The intuitive faculties through which he can learn to perceive divine reality are built during a lifetime; they are made of the single moments when man turns to God, not to demand, but to give.

Science deals with the created; religion, with the creative; art participates in the act of creation. But what deserves the name of "art"? Ever since the era of intellectualism began, men have disagreed on the greatness of a contemporary artist, and on the value of his work. Today we try to be fair, and are afraid lest we reject what future generations may revere. But, commendable as such broad-mindedness may be, it brings a foreign element into a sphere in which man's sense of beauty and harmony should rule supreme.

It would certainly be wrong to condemn a man to a life of poverty and frustration just because his work does not appeal to present taste, but neither should lack of aesthetic judgment be mistaken for fair play. Perhaps we could learn to strengthen such judgment, even to find a way of differentiating between what is truly great, though not yet appealing to present taste, and what is lacking in value now or ever. This could be achieved by making the following distinction: not only art, but each of the main principles of cultural life, comprises two opposite poles—one benefiting man's biological, the other his spiritual nature. Each of these poles serves a legitimate purpose; it is only unfortunate that they are not distinguished by name.

Science may exploit nature—or serve her and truth. Religion can be an incessant demand—or self-effacing devotion. And art? It can be a means of self-expression, a way of freeing the artist's soul from instincts and emotions he is unable to bear. Such skill is beneficial for the person who masters it, for it provides an outlet for forces that, dammed up, would threaten his emotional balance. It is not without danger, however, to those who accept it in uncritical enthusiasm, for it may contaminate them with the illness of which it frees the artist.

How can the average man learn to distinguish between these two forms of art? By becoming observant of their effect on his emotions. Although it may last only for moments, such an effect must take place—provided, of course, a person's artistic interest is at all genuine. In general it can be characterized thus: the creative element in art lifts a person beyond the narrow confines of selfhood, while its purely exhibitionistic element tends to draw him deeper into his biological organism. Probably every work of art is composed of both of these; but invariably one of them takes the lead. Even among the greatest artists, the urge for self-expression has exceeded at times the purely creative, and therefore healing, impulse. Goethe's *The Sufferings of Young Werther,* unquestionably the most famous novel of its time, may serve as an example. By writing it, the poet healed himself of mental anguish and possibly worse. But in later years he was deeply dismayed when the tragic effect of this book became known to him, and when he learned that a "Werther fever" had seized the public, often leading to mental derangement and suicide.

Yet art can also be of a different kind. It can be the manifestation of a power all but lost today—a power that lends expression to the creative vision in man. In contrast to the self-exhibiting artist who finds relief by setting free what he cannot master, the creative artist suffers the agonies of giving birth. But while he suffers, he brings healing to the world.

What is healing? It is a step toward the perfection of the imperfect. Perfection, however, is not to be found in the world of the senses; it is a reality only to the intuitive perception of a few, just as the world of Ideas was a reality to Plato. The true artist is to some extent endowed with such perception, and labors to re-create the physical world in the image of creative thought. Or, as John Brown put it: "Very sacred is the vocation of the artist, who has to do directly with the works of God, and interpret the teachings of creation to mankind."[11]

Yes, the artist is not only a healer himself; he teaches and interprets the secrets of healing to those who receive his message with an open heart. In ancient Greece all creative art was considered sacred; it was revered as the bond between the divine and the corruptible part of the human psyche, between spirit and soul. In cultural life it forms a bridge between intuition and intellect, between religion and science; and it is no coincidence that the science of medicine is still called an art. What artistic experience can give to man is insight into the nature of healing. It is capable of gradually awakening in him understanding for harmony, for the factors disturbing, and the means of restoring it. If a person undergoing this type of intuitive training is also compassionate, he need not be a physician in order to heal. Every conversation he holds, every action he performs, will restore some harmony to the unbalanced soul life of modern man.

We do not claim that our suggestions will make seers of those who follow them. But this we know from actual experience: he who learns to forget himself in moments of self-effacing reverence, will attain at least a measure of intuitive perception. Thanks to this perception, he will come to know that a world of qualitative reality exists, a world that can harbor and sustain his individuality even when his heart has ceased to beat. Without such knowledge, neither sermons nor exhortations are of much avail; and his loud proclamations of faith recall a frightened child whistling in the dark.

CHAPTER XV

CONCLUSION

The course of history is determined to a far greater degree by ideas than by economic and military forces. The tremendous strength of Egypt was no match for the ideas of Moses, and the world power of Rome crumbled before Christianity. Nazism could never have prevailed in Germany, had Nietzsche's philosophy not been preferred to Goethe's, and communism could not have misled millions, had not the ideologies of Marx and Engels supplanted the lofty ideas of Tolstoi and Soloviev.

And how is it with us? We pride ourselves on having at least one great idea: freedom. And we are surprised that its light has failed to gather the peoples of the world to our side. But the truth is that, while still the world's champions of liberty, we have never succeeded in conceiving a clear idea of freedom. Actually we have done the opposite: we have promulgated a materialistic world concept which is far more inducive to the emergence of a state-controlled, than to a free, society.

What is free choice? One that offers two essential possibilites whose powers of attraction, though different in quality, are equal in degree. If man is a free being at all, his nature must contain, as pointed out earlier, at least two potentialities between which he can choose. He is a threefold being inasmuch as his ego stands as a free agent between the spiritual and natural currents which constitute part of his being. Were he, as most of our schools teach, the product of "emergent evolution" from one evolving stream of biological unfoldment, all ideas of freedom would be mere illusion. He then would be possessed of no more freedom than a tree which grows, bears fruit, and moves in the wind, predetermined by the seed from which it springs, and controlled by the conditions which surround it.

Capacity for freedom can exist only in a threefold being; and man is exactly such an entity. His innermost core, capable of moral choice, is suspended between a material and a non-material world. In his mind two currents meet, one rising from the depths, the other descending from the heights. Through intuitive perception he receives his religious, artistic, and comprehending cognitions. From below, the dynamics of matter, the regenerative powers of plant life, and the biological instincts of the animal kingdom carry their forces into the structure of his brain.

Modern psychology either disregards the former entirely, or arbitrarily classifies it as part of the latter. Thus discarding the vital polarity of human nature, it has distorted man's image of himself and unwittingly barred his quest for self-knowledge. The mind, as it has emerged in the history of our era, is a product of two evolutionary currents. One has been the subject of Biblical Genesis and the myths of all peoples; the other is the topic of scientific theory on biological evolution.

Maybe the most frequently heard objection to the mythological and Biblical views on man's celestial origin is the following: if they were true, how could the primitiveness of early human races be explained? We might be able to answer this question if we learn to look at evolution as if it were the work of a creative artist. When a sculptor strives toward perfection, his studio may well be littered with primitive forerunners of his final accomplishment. However, from the beginning it was the same living idea which descended deeper and deeper into the material substance of its work.

Could not the mystery of evolution be visualized in the same light? If so, it would not be accidental changes which have given birth to present-day man, but the human spirit itself, seeking expression in progressively suitable forms. Its workshop is filled with imperfect and discarded shapes which may well fit into Darwinian concepts and may even contain "the missing link." What matters is that we recognize the existence of two evolutionary currents, one concerning the creative, the other the created. Recognition of both and strict distinction between them would contribute greatly to a better understanding of the world as well as of ourselves. In the dawn of racial consciousness we can conceive of an awakening phase of evolution during which man's body was being molded into a proper vessel for his spirit. Since the organ of which the mind took its first hold is in all probability the brain, it is not surprising that primordial man, while subhuman in his bodily formation, had a brain of remarkable size. Once, however, his physical instrument had become capable of formulating thoughts, these thoughts reflected spiritual rather than biological concepts. They appeared in legends which told of a past of unearthly perfection, of a nonmaterial, unegotistic state of consciousness, called the Garden of Eden, Krita Yuga, or the Golden Age.

The origin of some of the world's greatest legends is lost in the darkness of the past, and was already forgotten when history began. Indeed, so old are they that their emergence must be attributed to eras when—according to present teaching—man's desires should have been those of an animal just emerging from the jungle. But what is it an animal desires? Food, shelter, spoils, and hunting grounds. Are such desires not closer to the dreams of modern men than to ancient paeans of justice, compassion, and self-sacrifice? Today we see greatness in designs to exploit the planets and to conquer outer space; our ancestors looked up to the starry heavens and felt what only the human spirit can feel: awe for their creator.

It may be true that our deeds are more humane than those of ancient men, but their dreams, at least, were less carnal than ours. This alone should make us pause and wonder if the origin of the human mind ought not to be sought in the realm of the spirit rather than in the brain cells of a prehistoric ape.

It stands to reason that, the more firmly the human spirit took hold of its vessel, the more diversified man's way of self-expression became. His consciousness moved from its inner to its outer pole. In the imagery of Genesis, when his eyes were opened to the physical world, his intuitive vision dwindled. Thus freed of the overpowering awareness of a divine presence, he could determine his own fate, and become like a god in his knowledge of good and evil and in his choice between them.

In that remote era to which the oldest traditions refer, man's physiological organism may not have had the advanced form it has now; the instincts rising from its still untamed biological nature may have been far more ferocious and unruly than they are today. But in rare moments the human spirit, not so deeply buried in matter as ours is today, could still break its fetters and attain a glimpse into the world of its origin. Consequently, it was antiquity, not the modern age, which conceived of most of the great ideals and spiritual values that support the free world to our day.

In ancient mythology, the coexistence of the two still unmerged currents in human nature found its symbol in the Centaur, a being half sage, half beast. It is hardly a coincidence that the last representative of that stage of consciousness was the teacher of Hercules. Hercules, in turn, was to the Greeks the archetype of man to be—his tasks and trials representing the struggle of the human spirit against instincts and desires arising from his lower nature.

Once the human race had set out on the journey leading from the intuitive pole of consciousness to the predominantly sense-directed, intellectual one, its course could not be arrested. For brief intervals it seemed to pause at points of equilibrium, called the classical periods of national and racial cultures. But then, before man had time to harvest the fruits of those sunlit hours, his unconscious longing carried him on toward the goal of his original choice. Only today do we approach a crossroad in the history of consciousness, for we have all but mastered the world of senses and are emerging at the far limits of matter, where substance dissolves into subatomic nothingness.

The Serpent's promises to Eve have come close to fulfillment: her offspring has become powerful as a god on earth and grown wise in the ways of good and evil. Man's break-through into a world beneath the solidity of matter, his initial steps away from his legitimate domain into outer space, mark the end of a long chapter in his destiny. Today, a new one is to be written, and the scribe is man himself. For if freedom is to be won, he must take the reins of destiny into his own hands.

The just closing chapter in the history of consciousness has set the stage for a new scene in the climaxing drama of moral independence. So far it was man's subconscious longing for freedom which governed the course of his evolution. During this course intuitive awareness of a superhuman wisdom had to dim to the point where it permitted him the freedom to err. Good and evil had to be experienced so as to make moral choice a matter of freedom rather than of unquestioning obedience. The world in which man lives had to be reduced to its merely mechanical aspects so that in good conscience he could deal with it as if it were made of unfeeling stone.

The new chapter will reveal the use he will make of the godlike independence his ancestors so fervently sought; and the crucial question is whether or not he has learned to recognize the challenge of today.

If individual experience with people from various walks of life and of different nationalities and upbringing is at all indicative, we would not hesitate to draw the following conclusion: a change is occurring in the vast majority of modern men. In the deepest layer of their consciousness still accessible to the psychologist, lust for power and intellectual curiosity seem to become less compelling. Instead, there is a growing longing for a meaningful existence, a craving for giving and receiving love, for breaking through the isolation of loneliness. Thus, since history eventually brings to fruition what lives as longing in the human heart, man's future could become bright indeed, except for one serious obstacle. This obstacle is not lack of good will but a growing inability to recognize moral values. True, millenniums of historical experience have given the human race a vast knowledge of good and evil, but such knowledge is not identical with a capacity for moral judgment.

Right and wrong, in their practical as well as in their moral sense, are qualitative answers to a specific challenge of life. What was right yesterday cannot be entirely right today, due to the inevitable change in the nature of the challenge. People who in our time try to depend on moral abstractions, will find themselves in constant conflicts owing to the increasing incidence of unprecedented situations. Those who believe that experience and intellectual analysis—in other words, knowledge—give them judgment as to right and wrong in a new situation, are badly mistaken. While such knowledge offers a solid launching platform, it is the free flight of moral imagination (*moralische Phantasie* in the sense of Goethe) which is the supreme and only true judge of right and wrong in any new situation. Yet moral imagination can be reliable only when harmoniously balanced between the creative-intuitive and the intellectual-sensual wings of human nature. In times long past, when intuitive experience was overwhelmingly strong, it left no room for moral freedom, while the predominantly sense-directed and analytical consciousness of today reduces the scope of moral vision.

Lack of vision is the chief characteristic of our generation, whose ideals have become shadowy abstractions. Thus words like "freedom," "compassion," and "love" can now be heard everywhere, denoting different and often conflicting concepts. Why? Because their true reality is as obscure to us as color to the color blind. People like Marx, Engels, and Lenin are worthy examples of the modern visionary without vision. But those of us who reject their dogmas are also wanting. Quick as we are to denounce the errors in materialistic ideologies, we are neither capable of clearly defining their true nature nor of combating them with ideas of our own.

Because of our lack of vision, we are adrift in the rapids, frantically dodging ultimate disaster, without clear sight of a goal ahead or of the course to steer. For the same reason our political leaders seem devoid of initiative: they have resigned themselves to warding off the designs of their enemies, or even to imitating them.

Yet can we censure our statesmen too severely? Original action requires a degree of intuition which not only our politicians but our whole generation lacks. And still—even without initiative, without creative thinking—the present political crisis may. pass. There are several reasons why a guarded optimism as to a possible end to the cold war seems permissible today. Russia's economic situation is rapidly improving. The challenge of hunger and poverty which has kept a large number of her idealists emotionally engaged is receding. The lure of space travel will hardly exert too strong an influence on a nation which has traditionally worshiped its "sacred" soil. However, the greatest hope that the Bolshevic plot to dehumanize humanity will fail, lies in the average Russian himself, who is, possibly, the most warmhearted and intuitively gifted individual on the face of the earth.

The cry of a renaissance in religion has become so loud among its peasantry, that the Kremlin will not be able to silence it for long. To all this comes the increasing threat of China's mushrooming population and Russia's hereditary distrust of her Eastern neighbor. China herself is not yet ready to challenge the rest of the world openly, and will not for a long time, provided, of course, Western politics succeed in isolating her. For all parties involved, the cost of a continued armament race may prove so exorbitant, and a nuclear war so unthinkable, that a long-lasting period of grace may well supplant the cold war of today. But what will happen then? According to the cheerleaders in our midst our future will be wonderful indeed. Four-hour working days, allowing more time for the needs of our not too rich inner life. Boredom to be stilled by more crime, more narcotic addiction, more abnormalities—perhaps interrupted by occasional vacation trips to the moon. Pills to nourish the exploding population. Bigger and faster vehicles to carry man from one city to the next, each resembling the other to a dot. Assuming that peaceful coexistence becomes possible, will it solve the problem of our age? We have failed to make use of two victories; are we prepared to make use of another one, should it be achieved?

One thing seems certain to the student of human consciousness and its history: we have reached a state of evolution in which no lasting good can be expected for the future unless it is of our own and fully conscious making. Yet in order to build a better future we must first diagnose the ills of the present, ills which affect the individual everywhere, whether he be of American, European, or Asian extraction. The usual diagnosis heard so often as to sound almost convincing by sheer repetition, may be expressed in these words: man's moral development has not kept pace with his intellectual-scientific progress, and this is the source of his present predicament.

Yet, is this altogether true? Not to one who, owing to his vocation, sees many souls unveiled. Actually, the amount of good buried under layers of time-honored prejudices, resentments, and ideological misconceptions is so great that the world could be a paradise, were the hidden qualities of modern man released from their bondage. Compared with the pre-Christian and medieval personality—as his soul life is revealed in countless biographical, philosophical, and even theological writings —modern man appears to have developed so much more understanding, compassion, and generosity toward his fellow creatures that, to us at least, his moral evolution seems to have exceeded his technological progress. Just compare the modern attitude toward the conquered and the handicapped, and toward criminals and animals, with ancient and medieval customs! Compare the behavior of the average soldier of today with his ancient or medieval predecessor. Today it is a major military problem to persuade the soldier in battle to destroy his enemy or to refrain from fraternizing and sharing too freely with the conquered foe while, a few hundred years ago, the coveted reward of a victorious army was the license to commit unspeakable cruelties. No, so far at least, there has been no standstill in the moral development of the average individual.

In our time the worst cruelties are not perpetrated by the individual but by the organization which in itself is analytical intellect incarnate. The military and political leader of today, as an individual, is usually altogether opposed to cruelty. But, whenever he organizes campaigns, he becomes "organization man," incapable of visualizing the human consequences of his decisions. Thus horrors in our time, such as the suffering and death of tens of thousands of civilians from bombs thrown on nonmilitary targets, are not so much the consequence of individual immorality as of impersonal analytical intellect gone berserk.

Were there an actual lag in moral development in modern

man, our situation would be hopeless. For such a lag could not be corrected by any remedy known—a fact shown in the utter futility of the moral exhortations to which we have been exposed. But, fortunately, the illness of our time is *not* incurable, and the remedies for it are available to all.

Neither moral exhortations nor religious sentimentality can meet the needs of our age. Modern youth, increasingly imperceptive of intangible reality, seeks to fill the vacuum within with all the thrills and pleasures of an otherwise meaningless existence. Against this madness born of spiritual starvation, only one remedy remains: resuscitation and training of the dormant faculties which alone can convey a sense of purpose and the certainty of a spiritual reality.

The methods for such training can be found in an expanded knowledge of the human psyche, a knowledge potentially as precise as the one governing our scientific-intellectual education. Actually, it is a deep-seated fear which is blocking such a course, the fear that it may end in disillusionment. We, in the free world, are still cherishing our time-honored ideals, but we are secretly afraid that on close inspection they may prove to be illusions born of ancient superstitions.

Those who consider the training of intuitive perception an escape from practical reality had better take a closer look at Communist long-range policy. The Soviet dialectician is making every effort to apply educational methods designed to close man's vision forever to the existence of a nonmaterial reality. He has been partly successful, so successful indeed, that inside Russia police terror could be relaxed, and the conviction spread among many peoples that the West's spiritual claims are made in bad faith; not that we should export our ideals, but present the world with methods of self-education and pedagogy enabling human beings all over the globe to perceive truth for themselves. Neither iron nor bamboo curtains could block such a move and, once even a glimpse of an intuitively perceptible reality could be attained, communism would lose its hold on the human mind. But we must develop the courage to test what we claim to hold true, for ideological sentimentality can never win the battle of ideas against materialistic conviction.

Or is it true that man is doomed to inner blindness? If so,

how can we account for the fact that all our creeds and great
ideals have come from those who claimed perception of the
sensually imperceptible and knowledge of the intellectually
unknowable? True, the sages and seers of old were exceptional
beings, but they were mortals just as we. Still closer to a predominantly intuitive consciousness, their intuitive vision was
less hampered than ours. Yet is it not a goal of evolution to give
to many what was once the privilege of a few? Evolution of
modern consciousness has led man forward toward the goal of
moral freedom. It has also carried him downward into shadowy
depths where the spark of his individuality can spread its own
light, away from the peaks on which its tiny flame would pale
before the blinding glare of a supernal Presence.

All through antiquity this painful but necessary course of
evolution was known to the teachers of mankind. In their
legends and myths, the Golden Age had long since given way
to the Age of Iron—Krita Yuga and the era of light, to Kali
Yuga, the time of darkness. Plato himself bemoaned his fate—
not for having been born too early, as one might expect, but for
having been born too late. Yet ancient wisdom saw necessity, not
evil, in man's earthbound course. The gods who had led this
course were neither good nor bad, but innocent tools of a
wisdom beyond their own.

With the birth of Christianity a change occurred in the consciousness of the time. Man was now considered in danger of
final separation from God owing to the "original sin," a
danger which Christ alone could avert. This concept which,
in later centuries, was to cause a great deal of theological confusion and to cast doubt on "divine justice" itself, merely
expressed the fact that deep down in his soul every human
being still longed for moral independence, experience of good
and evil, and godlike power over a material world. Without
abandonment of human freedom, the course man had set for
himself could be halted under one condition only: replace-
ment of his proud defiance of divine tutelage by compassionate
love for his Creator.

Christ's life, his suffering and death, fulfilled this condition,
provided he was accepted as God incarnate. Early Christian and

medieval thinkers took Jesus' life as a portent, warning mankind that the time was near when historical evolution had to
change its course lest it carry future generations into a land of
no return. Thus apprehension for the ultimate fate of the human soul replaced the philosophic serenity of paganism. A sense
of urgency developed, a feeling that the time beyond reversal,
"the day of judgment," was close at hand. From then on, the
course of evolution was not thought to be dictated by necessity
any more, but by the individual's choice between love of God
and love of unlimited independence. Thus it became a moral
problem—and the power which drew the human mind ever
deeper into materialistic concepts was called the devil.

Much was known to the teachers of ancient and medieval
schools for which we, today, proudly claim authorship. Only
their language was different, and carefully veiled so as to keep
too potent knowledge from those who might misuse it. An
atomic world concept was already taught by Democritus in the
fourth century, and almost certainly based on far older sources.
Beneath the atom was chaos, nothingness. In the imaginative
language the medieval scholar warned against one-sided analytical thinking, which might mislead man into the belief that in
and below these smallest building stones were to be found the
secrets of existence. To him, it was the devil who tried to make
the journey of evolution irreversible by tying human consciousness too strongly to the perishable world of matter. For
beneath the atom was the maelstrom into which human consciousness could disintegrate. This is the sphere which the
medieval thinkers place beneath the earth. Only "earth" in the
ancient alchemistic sense did not signify the rind of our planet,
but of matter, and "underworld" not the glowing center of the
earth but the subatomic melting pot of physical existence. Thus
those who originally warned of an area of dissolution below
the earth, were not so naïve as to look for it beneath the
ground under their feet. Their repeated warning to mankind
was that the human soul too closely bound to matter, and
becoming incapable of soaring above it, could be drawn into
a process of dissolution. This they called "hell."

Before too lightly dismissing concepts born of the consciousness of a different time, we might ask ourselves whether their apparent obsolescence is not due to the changing forms of expression rather than to the message they were to convey. Today we are inclined to use simple and casual terms and, where possible, understatements. With just a little imagination, however, it should be easy to recognize some of the phenomena of our time in the apocalyptic language of earlier generations.

Let us consider just two of these phenomena: the unprecedented destructiveness of recent technological inventions and the menace of ideological despotism. Either of them may bring irrevocable disaster to man, one threatening his physical existence, the other his spiritual mission on earth. Our generation with all its power and cleverness does not seem capable of banishing these specters of doom.

The reason for this helplessness is a failure on the part of our leaders to penetrate to the common cause of these symptoms. This cause is human consciousness submerged too deeply in intellectual and materialistic thought habits. The dialectician whose intuitive perception has grown so dim that he can see no more in man than a highly developed animal will, if strictly consistent, come to authoritarian convictions. His ethics are those of an animal breeder who feels justified in eliminating from his herd whatever stands in the way of biological aims.

In the field of science, our training neglects the creative-intuitive aspect of the student's mind. Consequently, unchecked analytical tendencies gain control over his actions, and force his inventive genius ever deeper into the sphere of dissolution. Unfortunately, this tendency, actually determined by a lack of inner balance, is considered today a noble expression of intellectual freedom.

Such are the portents which make us believe that the ancient path of our evolutionary eon may soon have to be abandoned for another course. Like a rocket from outer space, human consciousness at first appeared glimmering in a starry light, and its coming was heralded in myths and legends. The deeper it penetrated into the atmosphere of matter the brighter shone its light, and its course became recorded history. Today its near-impact is portended by the flash of nuclear explosions, the clash of mind and matter. Analytical intellect is the power that propels man toward the conquest of the earth. However, should it strike ground in full force, it will smash what it wanted to possess, and itself be drawn into the holocaust.

The only force that can break the fall of human consciousness and make it gain its goal intact, is the uplifting power of intuition. This power was throttled to speed the journey; now it must be revived, or the journey will end in disaster. All through the ages great men have labored to keep inner experience alive. In religion, art, and philosophy they have borne witness to the existence of a nonmaterial world, a world accessible to intuitive experience, just as the outer world is perceptible to the senses. Mankind has felt their truth and paid them homage. Yet their aim was not to be admired, but to be heard. While man feels greatness, he cannot comprehend it any more, for his intuitive capacities have waned to a point where qualitative reality appears no more than aesthetic symbolism.

This book was written for one purpose only: to awaken in the individual a spark of immediate intuitive experience, which alone can give proof for the existence of a creative world, as real as the created. Should this spark be kindled, the words of the great teachers might be accepted, not just as allegorical but as factual expressions of an intuitively perceptible reality.

Yet more than this is needed. To attain equilibrium, man must become aware of the focal point of his being, and laboriously strengthen its tiny flame until it waxes into a steady light. Those who deny the reality of the physical world, identifying themselves with a mystical "superself," are only too prone to lose themselves in a maze of illusions; those misled by modern psychology to seek themselves in the realm of biological forces—and the unwary victims of an education based on such convictions—incur another danger. Their unrecognized and therefore unguarded selfhood is readily overcome by the storms of passion which in our time more than ever may rise from man's unconscious mind. And a person who has so far lived a normal life, may suddenly find himself turned into a fiend.

Both the Eastern mystical and the Western analytical approach to psychology have their merits, but they help little in man's quest for inner stability. Where, then, can it be found? In the art and philosophy of the age from which Occidental civilization emerged, the Classical Age of Greece.

Many are the treasures of the Hellenes left to posterity, but the greatest of them is their message of equipoise, of the Golden Mean. Everywhere in Hellas, in her sculptures, drama, and philosophy, in the training of her statesmen, scientists, and athletes, the goal was harmony between spirit and body, between intuition and intellect, between goodness and beauty.

The Greeks did not live what they preached; passing the halfway mark between the two poles of a historical eon, their minds could grasp the divine idea of man, yet their course continued earthbound. But what was then at best a prophetic dream, can today become living reality. For if modern man were to deepen his interest in the wisdom of classical Greece, and let its message resound in his heart, he would find what he so fervently seeks: the central core of his own being.

It is no coincidence that that era preceded the emergence of the creed which became the foremost religion of Occidental culture. Just as the individual must grow aware of his innermost self before the idea of pure love can take root in his soul, the human race had to experience its state of equipoise before it was ready to receive the seed of Christianity.

Individuals have at all times found their way to spiritual fulfillment, but humanity as a whole has only now reached its crossroads to moral choice. The course it will pursue must continue forward toward growing individualism and technological power. But whether it will turn upward or end in a holocaust will depend on the concepts man forms of himself and conveys to his children. True self-recognition emerges from an equilibrium between analytical intellect and comprehending intuition. To achieve such equilibrium we must seek to strengthen our dormant qualities of intuition without weakening our hard-won intellectual faculties. The way to this all-important goal is to reverse consciously and systematically—if only for minutes—our habitually utilitarian approach to the

natural, the divine, and the artistic, into an attitude of unselfish devotion. Such an attitude will gradually open the
clogged channels through which the creative forces flow into
the human soul, to kindle her intuitive perception.

When these channels are opened, nature can create in us
the power to transform scientific knowledge into comprehending wisdom. The gift of the divine is a gradual change from
abstract creed to living religion, from uneasy belief to immediate experience. The artist seeks to achieve in the outer
world what our ego should do within: the building of a bridge
between the perfect thought of creation and the imperfect
form of the created. This is healing in its deepest sense.

Man is the bridge between two planes, a bridge whose pylons
stand on different levels of existence. In ancient myths his soul
was likened to the rainbow whose arch became the symbol of a
link between two worlds.

The reins of destiny are now in our hands; whether we shall
win or lose the struggle for a better future will depend on our
vision of ourselves and on the basic choice we are going to make.

The new frontier of our age does not lie in outer space but
in the human soul. All the bewildering events of this era
are mere portents. They give warning that the torch of individual consciousness can no longer shed sufficient light and
meaning on the vast expanse of man's material domains. New
resources must be opened in the human soul, if man is not to
lose himself in the conquest of outer space or turn his heart
to stone while building a civilization of robots.

We are living in a stage of history as much in need of inner
exploits as the fifteenth century was of geographical exploration. But the oceans and mountains which must be crossed on
this quest are not visible to physical senses and cannot be
found on maps and globes. To find them we must restore the
sight within, the sight which began to wane millenniums ago.
There is no alternative, for "where there is no vision, the
people perish."

Notes

Chapter II. PSYCHOLOGICAL UNDERCURRENTS IN OUR TIME

1. John Dewey, *A Common Faith*, p. 8.
2. Charles W. Lowry, *Communism and Christ*, p. 31.
3. John H. Hallowell, *Main Currents in Modern Political Thought*, p. 514.

Chapter III. THE THREE DIMENSIONS OF REALITY

1. Vannevar Bush, in an address at the Massachusetts Institute of Technology, Oct. 5, 1953.
2. John Dewey, *Human Nature and Conduct*, p. 176.
3. *Ibid.*, p. 176.
4. Sir William Hamilton, *Lectures on Metaphysics*, Lecture XI, p. 132.
5. Dewey, *Human Nature and Conduct*, p. 169.
6. Dewey, *Psychology*, p. 410.
7. As quoted by Harold Lamb in *Theodora and the Emperor*, p. 266.

Chapter IV. TRAINING FOR TRUTH

1. Arthur M. Abell, *Talks with Great Composers*, p. 58.
2. Nina Berberowa, *Tschaikovsky*, pp. 205, 212.
3. *Ibid.*, p. 14.
4. Abels, *op. cit.*, p. 137.
5. Lic. Emil Bock, *Studies in the Gospels*, Lecture IX, p. 103.
6. W. F. Albright, as quoted by Edmund Wilson in *The Scrolls from the Dead Sea*, p. 103.

Chapter V. NATURAL PHENOMENA IN THE MIRROR OF THE HUMAN MIND

1. Robert Ulich, *The Human Career*, pp. 49, 50.
2. Herbert Dingle, ed., *A Century of Science*, p. 315.

3. R. Beutner, *Life's Beginning on the Earth,* p. 91.
4. *Ibid.,* p. 222.
5. *Life* magazine, Sept. 7, 1953, p. 59.
6. Lecture by Prof. Harlow Shapley, held at Adelphi College, Feb. 2, 1958.
7. Dingle, ed., *op. cit.,* p. 315.
8. *The Weekly Review Ltd.* (London), quoting *World Science Review,* quoting Prof. H. S. D. Garven.
9. *Goethe's Botanical Writings,* trans. by Bertha Muller, p. 217.
10. *Ibid.,* p. 218.

Chapter VI. *THE HUMAN SELF BETWEEN THE CREATIVE AND THE CREATED*

1. Earl C. Kelley and Marie I. Rasey, *Education and the Nature of Man,* p. 22.
2. *Aviation Week,* 1958, Vol. 69, No. 1, p. 60.
3. *The Weekly Review Ltd.* (London), quoting *World Science Review,* quoting Prof. H. S. D. Garven.

Chapter VII. *THE EVOLUTION OF CONSCIOUSNESS AND ITS REFLECTION IN LEGENDS*

1. Funk and Wagnalls *Standard Dictionary of Folklore,* Vol. II, p. 1121.
2. Erich Neumann, *The Origins and History of Consciousness,* p. xviii.
3. Funk and Wagnalls, *op. cit.,* Vol. II, p. 1121.
4. Stewart Easton, *The Heritage of the Past,* p. 14.
5. Loren C. Eiseley, "Was Darwin Wrong About the Human Brain?" in *Harper's Magazine,* November 1955.
6. Easton, *op. cit.,* p. 11.
7. Ovid, *Metamorphoses.*
8. Carl Gustav Jung, *Psychology and Religion,* p. 11.
9. Kelley and Rasey, *Education and the Nature of Man,* p. 8.
10. C. W. Ceram, *Gods, Graves and Scholars,* p. 320.
11. *Ibid.,* p. 318.
12. Gustav Schwab, *Gods and Heroes,* p. 52.
13. *Ibid.,* p. 57.
14. *Ibid.,* p. 303.
15. Frederick Hiebel, *The Gospel of Hellas,* pp. 145–46.
16. Jung, *Psychology and Religion,* pp. 4, 6.
17. Hiebel, *op. cit.,* pp. 28, 29.

Chapter VIII. *MEDIEVAL ETHICS*

1. Carl Gustav Jung, *Psychology and Religion,* p. 52.
2. Dagobert D. Runes, *The Dictionary of Philosophy,* p. 8.
3. Funk and Wagnalls *Standard Dictionary of Folklore,* Vol. II, p. 1121.
4. Jung, *Psychology and Alchemy,* pp. 299–300.
5. *Ibid.,* p. 265.
6. Jung, *Psychology and Alchemy,* p. 260.

Chapter IX. *MORAL IMAGINATION*

1. *Goethe's Botanical Writings,* trans. by Bertha Muller, p. 12.
2. *Idem.*
3. Russell W. Davenport, *The Dignity of Man,* p. 195.
4. *Ibid.,* p. 141.
5. *The Writings of Ralph Waldo Emerson* (Modern Library), p. 40.
6. *Ibid.,* pp. 331–32.
7. Rudolf Steiner, *Philosophy of Spiritual Activity,* p. 153.
8. Davenport, *op. cit.,* p. 46.
9. *Ibid.,* p. 47.
10. Homer Jacobson, in *The American Scientist,* January 1955, pp. 119–27.
11. G. E. Hutchinson, *ibid.,* January 1955, pp. 144–49.
12. Pico della Mirandola, as quoted by Erich Fromm as one of the guide lines of his *Escape from Freedom.*
13. Norbert Wiener, *The Human Use of Human Beings,* pp. 185–86.

Chapter X. *THE HYDRA'S HEAD*

1. Address to the Central Committee on Atheist Propaganda by Khrushchev, Nov. 10, 1954.
2. A. R. MacAndrew, "Boredom in Soviet Culture," in *The New York Herald Tribune,* May 30, 1956.
3. Russell W. Davenport, *The Dignity of Man,* p. 185.

Chapter XI. *AN ASPECT OF CRIME*

1. Oderis Vitalis, as quoted by Harold Lamb in *The Crusaders,* p. 50.
2. Kelley and Rasey, *Education and the Nature of Man,* p. 118.
3. John B. Martin, "Why Did They Kill?" in *The Saturday Evening Post,* July 5, 1952.

Chapter XII. *PREREQUISITES OF LOVE*

1. Kelley and Rasey, *Education and the Nature of Man*, p. 23.
2. *Idem.*
3. *Ibid.*, p. 30.
4. Part of this chapter was used in a lecture held by the author at The Myrin Institute, Inc., at Adelphi College, Garden City, N.Y., on April 13, 1954, and published in the Institute's *Proceedings*, No. 2, "The Influence of Psychology on Education," pp. 23–24.

Chapter XIII. *INFORMATION AND EDUCATION*

1. Mary H. B. Wollner, "Back to the Classics," in *Today's Health*, Vol. 35, No. 9, September 1957.
2. Peter F. Drucker, "The New Philosophy Comes to Life," section entitled "The Purposeful Universe," in *Harper's Magazine*, August 1957.

Chapter XIV. *TRAINING IN INTUITION*

1. Frederick Hiebel, *The Gospel of Hellas*, p. 110.
2. Will Durant, *The Story of Our Civilization*, Vol. II, p. 163.
3. Hiebel, *op. cit.*, p. 243.
4. Durant, *op. cit.*, p. 516.
5. Bruno Walter, *Von der Musik und vom Musizieren*, Epilogue.
6. Durant, *The Age of Faith*, p. 797.
7. *Idem.*
8. Johannes Jorgensen, *St. Francis of Assisi*, p. 42.
9. Durant, *The Age of Faith*, p. 800.
10. Archbishop O'Boyle, "Is Our Religious Revival Real?" in *McCall's*, June 19, 1955, p. 25.
11. Tyron Edwards, *The New Dictionary of Thoughts*, p. 31.

Bibliography

Abell, Arthur M.   *Talks with Great Composers,* Philosophical Library, New York, 1955.

Berberowa, Nina.   *Tchaikovsky,* Gustav Kiepenheuer, Berlin, 1941.

Beutner, R.   *Life's Beginning on the Earth,* The Williams and Wilkins Co., Baltimore, 1938.

Bock, Lic. Emil.   *Studies in the Gospels,* The Christian Community Press, London, Lecture IX, p. 103.

———.   *The Three Years. The Life of Christ between Baptism and Ascension,* The Christian Community Press, London, 1955.

Bush, Vannevar.   Address at the Massachusetts Institute of Technology, Oct. 5, 1953.

Ceram, C. W.   *Gods, Graves and Scholars,* Alfred A. Knopf, New York, 1951.

Davenport, Russell W.   *The Dignity of Man,* Harper & Brothers, New York, 1955.

Dewey, John.   *A Common Faith,* Yale University Press, New Haven, 1934.

———.   *Human Nature and Conduct,* The Modern Library, New York, 1922.

———.   *Psychology,* American Book Co., New York, 1891.

Dingle, Herbert (ed.).   *A Century of Science,* Roy Publishers, New York, 1951.

Durant, Will.   *The Story of Our Civilization,* Simon & Schuster, New York, 1950.

———.   *The Age of Faith,* Simon & Schuster, New York, 1950.

Easton, Stewart.   *The Heritage of the Past,* Rinehart & Co., Inc., New York, 1955.

Edmunds, L. Francis.   *Rudolf Steiner Education—A Brief Exposition,* Mandley & Unett Limited, Newcastle, Staffs, 1956.

———.   *The Scientific and the Moral in Education*—Proceedings No. 6, 1956, The Myrin Institute, Inc., at Adelphi College, Garden City, New York.

Emerson, Ralph W.   *The Writings of Ralph Waldo Emerson,* Modern Library, Random House, New York, 1940.

Exman, Eugene.   *The World of Albert Schweitzer,* Harper & Brothers, New York, 1955.

Fromm, Erich.   *Escape from Freedom,* Rinehart & Co., New York & Toronto, 1941.

Funk and Wagnalls.   *Standard Dictionary of Folklore,* Funk & Wagnalls Co., New York, 1949.

Hallowell, John H.   *Main Currents in Modern Political Thought,* Henry Holt & Co., New York.

Hamilton, Sir William.   *Lectures on Metaphysics,* Sheldon & Co., New York, 1883. Lecture II, p. 31.

Harwood, Cecil.   *Portrait of a Waldorf School*—Proceedings No. 4, 1956, The Myrin Institute, Inc., at Adelphi College, Garden City, New York.

———.   *The Recovery of Man in Childhood—A Study in the Educational Work of Rudolf Steiner,* Hodder & Stoughton, London, 1958.

Hiebel, Frederick.   *The Gospel of Hellas,* Anthroposophic Press, New York, 1949.

Jung, Carl Gustav.   *Psychology and Religion,* Yale University Press, 1938.

———.   *Psychology and Alchemy,* Pantheon Books, New York, 1953.

Kelley, Earl C., and Rasey, Marie I.   *Education and the Nature of Man,* Harper & Brothers, New York, 1952.

Krutch, Joseph Wood.   *The Measure of Man,* Bobbs-Merrill Co., Inc. New York, 1954.

Lamb, Harold. *Theodora and the Emperor,* Doubleday & Co., Inc., Garden City, New York, 1952, p. 266.

———. *The Crusaders,* Doubleday & Co., Inc., Garden City, New York, 1930.

Lehrs, Ernst. *Man or Matter,* Harper & Brothers, New York, 1958.

Lowry, Charles W. *Communism and Christ,* Morehouse-Gorham Co., New York, 1953.

Neumann, Erich. *The Origins and History of Consciousness,* Pantheon Books, Inc., New York, 1954.

Muller, Bertha. *Goethe's Botanical Writings,* University of Hawaii Press, 1952.

Pfeiffer, Ehrenfried E. *Sensitive Crystallization Processes—A Demonstration of Formative Forces in the Blood,* Verlag Emil Weise, Dresden, 1936.

Poppelbaum, Hermann. *Man's Eternal Biography,* Adonis Press, New York, 1946.

Powers, Thomas E. *First Questions on the Life of the Spirit,* Harper & Brothers, New York, 1959.

Rittelmeyer, Friedrich. *Rudolf Steiner Enters My Life,* The Christian Community Press, London, 1954.

Runes, Dagobert D. *The Dictionary of Philosophy,* Philosophical Library, New York.

Schwab, Gustav. *Gods and Heroes,* Pantheon Books, Inc., New York, 1950.

Schweitzer, Albert. *Out of My Life and Thought,* Henry Holt, New York, 1933, revised 1949.

Shepherd, A. P. *A Scientist of the Invisible. An Introduction to the Life and Work of Rudolf Steiner,* Hodder & Stoughton, London, 1954.

Steffen, Albert. *Burning Problems,* Verlag füer schöene Wissenschaften, Dornach, Switzerland, 1957.

Steiner, Rudolf. *Goethe the Scientist,* Anthroposophic Press, Inc., New York, 1950.

————. *Philosophy of Spiritual Activity*, Rudolf Steiner Publication Co., London, 1953.

————. *Knowledge of the Higher Worlds and Its Attainment*, Anthroposophic Press, Inc., New York, 1947.

————. *The Redemption of Thinking, A Study in the Philosophy of Thomas Aquinas*, Hodder & Stoughton, London, 1956.

Ulich, Robert.   *The Human Career*, Harper & Brothers, New York, 1955.

Wachsmuth, Guenther.   *The Life and Work of Rudolf Steiner*, Whittier Books, Inc., New York, 1955.

Walter, Bruno.   *Von der Musik und vom Musizieren*, S. Fischer Verlag, Frankfurt, Germany, 1957. (English translation to be published by Norton.)

Wiener, Norbert.   *The Human Use of Human Beings*, Doubleday & Co., Inc., Garden City, New York, 1954.

Wilson, Edmund.   *The Scrolls from the Dead Sea*, Oxford University Press, New York, 1955.

Wollner, Mary H. B.   "Back to the Classics," in *Today's Health*, American Medical Association, Vol. 35, No. 9, September 1957.

Zeylmans van Emmichoven, F. W.   *Hygiene of the Soul*, Whittier Books, Inc., New York, 1955.

Index

Set in Linotype Baskerville
Format by René Cleveland
Manufactured by The Riverside Press
Published by HARPER & BROTHERS, *New York*